SELECTIONS FROM THE KUR-AN

SELECTIONS FROM THE KUR-AN

EDWARD WILLIAM LANE

A New Edition, Revised and Enlarged
With an Introduction

BY
STANLEY LANE POOLE

GYAN

Published by

Gyan Publishing House
5, Ansari Road
Daryaganj, New Delhi-110002
Phone: 011-47034999, 9811692060
E-mail: books@gyanbooks.com

Distribution Network
gyanbooks.com
India, USA, Canada, UK, Australia, France

ISBN : 978-81-212-3997-4 (PB)
First Published, London, 1890

2nd Impression 2020

Printed at: Gyan Press, Delhi.

Selections from the Kur-an
Author: Edward William Lane

SELECTIONS FROM THE KUR-AN.

BY

EDWARD WILLIAM LANE,

HON. DOCTOR OF LITERATURE, LEYDEN;
CORRESPONDENT OF THE INSTITUTE OF FRANCE;
HON. MEMBER OF THE GERMAN ORIENTAL SOCIETY, THE ROYAL ASIATIC SOCIETY,
THE ROYAL SOCIETY OF LITERATURE, ETC.;
AUTHOR OF "THE MODERN EGYPTIANS," AND "AN ARABIC-ENGLISH LEXICON;"
TRANSLATOR OF "THE THOUSAND AND ONE NIGHTS."

A New Edition, Revised and Enlarged,

WITH AN INTRODUCTION,

BY

STANLEY LANE POOLE.

LONDON:
KEGAN PAUL, TRENCH, TRÜBNER, & CO., LTD.
1890.

PREFACE.

THERE are several translations of the Kurán in several languages; but there are very few people who have the strength of mind to read any of them through. The chaotic arrangement and frequent repetitions, and the obscurity of the language, are sufficient to deter the most persistent reader, whilst the nature of a part of its contents renders the Kurán unfit for a woman's eye.

Yet there always has been a wish to know something about the sacred book of the Mohammadans, and it was with the design of satisfying this wish,

that Mr. Lane arranged the 'Selections' which were published in 1843. In spite of many printer's errors, due to the author's absence from England, the book was so far successful that the edition was exhausted, and it is now very difficult to obtain a copy. But partly owing to the obstructions to the reading offered by an interwoven native commentary, and partly by reason of the preference shown for the doctrinal over the poetical passages, the book went into scholars' hands rather than into the libraries of the general reading public. It has proved of considerable service to students of Arabic, who have found it the most accurate rendering in existence of a large part of the Ḳuran; and even native Muslims of India, ignorant of Arabic, have used Lane's 'Selections' as their Bible.

In this edition I have endeavoured rather to carry out the original intention of the translator. Experience has shown that the first plan was over-learned to commend itself to the average reader, for whom Mr. Lane had destined the book; in this edition I have therefore omitted many of the notes, which will not be missed by the reader for whom the book is intended, and for which the Arabic scholar has only to refer to the first edition, or to Sale's *Koran*, whence most of them were derived. Again, the text of the first edition was obscured and interrupted by an interwoven commentary, which destroyed the pleasure of the language and often made the meaning less intelligible than before. This commentary has been thinned. Where it added nothing to the text, it has been erased; where it gave a curious or valuable explanation, it has been thrown into a footnote; where it merely supplied a necessary word to complete the sense, that word has been left in the text distinguished by a different type.[1] Once more, the early and wilder *soorahs* were almost wholly omitted in the first edition, whilst the later more dogmatic and less poetical *soorahs* were perhaps too fully represented. I have endeavoured to establish the balance between the two.

---

[1] See prefatory note, p. 2.

In this edition the Selections are divided into two parts. The first is Islám; the second, other religions as regarded in Islám. In the first are grouped, under distinctive headings, the more important utterances of Moḥammad on what his followers must believe and do; in the second are his versions of the history of the patriarchs and other personages of the Jewish and Christian writings.

It is only in the First Part that I have made much alteration, either by adding fresh extracts (distinguished by a sign), or by making a few merely verbal alterations in the original extracts, or by the suppression or transposition of the commentary. Any alterations that go beyond this—new renderings, for instance—are duly recorded in the footnotes.

The Second Part is almost unchanged from the first edition. In this part the interwoven commentary is left entire, for the traditions of the commentators about Abraham and Moses and Christ are as curious as the traditions of Moḥammad, and about as credible; and the narrative style of the Second Part allows the introduction of parentheses more easily than the rhetorical form which many of the extracts in the First Part present.

Mr. Lane's Introduction was abridged from Sale's Preliminary Discourse, with but little addition from his own knowledge. Sale's Discourse abounds in information, but it is too detailed and lengthy for the purpose of this volume. I have, then, substituted a short sketch of the beginnings of Islám. I have tried to bring home to the reader the little we know of the early Arabs; then to draw the picture of the great Arab prophet and his work; to show what are the salient points of Islám; and finally to explain something of the history of the Ḳurán and its contents. I am conscious of having drawn the picture with a weak hand, but I hope the sketch may serve as a not quite useless introduction to a volume of typical selections from a book which, in the peculiar character of its contents and the extraordinary power of its influence, has not its parallel in the world.

S. L. P.

June 1878.

CONTENTS.

INTRODUCTION.

PART THE FIRST.

PART THE SECOND.

INTRODUCTION.

I.—*THE ARABS BEFORE MOḤAMMAD.*

> 'Oh, our manhood's prime vigour! No spirit feels waste,
> Not a muscle is stopped in its playing nor sinew unbraced.
> Oh, the wild joys of living! the leaping from rock up to rock,
> The strong rending of boughs from the fir-tree, the cool silver shock
> Of the plunge in the pool's living water, the hunt of the bear,
> And the sultriness showing the lion is couched in his lair.
> And the meal, the rich dates yellowed over with gold-dust divine,
> And the locust flesh steeped in the pitcher, the full draught of wine,
> And the sleep in the dried river-channel where bulrushes tell
> That the water was wont to go warbling so softly and well.
> How good is man's life, the mere living! how fit to employ
> All the heart and the soul and the senses for ever in joy!'
>
> —BROWNING, *Saul.*

BETWEEN Egypt and Assyria, jostled by both, yielding to neither, lay a strange country, unknown save at its marches even to its neighbours, dwelt-in by a people that held itself aloof from all the earth—a people whom the great empires of the ancient world in vain essayed to conquer, against whom the power of Persia, Egypt, Rome, Byzantium was proven impotence, and at whose hands even the superb Alexander, had he lived to test his dream, might for once have learnt the lesson of defeat. Witnessing the struggle and fall of one and another of the great tyrannies of antiquity, yet never entering the arena of the fight;—swept on its northern frontier by the conflicting armies of Khusru and Cæsar, but lifting never a hand in either cause;—Arabia was at length to issue forth from its silent mystery, and after baffling for a thousand years the curious gaze of strangers, was at last to draw to itself the fearful eyes of all men. The people of whom almost nothing before could certainly be asserted but its existence was finally of its own free will to throw aside the veil, to come forth from its fastnesses, and imperiously to bring to its feet the kingdoms of the world.

It is not all Arabia of which I speak. The story to tell has nothing as yet to say to the 'happy' tilled lands of the south, nor to the outlying princedoms of El-Ḥeereh and Ghassan bordering the territories and admitting the suzerainty of Persia and Rome. These lands were not wrapped in mystery: the Himyerite's kingdom in the Yemen, the rule of Zenobia at Palmyra, were familiar to the nations around. But the cradle of Islám was not here.

Along the eastern coast of the Red Sea, sometimes thrusting its spurs of red sandstone and porphyry into the waves, sometimes drawing away and leaving a wide stretch of lowland, runs a rugged range of mountain. One above another, the hills rise from the coast, leaving here and there between them a green valley, where you may see an Arab settlement or a group of Bedawees watering their flocks. Rivers there are none; and the streams that gather from the rainfall are scarcely formed but they sink into the parched earth. Yet beneath the dried-up torrent-beds a rivulet trickles at times, and straightway there spreads a rich oasis dearly prized by the wanderers of the desert. All else is bare and desolate. Climb hill after hill, and the same sight meets the eye—barren mountain-side, dry gravelly plain, and the rare green valleys. At length you have reached the topmost ridge; and you see, not a steep descent, no expected return to the plain, but a vast desert plateau, blank, inhospitable, to all but Arabs unindwellable. You have climbed the Ḥijáz—the 'barrier' —and are come to the steppes of the Nejd—the 'highland.' In the valleys of this barrier-land are the Holy Cities, Mekka and Medina. Here is the birthplace of Islám: the Arab tribes of the Ḥijáz and the Nejd were the first disciples of Moḥammad.

One may tell much of a people's character from its

home. Truism as it seems, there is yet a meaning in the saying that the Arabs are peculiarly the people of Arabia. Those who have travelled in this wonderful land tell us of the quickening influence of the air and scene of the desert. The fresh breath of the plain, the glorious sky, the still of the wide expanse, trod by no step but your own, looked upon only by yourself and perhaps yonder solitary eagle or the wild goat leaping the cliffs you have left behind, the absolute stillness and aloneness, bring about a strange sense of delight and exultation, a bounding-up of spirits held in long restraint, an unknown nimbleness of wit and limb. The Arabs felt all this and more in their bright imaginative souls. A few would settle in villages, and engage in the trade which came through from India to the West; but such were held in poor repute by the true Bedawees, who preferred above all things else the free life of the desert. It is a relief to turn from the hurry and unrest of modern civilisation, from the never-ending strife for wealth, for 'position,' for pleasure, even for knowledge, and look for a moment on the careless life of the Bedawee. He lived the aimless, satisfied life of some child; he sought no change; he was supremely content with the exquisite sense of simple existence; he was happy because he lived. He wished no more. He dreaded the dark After-death; he thrust it from his thoughts as often as it would force itself unwelcome upon him. Utterly fearless of man and fortune, he took no thought for the morrow: whatever it brought forth, he felt confidently his strength to enjoy or endure; only let him seize the happiness of to-day while it shall last, and drain to the dregs the overbrimming cup of his life. He was ambitious of glory and victory, but it was not an ambition that clouded his joy. Throughout a life that was full of energy, of passion, of strong endeavour after his ideal of desert perfectness, there was yet a restful sense of satisfied enjoyment, a feeling that life was of a surety well worth living.

For the Arab had his ideal of life. The true son of the desert must in the old times do more than stretch his limbs contentedly under the shade of the overhanging rock. He must be brave and chivalrous, generous, hospitable; ready to sacrifice himself and his substance for his clan; prompt to help the needy and the traveller; true to his word, and, not least, eloquent in his speech.

Devotion to the clan was the strongest tie the Arab possessed. Though tracing their descent from a common traditional ancestor, the great northern family of Bedawees was split up into numerous clans, owning no central authority, but led, scarcely governed, each by its own chief, who was the most valiant and best-born man in it. The whole clan acted as one being; an injury done to one member was revenged by all, and even a crime committed by a clansman was upheld by the whole brotherhood. Though a small spark would easily light-up war between even friendly clans, it was rarely that those of kin met as enemies. It is told how a clan suffered long and oft-repeated injuries from a kindred clan without one deed of revenge. 'They are our brothers,' they said; 'perhaps they will return to better feelings; perhaps we shall see them again as they once were.' To be brought to poverty or even to die for the clan, the Arab deemed his duty—his privilege. To add by his prowess or his hospitality or his eloquence to the glory of the clan was his ambition.

A mountain[1] we have where dwells he whom we shelter there,
  lofty, before whose height the eye falls back blunted:
Deep-based is its root below ground, and overhead there soars
  its peak to the stars of heaven whereto no man reaches.
A folk are we who deem it no shame to be slain in fight,
  though that be the deeming thereof of Salool and 'Ámir;
Our love of death brings near to us our days of doom,
  but their dooms shrink from death and stand far distant.
There dies among us no lord a quiet death in his bed,
  and never is blood of us poured forth without vengeance.

---

[1] *i.e.*, the glory of the clan.

Our souls stream forth in a flood from the edge of the whetted swords:
 no otherwise than so does our spirit leave its mansion.
Pure is our stock, unsullied : fair is it kept and bright
 by mothers whose bed bears well, and fathers mighty.
To the best of the uplands we wend, and when the season comes
 we travel adown to the best of fruitful valleys.
Like rain of the heaven are we : there is not in all our line
 one blunt of heart, nor among us is counted a niggard.
We say nay when so we will to the words of other men,
 but no man to us says nay when we give sentence.
When passes a lord of our line, in his stead there rises straight
 a lord to say the say and do the deeds of the noble.
Our beacon is never quenched to the wanderer of the night,
 nor has ever a guest blamed us where men meet together.
Our Days[1] are famous among our foemen, of fair report,
 branded and blazed with glory like noble horses.
Our swords have swept throughout all lands both west and east,
 and gathered many a notch from the steel of hauberk-wearers;
Not used are they when drawn to be laid back in the sheaths
 before that the folk they meet are spoiled and scattered.
If thou knowest not, ask men what they think of us and them
 —not alike are he that knows and he that knows not.
The children of Ed-Dayyán are the shaft of their people's mill,
 —around them it turns and whirls, while they stand midmost.[2]

The renown of the clan was closely wrapped up with the Arab chieftain's personal renown. He was keenly sensitive on the point of honour, and to that notion he attached a breadth of meaning which can scarcely be understood in these days. Honour included all the different virtues that went to make up the ideal Bedawee. To be proved wanting in any of these was to be dishonoured. Above all things, the man who would 'keep

---

1 Battles.

2 This and the other verses quoted in this chapter are taken from the translations of old Arab poetry contributed by Mr. C. J. Lyall to the *Journal of the Royal Asiatic Society of Bengal* (*Translations from the Ḥamáseh and the Aghánî; The Mo'allaqah of Zuheyr*). They imitate the metres of the original Arabic verse, but are nevertheless as literal as need be. The transliteration of proper names in the verses (and in other quotations) has been assimilated to the system adopted by Mr. Lane, from which in this work I only depart in the case of names which by frequent use have become almost the property of the English language.

his honour and defile it not' must be brave and hospitable—

> A rushing rain-flood when he gave guerdons :
> when he sprang to the onset, a mighty lion.

The Arab warrior was a mighty man of valour. He would spend whole days in the saddle, burdened with heavy armour, in the pursuit of a foe, seeking the life of the slayer of his kin, or sweeping down upon the caravan of rich merchandise which his more peaceful countrymen of the towns were carrying through the deserts. The Arab lived mainly by plunder. His land did not yield him food—unless it were dates, the Bedawee's bread—and he relied on the success of his foraging expeditions for his support. These he conducted with perfect good-breeding; he used no violence when it could be avoided; he merely relieved the caravan from the trouble of carrying any further the goods that he was himself willing to take charge of, urging, if necessary, the unfair treatment of his forefather Ishmael as an excellent reason for pillaging the sons of Isaac. 'When a woman is the victim, no Bedouin brigand, however rude, will be ill-mannered enough to lay hands upon her. He begs her to take off the garment on which he has set his heart, and he then retires to a distance and stands with eyes averted, lest he should do violence to her modesty.'

The poems of the early Arabs are full of the deeds of their warriors, the excitement of the pitched battle, the delight of the pursuit, the nightly raid on the camp, the trial of skill between rival chiefs, and the other pictures of a warrior's triumph. Here we find little of the generosity of war: mercy was rarely exercised and hatred was carried to its extremest limits; quarter was neither asked nor given; to despatch a wounded man was no disgrace; the families of the vanquished were enslaved. Notwithstanding his frank genial nature, the Arab was of a dangerously quick temper, derived, he boasted, from the flesh he lived-on of the camel, the surliest and most ill-conditioned of beasts. If he conceived himself insulted, he was bound to revenge himself to the full, or he would have been deemed dishonoured for ever. And since his fiery temper easily took offence, the history of the early Arabs is full of the traditions of slight quarrels and their horrible results—secret assassination and the long-lasting blood-feud.

Many the warriors, noon-journeying, who, when
night fell, journeyed on and halted at dawning—
Keen each one of them, girt with a keen blade
that when one drew it flashed forth like the lightning—
They were tasting of sleep by sips, when, as
they nodded, thou didst fright them, and they were scattered.
Vengeance we did on them : there escaped us
of the two houses none but the fewest.
And if Hudheyl[1] broke the edge of his[2] sword-blade—
many the notch that Hudheyl gained from him!
Many the time that he made them kneel down on
jagged rocks where the hoof is worn with running!
Many the morning he fell on their shelter,
and after slaughter came plunder and spoiling!
Hudheyl has been burned by me, one valiant
whom Evil tires not though they be wearied—
Whose spear drinks deep the first draught, and thereon
drinks deep again of the blood of foemen.
Forbidden was wine, but now it is lawful :
hard was the toil that made it lawful!
Reach me the cup, O Sawád son of 'Amr!
my body is spent with gaining my vengeance.
To Hudheyl we gave to drink Death's goblet,
whose dregs are disgrace and shame and dishonour.
The hyena laughs over the slain of Hudheyl, and
the wolf—see thou—grins by their corpses,
And the vultures flap their wings, full-bellied
treading their dead, too gorged to leave them.

The contempt which the Arab, with a few noble exceptions, felt for the gentler virtues is seen in these lines:—

Had I been a son of Mázin, there had not plundered my herds
the sons of the Child of the Dust, Dhuhl son of Sheybán!

---

[1] A tribe.

[2] The subject of the poem, mentioned in the second hemistich of the third verse as 'thou,' whose death the supposed author ('one valiant') avenged.

There had straightway arisen to help me a heavy-handed kin,
good smiters when help is needed, though the feeble bend to the
Men who, when Evil bares before them his hindmost teeth, [blow:
fly gaily to meet him, in companies or alone.
They ask not their brother, when he lays before them his wrong
in his trouble, to give them proof of the truth of what he says.
But as for my people, though their number be not small,
they are good for nought against evil, however light it be;
They requite with forgiveness the wrong of those that do them wrong,
and the evil deeds of the evil they meet with kindness and love;
As though thy Lord had created among the tribes of men
themselves alone to fear Him, and never one man more.
Would that I had in their stead a folk who, when they ride forth,
strike swiftly and hard, on horse or on camel borne!

A point on which the temper of the Bedawee was easily touched was his family pride. The Arab prized good blood as much in men as in his horses and camels. In these he saw the importance of breed, and in men he firmly believed the same principle held good. With the tenacious memory of his race, he had no difficulty in remembering the whole of a complicated pedigree, and he would often proudly dwell on the purity of his blood and the gallant deeds of his forefathers. He would challenge another chief to prove a more noble descent, and hot disputes and bitter rivalries often came of these comparisons.

But if noble birth brought rivalry and hatred, it brought withal excellent virtues. The Arab nobleman was not a man who was richer and more idle and luxurious than his inferiors: his position, founded upon descent, depended for its maintenance on personal qualities. Rank brought with it onerous obligations. The chief, if he would retain and carry on the repute of his line, must not only be fearless and ready to fight all the world; he must be given to hospitality, generous to kith and kin, and to all who cry unto him. His tent must be so pitched in the camp that it shall not only be the first that the enemy attacks, but also the first the wayworn stranger approaches; and at night fires must be kindled hard by to guide wanderers in the desert to his hospitable entertainment. If a man came to an Arab noble's tent and said, 'I throw myself on your honour,' he was safe from his enemies until they had trampled on the dead body of his host. Nothing was baser than to give up a guest; the treachery was rare, and brought endless dishonour upon the clan in which the shame had taken place. The poet extols the tents—

Where dwells a kin great of heart, whose word is enough to shield
whom they shelter when peril comes in a night of fierce strife and storm;
Yea, noble are they: the seeker of vengeance gains not from them
the blood of his foe, nor is he that wrongs them left without help.

The feeling lasted even under the debased rule of Muslim despots; for it is related that a governor was once ordering-out some prisoners to execution, when one of them asked for a drink of water, which was immediately given him. He then turned to the governor and said, 'Wilt thou slay thy guest?' and was forthwith set free. A pledge of protection was inferred in the giving of hospitality, and to break his word was a thing not to be thought upon by an Arab. He did not care to give an oath; his simple word was enough, for it was known to be inviolable. Hence the priceless worth of the Arab chief's word of welcome: it meant protection, unswerving fidelity, help, and succour.

There was no bound to this hospitality. It was the pride of the Arab to place everything he possessed at the service of the guest. The last milch-camel must be killed sooner than the duties of hospitality be neglected. The story is told of Ḥátim, a gallant poet-warrior of the tribe of Ṭayyi, which well illustrates the Arab ideal of hostship. Ḥátim was at one time brought to the brink of starvation by the dearth of a rainless season. For a whole day he and his family had eaten nothing, and at night, after soothing the children to sleep by telling them some of those stories in which the Arabs have few rivals, he was trying by his cheerful conversation to make his wife forget her hunger. Just then they heard steps without, and a corner of the tent was raised. 'Who is there?' said Ḥátim. A woman's voice replied, 'I am such a one, thy neighbour. My children have nothing to eat, and are howling like young wolves, and I have come to beg help of thee.' 'Bring them here,' said Ḥátim. His wife asked him what he would do, for if he could not feed his own children, how should he find food for this woman's? 'Do not disturb thyself,' he answered. Now Ḥátim had a horse renowned far and wide for the purity of his stock and the fleetness and beauty of his paces. He would not kill his favourite for himself nor even for his own children; but now he went out and slew him, and prepared him with fire for the strangers' need. And when he saw them eating with his wife and children, he exclaimed, 'It were a shame that you alone should eat whilst all the camp is perishing of hunger;' and he went and called the neighbours to the meal, and in the morning there remained of the horse nothing but his bones. But as for himself, wrapped in his mantle, he sat apart in a corner of the tent.

This Ḥátim is a type of the Arab nature at its noblest. Though renowned for his courage and skill in war, he never suffered his enmity to overcome his generosity. He had sworn an oath never to take a man's life, and he strictly observed it, and always withheld the fatal last blow. In spite of his clemency, he was ever successful in the wars of his clan, and brought back from his raids many a rich spoil, only to spend it at once in his princely fashion. His generosity and faithful observance of his word at times placed him in positions of great danger; but the alternative of denying his principles seems never to have occurred to his mind. For instance, he had imposed upon himself as a law never to refuse a gift to him that asked it of him. Once, engaged in single combat, he had disarmed and routed his opponent, who then turned and said, 'Ḥátim, give me thy spear.' At once he threw it to him, leaving himself defenceless; and had he not met an adversary worthy of himself, this had been the last of his deeds. Happily Ḥátim was not the only generous warrior of the Arabs, and his foe did not avail himself of his advantage. When Ḥátim's friends remonstrated with him on the rashness of an act which, in the spirit of shopkeepers, they regarded as quixotic, Ḥátim said, 'What would you have me to do? He asked of me a gift!'

It was Ḥátim's practice to buy the liberty of all captives who sought his aid: it was but another application of the Arab virtue of hospitality. Once a captive called to him when he was on a journey and had not with him the means of paying the ransom. But he was not wont to allow any difficulties to baulk him of the exercise of his duty, and he had the prisoner released, stepping meanwhile into his chains until his own clan should send the ransom.

Brave, chivalrous, faithful, and generous beyond the needful of Arab ideal—so that his niggard wife, using the privilege of high dames, repudiated him because he was ever ruining himself and her by his open hand—Ḥátim filled up the measure of Arab virtue by his eloquence, and such of his poems as have come down to us reflect the nobility of his life. As a youth he had shown a strong passion for poetry, and would spare no means of doing honour to poets. His grandfather, in despair at the boy's extravagance, sent him away from the camp to guard the camels, which were pastured at a distance. Sitting there in a state of solitude little congenial to his nature, Ḥátim lifted his eyes and saw a caravan approaching. It was the caravan of three great poets who were travelling to the court of the King of El-Ḥeereh. Ḥátim begged them to alight and to accept of refreshment after the hot and dreary journey. He killed them a camel each, though one would have more than sufficed for the three; and in return they wrote him verses in praise of himself and his kindred. Overjoyed at the honour, Ḥátim insisted on the poets each accepting a hundred camels; and they departed with their gifts. When the grandfather came to the pasturing and asked where the camels were gone, Ḥátim answered, 'I have exchanged them for a crown of honour, which will shine for all time on the brow of thy race. The lines in which great poets have celebrated our house will pass from mouth to mouth, and will carry our glory over all Arabia.'[1]

This story well illustrates the Arab's passionate love of poetry. He conceived his language to be the finest in the world, and he prized eloquence and poetry as the goodliest gifts of the gods. There were three great events in Arab life, when the clan was called together and great feastings and rejoicings ensued. One was the birth of a son to a chief; another the foaling of a generous mare; the third was the discovery that a great poet had risen up among them. The advent of the poet meant the immortality of the deeds of the clansmen and the everlasting contumely of their foes; it meant the raising up of the glory of the tribe over all the clans of Arabia, and the winning of triumphs by bitterer weapons than sword and spear—the weapons of stinging satire and scurrilous squib. No man might dare withstand the power of the poets among a people who were keenly alive to the point of an epigram, and who never forgot an ill-natured jibe if it were borne upon musical verse. Most of the great heroes of the desert were poets as well as warriors, and their poesy was deemed the chiefest gem in their crown, and, like their courage, was counted a proof of generous birth. The Khalif 'Omar said well, 'The kings of the Arabs are their orators and poets, those who practise and who celebrate all the virtues of the Bedawee.'

This ancient poetry of the Arabs is the reflection of the people's life. Far away from the trouble of the world, barred by wild wastes from the stranger, the Bedawee

---

[1] For these and other stories about Ḥátim, see Caussin de Perceval's *Essai sur l'Histoire des Arabes*, ii. 607–628: a book which is a treasury of Arab life, and abounds in those anecdotes which reveal more of the character of the people than whole volumes of ethnological treatise.

lived his happy child's life, enjoying to the uttermost the good the gods had sent him, delighting in the face that Nature showed him, inspired by the glorious breath of the deserts that were his home. His poetry rings of that desert life. It is emotional, passionate, seldom reflective. Not the end of life, the whence and the whither, but the actual present joy of existence, was the subject of his song. Vivid painting of nature is the characteristic of this poetry: it is natural, unpolished, unlaboured. The scenes of the desert—the terrors of the nightly ride through the hill-girdled valley where the Ghools and the Jinn have their haunts; the gloom of the barren plain, where the wolf, 'like a ruined gamester,' roams ululating; the weariness of the journey under the noonday sun; the stifling of the sand-storm, the delusions of the mirage; or again, the solace of the palm-tree's shade, and the delights of the cool well;—such are the pictures of the Arab poet. The people's life is another frequent theme: the daily doings of the herdsman, the quiet pastoral life, on the one hand; on the other, the deeds of the chiefs—war, plunder, the chase, wassail, revenge, friendship, love. There were satires on rival tribes, panegyrics on chiefs, laments for the dead. This poetry is wholly objective, artless, child-like; it is the outcome of a people still in the freshness of youth, whom the mysteries and complications of life have not yet set a-thinking. 'Just as his language knows but the present and the past, so the ancient Arab lived but in to-day and yesterday. The future is nought to him; he seizes the present with too thorough abandonment to have an emotion left for anything beyond. He troubles himself not with what fate the morrow may bring forth, he dreams not of a beautiful future,—only he revels in the present, and his glance looks backward alone. Rich in ideas and impressions, he is poor in thought. He drains hastily the foaming cup of life; he feels deeply and passionately; but it is as if he were never conscious of the coming of the thoughtful age which, while it surveys the past, as often turns an anxious look to the unknown future.'

It is very difficult for a Western mind to enter into the real beauty of the old Arab poetry. The life it depicts is so unlike any we can now witness, that it is almost removed beyond the pale of our sympathies. The poetry is loaded with metaphors and similes, which to us seem far-fetched, though they are drawn from the simplest daily sights of the Bedawee. Moreover, it is only in fragments that we can read it; for the change in the whole character of Arab life and in the current of Arab ideas which followed the conquests of Islám extinguished the old songs, which were no longer suitable to the new conditions of things; and as they were seldom recorded in writing, we possess but a little remnant of them.[1] Yet 'these fragments may be broken, defaced, dimmed, and obscured by fanaticism, ignorance, and neglect; but out of them there arises anew all the freshness, bloom, and glory of desert-song, as out of Homer's epics rise the glowing spring-time of humanity and the deep blue heavens of Hellas. It is not a transcendental poetry, rich in deep and thoughtful legend and lore, or glittering in the many-coloured prisms of fancy, but a poetry the chief task of which is to paint life and nature as they really are; and within its narrow bounds it is magnificent. It is chiefly and characteristically full of manliness, of vigour, and of a chivalrous spirit, doubly striking when compared with the spirit of abjectness and slavery found in some other Asiatic nations. It is wild and vast and monotonous as the yellow seas of its desert solitudes; it is daring and noble, tender and true.'[2]

---

[1] The later Arabic poets were mostly incapable of the genius of the old singers: the times had changed, and the ancient poetry appeared almost as exotic to their ideas as it does to our own. No greater mistake can be made than to judge of the old poets by such a writer as Behá-ed-deen Zoheyr, of whom Professor E. H. Palmer has lately given us so beautiful a version. There is nothing in common between El-Behá and 'Antarah—scarcely even the language.

[2] Deutsch, *Lit. Remains*, 453, 454: cp. Nöldeke, *Beiträge zur Kennt. d. Poesie d. alten Araber*, xxiii., xxiv.

There was one place where, above all others, the Ḳaṣeedehs of the ancient Arabs were recited: this was 'Okáḍh, the Olympia of Arabia, where there was held a great annual Fair, to which not merely the merchants of Mekka and the south, but the poet-heroes of all the land resorted. The Fair of 'Okáḍh was held during the sacred months,—a sort of 'God's Truce,' when blood could not be shed without a violation of the ancient customs and faiths of the Bedawees. Thither went the poets of rival clans, who had as often locked spears as hurled rhythmical curses. There was little fear of a bloody ending to the poetic contest, for those heroes who might meet there with enemies or blood-avengers are said to have worn masks or veils, and their poems were recited by a public orator at their dictation. That these precautions and the sacredness of the time could not always prevent the ill-feeling evoked by the pointed personalities of rival singers leading to a fray and bloodshed is proved by recorded instances; but such results were uncommon, and as a rule the customs of the time and place were respected. In spite of occasional broils on the spot, and the lasting feuds which these poetic contests must have excited, the Fair of 'Okáḍh was a grand institution. It served as a focus for the literature of all Arabia: every one with any pretensions to poetic power came, and if he could not himself gain the applause of the assembled people, at least he could form one of the critical audience on whose verdict rested the fame or the shame of every poet. The Fair of 'Okáḍh was a literary congress, without formal judges, but with unbounded influence. It was here that the polished heroes of the desert determined points of grammar and prosody; here the seven Golden Songs were recited, although (alas for the charming legend!) they were *not* afterwards 'suspended' on the Kaạbeh; and here 'a magical language, the language of the Ḥijáz,' was built out of the dialects of Arabia, and was made ready to the skilful hand of Moḥammad, that he might conquer the world with his Kurán.

The Fair of 'Okáḍh was not merely a centre of emulation for Arab poets; it was also an annual review of Bedawee virtues. It was there that the Arab nation once-a-year inspected itself, so to say, and brought forth and criticised its ideals of the noble and the beautiful in life and in poetry. For it was in poetry that the Arab—and for that matter each man all the world over—expressed his highest thoughts, and it was at 'Okáḍh that these thoughts were measured by the standard of the Bedawee ideal. The Fair not only maintained the highest standard of poetry that the Arabic language has ever reached: it also upheld the noblest idea of life and duty that the Arab nation has yet set forth and obeyed. 'Okáḍh was the press, the stage, the pulpit, the Parliament, and the Académie Française of the Arab people; and when, in his fear of the infidel poets (whom Imra-el-Ḳeys was to usher to hell), Moḥammad abolished the Fair, he destroyed the Arab nation even whilst he created his own new nation of Muslims;—and the Muslims cannot sit in the places of the old pagan Arabs.

It is very difficult for the Western mind to dissociate the idea of Oriental poetry from the notion of amatory odes, and sonnets to the lady's eyebrow: but even the few extracts that have been given in this chapter show that the Arab had many other subjects besides love to sing about, and though the divine theme has its place in almost every poem, it seldom rivals the prominence of war and nature-painting, and it is treated from a much less sensual point of view than that of later Arab poets. Many writers have drawn a gloomy picture of the condition of women in Arabia before the coming of Moḥammad, and there is no doubt that in many cases their lot was a miserable one. There are ancient Arabic proverbs that point to the contempt in which woman's judgment and character were held by the Arabs of 'the Time of Ignorance,' and Moḥammad must have derived his mean opinion of women from a too general impression among his countrymen. The marriage tie was certainly very loose among the ancient Arabs. The ceremony itself was of the briefest. The man said *khiṭb* (*i.e.* I am an asker-in-marriage), and the giver-away answered *nikḥ* (*i.e.*, I am a giver-in-marriage), and the knot was thus tied, only to be undone with equal facility and brevity. The frequency of divorce among the Arabs does not speak well for their constancy, and must have had a degrading effect upon the women. Hence it is argued that women were the objects of contempt rather than of respect among the ancient Arabs.

Yet there is reason to believe that the evidence upon which this conclusion is founded is partial and one-sided. There was a wide gulf between the Bedawee and the town Arab. It is not impossible that the view commonly entertained as to the state of women in preïslamic times is based mainly on what Moḥammad saw around him in Mekka, and not on the ordinary life of the desert. To such a conjecture a curiously uniform support is lent by the ancient poetry of the desert; and though the poets were then—as they always are—men of finer mould than the rest, yet their example, and still more their poems passing from mouth to mouth, must have created a widespread belief in their principles. It is certain that the roaming Bedawee, like the mediæval knight, entertained a chivalrous reverence for women, although he, too, like the knight, was not always above a career of promiscuous gallantry; but there was always a certain glamour of romance about the intrigues of the Bedawee. He did not regard the object of his love as a chattel to be possessed, but as a divinity to be assiduously worshipped. The poems are full of instances of the courtly respect displayed by the heroes of the desert toward defenceless maidens, and the mere existence of so general an ideal of conduct in the poems is a strong argument for Arab chivalry: for with the Arabs the abyss between the ideal accepted of the mind and the attaining thereof in action was narrower than it is among 'more advanced' nations.

Whatever was the condition of women in the trading cities and villages, it is certain that in the desert woman was regarded as she has never since been among Muslims. The modern ḥareem system was there as yet undreamt of; the maid of the desert was unfettered by the ruinous restrictions of modern life in the East. She was free to choose her own husband, and to bind him to have no other wife than herself. She might receive male visitors, even strangers, without suspicion: for her virtue was too dear to her and too well assured to need the keeper. It was the bitterest taunt of all to say to a hostile clan that their men had not the heart to give nor their women to deny; for the chastity of the women of the clan was reckoned only next to the valour and generosity of the men. In those days bastardy was an indelible stain. It was the wife who inspired the hero to deeds of glory, and it was her praise that he most valued when he returned triumphant. The hero of desert song thought himself happy to die in guarding some women from their pursuers. Wounded to the death, 'Antarah halted alone in a narrow pass, and bade the women press on to a place of safety. Planting his spear in the ground, he supported himself on his horse, so that when the pursuers came up they knew not he was dead, and dared not approach within reach of his dreaded arm. At length the horse moved, and the body fell to the ground, and the enemies saw that it was but the corpse of the hero that had held the pass. In death, as in a life *sans peur et sans reproche*, 'Antarah was true to the chivalry of his race.

There are many instances like this of the knightly courtesy of the Arab chief in 'the Time of Ignorance.' In the old days, as an ancient writer says, the true Arab had but one love, and her he loved till death, and she him. Even when polygamy became commoner, especially in the towns, it was not what is meant by polygamy in a modern Muslim state: it was rather the patriarchal system of Abram and Sarai.

There is much in the fragments of the ancient poetry which reflects this fine spirit. It is ofttimes 'tender and true,' and even Islám could not wholly root out the real Arab sentiment, which reappears in Muslim times in the poems of Aboo-Firás. Especially valuable is the evidence of the old poetry with regard to the love of a father for his daughters. Infanticide, which is commonly attributed to the whole Arab nation of every age before Islám, was in reality exceedingly rare in the desert, and after almost dying out only revived about the time of Moḥammad. It was probably adopted by poor and weak clans, either from inability to support their children, or in order to protect themselves from the stain of having their children dishonoured by stronger tribes, and the occasional practice of this barbarous and suicidal custom affords no ground for assuming an unnatural hatred and contempt for girls among the ancient Arabs. These verses of a father to his daughter tell a different story:—

> If no Umeymeh were there, no want would trouble my soul,
> no labour call me to toil for bread through pitchiest night;
> What moves my longing to live is but that well do I know
> how low the fatherless lies, how hard the kindness of kin.
> I quake before loss of wealth lest lacking fall upon her,
> and leave her shieldless and bare as flesh set forth on a board.
> My life she prays for, and I from mere love pray for her death—
> yea death, the gentlest and kindest guest to visit a maid.
> I fear an uncle's rebuke, a brother's harshness for her;
> my chiefest end was to spare her heart the grief of a word.

Once more, the following lines do not breathe the spirit of infanticide:—

> Fortune has brought me down (her wonted way)
> from station great and high to low estate;
> Fortune has rent away my plenteous store:
> of all my wealth, honour alone is left.
> Fortune has turned my joy to tears: how oft
> did Fortune make me laugh with what she gave!
> But for these girls, the Ḳaṭa's downy brood,
> unkindly thrust from door to door as hard,
> Far would I roam and wide to seek my bread
> in earth that has no lack of breadth and length;

Nay, but our children in our midst, what else
but our hearts are they walking on the ground?
If but the wind blow harsh on one of them,
mine eye says no to slumber all night long.

Hitherto we have been looking at but one side of Arab life. The Bedawees were indeed the bulk of the race, and furnished the swords of the Muslim conquests; but there was also a vigorous town-life in Arabia, and the citizens waxed rich with the gains of their trafficking. For through Arabia ran the trade-route between East and West: it was the Arab traders who carried the produce of the Yemen to the markets of Syria; and how ancient was their commerce one may divine from the words of a poet of Judæa spoken more than a thousand years before the coming of Moḥammad.

Wedan and Javan from San'a paid for thy produce:
sword-blades, cassia, and calamus were in thy trafficking.
Dedan was thy merchant in saddle-cloths for riding;
Arabia and all the merchants of Kedar, they were the merchants of thy hand:
in lambs and rams and goats, in these were they thy merchants.
The merchants of Sheba and Raamah, they were thy merchants.
with the chief of all spices, and with every precious stone, and gold, they paid for thy produce.
Haran, Aden, and Canneh, the merchants of Sheba, Asshur and Chilmad were thy merchants;
They were thy merchants in excellent wares,
in cloth of blue and broidered work,
in chests of cloth of divers colours, bound with cords and made fast among thy merchandize.[1]

Mekka was the centre of this trading life, the typical Arab city of old times—a stirring little town, with its caravans bringing the silks and woven stuffs of Syria and the far-famed damask, and carrying away the sweet-smelling produce of Arabia, frankincense, cinnamon, sandal-wood, aloe, and myrrh, and the dates and leather

[1] Ezekiel xxvii. 19–24. The identifications of the various names with Arabian towns are partly conjectural, but the general reference is clearly to Arabia. Cf. the 'Speaker's' *Commentary*, vi. 122; and the interpretations of Hitzig, Movers, Tuch, and Ménant.

and metals of the south, and the goods that come to the Yemen from Africa and even India; its assemblies of merchant-princes in the Council Hall near the Kaabeh; and again its young poets running over with love and gallantry; its Greek and Persian slave-girls brightening the luxurious banquet with their native songs, when as yet there was no Arab school of music, and the monotonous but not unmelodious chant of the camel-driver was the national song of Arabia; and its club, where busy men spent their idle hours in playing chess and draughts, or in gossiping with their acquaintance. It was a little republic of commerce, too much infected with the luxuries aud refinements of the states it traded with, yet retaining enough of the free Arab nature to redeem it from the charge of effeminacy.

Mekka was a great home of music and poetry, and this characteristic lasted into Muslim times. There is a story of a certain stonemason who had a wonderful gift of singing. When he was at work the young men used to come and importune him, and bring him gifts of money and food to induce him to sing. He would then make a stipulation that they should first help him in his work; and forthwith they would strip off their cloaks, and the stones would gather round him rapidly. Then he would mount a rock and begin to sing, whilst the whole hill was coloured red and yellow with the variegated garments of his audience. Singers were then held in the highest admiration, and the greatest chiefs used to pay their court to ladies of the musical profession. One of them used to give receptions, open to the whole city, in which she would appear in great state, surrounded by her ladies-in-waiting, each dressed magnificently, and wearing 'an elegant artificial chignon.' It was in this town-life that the worse qualities of the Arab came out; it was here that his raging passion for dicing and his thirst for wine were most prominent. In the desert there was little opportunity for indulging in either luxury; but in a town which often welcomed a caravan bringing goods to the value of twenty thousand pound, such excesses were to be looked for. Excited by the song of the Greek slave-girl and the fumes of mellow wine, the Mekkan would throw the dice till, like the Germans of Tacitus, he had staked and lost his own liberty.

But Mekka was more than a centre of trade and of song. It was the focus of the religion of the Arabs. Thither the tribes went up every year to kiss the black stone which had fallen from heaven in the primeval days of Adam, and to make the seven circuits of the Kaạbeh naked,—for they would not approach God in the garments in which they had done their sins,—and to perform the other ceremonies of the pilgrimage. The Kaạbeh, a cubical building in the centre of Mekka, was the most sacred temple in all Arabia, and it gave its sanctity to all the district around. It had been, saith tradition, first built by Adam from a heavenly model, and then rebuilt from time to time by Seth and Abraham and Ishmael, and less reverend persons, and it contained the sacred things of the land. Here was the black stone, here the great god of red agate, Hubal, and the three hundred and sixty idols, one for each day of the year, which Moḥammad afterwards destroyed in onc day. Here was Abraham's stone and that other which marked the tomb of Ishmael, and hard by Zemzem, the god-sent spring which gushed from the sand when the forefather of the Arabs was perishing of thirst.

The religion of the ancient Arabs, little as we know of it, is especially interesting, inasmuch as the Arabs longest retained the original Semitic character, and hence probably the original Semitic religion: and so in the ancient religion of Arabia we see the religion once professed by Chaldeans, Canaanites, Phœnicians. This ancient religion 'rises little higher than animistic polydaemonism. It is a collection of tribal religions standing side by side, only loosely united, though there are traces of a once closer connection.'[1] The great objects of worship were the sun and the stars and the three moon-goddesses—El-Lát the bright moon, Menáh the dark, and El-'Uzzà the union of the two; whilst a lower cultus of trees, stones, and mountains, supposed to be dwelt-in by souls, shows that the religion had not yet quite risen above simple fetishism. At the time of Moḥammad the Arabs worshipped numerous images, which may have been merely a development from the previous stone-worship, or may have been introduced from intercourse with Christians. There are traces of a belief in a supreme God behind this pantheon, and the moon-goddesses and other divinities were regarded as daughters of *the most high God* (Alláh ta'ála)—a conception also possibly derived from Christianity. The various deities (but not the Supreme Allah) had their fanes, where human sacrifices, though rare, were not unknown; and their cultus was superintended by a hereditary line of seers, who were held in great reverence, but never developed into a priestly caste.

Besides the tribal gods, individual households had their special Penates, to whom was due the first and the last salám of the returning or outgoing host. But in spite of all this superstitious apparatus the Arabs were never a religious people. In the old days, as now, they were reckless, skeptical, materialistic. They had their gods and their divining-arrows, but they were ready to demolish both if the responses proved contrary to their wishes. A great majority believed in no future life nor in a reckoning-day of good and evil. If a few tied camels to the graves of the dead that the corpse might ride mounted to the judgment-seat, it must have been the exception; and if there are some doubtful traces of the doctrine of metempsychosis, this again must have been the creed of the very few.

---

[1] C. P. Tiele, *Outlines of the History of Religion:* tr. J. E. Carpenter, p. 63.

Christianity and Judaism had made but small impress upon the Arabs. There were Jewish tribes in the north, and there is evidence in the Ḳurán and elsewhere that the traditions and rites of Judaism were widely known in Arabia. But the creed was too narrow and too exclusively national to commend itself to the majority of the people. Christianity fared even worse. Whether or not St. Paul went there, it is at least certain that very little effect was produced by the preaching of Christianity in Arabia. We hear of Christians on the borders, and even two or three among the Mekkans, and bishops and churches are spoken of at Dhafár and Nejrán. But the Christianity that the Arabs knew was, like the Judaism of the northern tribes, a very imperfect reflection of the faith it professed to set forth. It had become a thing of the head instead of the heart, and the refinements of monophysite and monothelite doctrines gained no hold upon the Arab mind.

Thus Judaism and Christianity, though they were well known, and furnished many ideas and ceremonies to Islám, were never able to effect any general settlement in Arabia. The common Arabs did not care much about any religion, and the finer spirits found the wrangling dogmatism of the Christian and the narrow isolation of the Jew little to their mind. For there were before the time of Moḥammad men who were dissatisfied with the low fetishism in which their countrymen were plunged, and who protested emphatically against the idle and often cruel superstitions of the Arabs. Not to refer to the prophets, who, as the Ḳurán relates, were sent in old time to the tribes of 'Ád and Thamood to convert them, there was, immediately before the preaching of Moḥammad, a general feeling that a change was at hand; a prophet was expected, and women were anxiously hoping for male children if so be they might mother the Apostle of God; and the more thoughtful minds, tinged with traditions of Judaism, were seeking for what they called 'the religion of Abraham.' These men were called '*Ḥaneefs*,' or skeptics, and their religion seems to have consisted chiefly in a negative position, in denying the superstition of the Arabs, and in only asserting the existence of one sole-ruling God whose absolute slaves are all mankind, without being able to decide on any minor doctrines, or to determine in what manner this one God was to be worshipped. So long as the Ḥaneefs could give their countrymen no more definite creed than this, their influence was limited to a few inquiring and doubting minds. It was reserved for Moḥammad to formulate the faith of the Ḥaneefs in the dogmas of Islám. For the leader of these few 'skeptics' was Zeyd ibn 'Amr, to whom Moḥammad often resorted, and another, Waraḳah, was the cousin of the Prophet and his near neighbour: and thus the Ḥaneefs were the forerunners of the man who was to change the destinies of the Arabs.

We can no longer see the true Arab as he was in 'the Time of Ignorance,' and we cannot but regret our loss; for the Pagan Arab is a noble type of man, though there be nobler. There is much that is admirable in his high mettle, his fine sense of honour, his knightliness, his 'open-handed, both-handed,' generosity, his frank friendship, and his manly independent spirit; and the faults of this wild reckless nature are not to be weighed against its many excellencies. When Moḥammad turned abroad the current of Arab life, he changed the character of the people. The mixture with foreign nations, and the quiet town-life that succeeded to the tumult of conquest, gradually effaced many of the leading ideas of the old Arab nature, and the remnant that still dwell in the land of their fathers have lost much of that nobleness of character which in their ancestors covered a multitude of sins. Moḥammad in part destroyed the Arab and created the Muslim. The last is no amends for the first. The modern Bedawee is neither the one nor the other; he has lost the greatness of the old type without gaining that of the new. As far as the Arabs alone are concerned, Moḥammad effected a temporary good and a lasting harm. As to the world at large, that is matter for another chapter.

II.—*MOḤAMMAD:*

> For every fiery prophet in old times,
> And all the sacred madness of the bard,
> When God made music through them, could but speak
> His music by the framework and the chord;
> And as *he* saw it *he hath* spoken truth.
>
> —*The Holy Grail.*

A PROPHET for the Arabs must fulfil two conditions if he will bring with his good tidings the power of making them accepted: he must spring from the traditional centre of Arabian religion, and he must come of a noble family of pure Arab blood. Moḥammad fulfilled both. His family was that branch of the Ḳureysh which had raised Mekka to the dignity of the undisputed metropolis of Arabia, and which, though impoverished, still held the chief offices of the sacred territory. Moḥammad's grandfather was the virtual chief of Mekka; for to him belonged the guardianship of the Kaạbeh, and he it was who used the generous privilege of giving food and water to the pilgrims who resorted to the 'House of God.' His youngest son, after marrying a kinswoman belonging to a branch of the Ḳureysh, settled at Yethrib (Medina), died before the birth of his son (571), and this son, Moḥammad, lost his mother when he was only six years old. The orphan was adopted by his grandfather, 'Abd-el-Muṭṭalib; and a tender affection sprang up between the chief of eighty years and his little grandson. Many a day the old man might be seen sitting at his wonted place near the Kaạbeh, and sharing his mat with his favourite. He lived but two years more; and at his dying request, his son Aboo-Ṭálib took charge of

Moḥammad, for whom he too ever showed a love as of father and mother.

Such is the bare outline of Moḥammad's childhood; and of his youth we know about as little, though the Arabian biographies abound in legends, of which some may be true and most are certainly false. There are stories of his journeyings to Syria with his uncle, and his encounter with a mysterious monk of obscure faith; but there is nothing to show for this tale, and much to be brought against it. All we can say is, that Moḥammad probably assisted his family in the war of the Fijár, and that he must many a time have frequented the annual Fair of 'Oḳádh, hearing the songs of the desert chiefs and the praise of Arab life, and listening to the earnest words of the Jews and Christians and others who came to the Fair. He was obliged at an early age to earn his own living; for the noble family of the Háshimees, to which he belonged, was fast losing its commanding position, whilst another branch of the Ḳureysh was succeeding to its dignities. The princely munificence of Háshim and 'Abd-el-Muṭṭalib was followed by the poverty and decline of their heirs. The duty of providing the pilgrims with food was given up by the Háshimees to the rival branch of Umeyyeh, whilst they retained only the lighter office of serving water to the worshippers. Moḥammad must take his share in the labour of the family, and he was sent to pasture the sheep of the Ḳureysh on the hills and valleys round Mekka; and though the people despised the shepherd's calling, he himself was wont to look back with pleasure to these early days, saying that God called never a prophet save from among the sheepfolds. And doubtless it was then that he developed that reflective disposition of mind which at length led him to seek the reform of his people, whilst in his solitary wanderings with the sheep he gained that marvellous eye for the beauty and wonder of the earth and sky which resulted in the gorgeous nature-painting of the Ḳurán. Yet he was glad to change this menial work for the more lucrative and adventurous post of camel-driver to the caravans of his wealthy kinswoman Khadeejeh; and he seems to have taken so kindly to the duty, which involved responsibilities, and to have acquitted himself so worthily, that he attracted the notice of his employer, who straightway fell in love with him, and presented him with her hand. The marriage was a singularly happy one, though Moḥammad was scarcely twenty-five and his wife nearly forty, and it brought him that repose and exemption from daily toil which he needed in order to prepare his mind for his great work. But beyond that, it gave him a loving woman's heart, that was the first to believe in his mission, that was ever ready to console him in his despair and to keep alive within him the thin flickering flame of hope when no man believed in him—not even himself—and the world was black before his eyes.

We know very little of the next fifteen years. Khadeejeh bore him sons and daughters, but only the daughters lived. We hear of his joining a league for the protection of the weak and oppressed, and there is a legend of his having acted with wise tact and judgment as arbitrator in a dispute among the great families of Mekka on the occasion of the rebuilding of the Kaạbeh. During this time, moreover, he relieved his still impoverished uncle of the charge of his son 'Alee—afterwards the Bayard of Islám,—and he freed and adopted a certain captive, Zeyd; and these two became his most devoted friends and disciples. Such is the short but characteristic record of these fifteen years of manhood. We know very little about what Moḥammad did, but we hear only one voice as to what he was. Up to the age of forty his unpretending modest way of life had attracted but little notice from his townspeople. He was only known as a simple upright man, whose life was severely pure and refined, and whose true desert sense of honour and faith-keeping had won him the high title of El-Emeen, 'the Trusty.'

Let us see what fashion of man this was, who was about to work a revolution among his countrymen, and change the conditions of social life in a vast part of the world. The picture[1] is drawn from an older man than we have yet seen; but Moḥammad at forty and Moḥammad at fifty or more were probably very little different. 'He was of the middle height, rather thin, but broad of shoulders, wide of chest, strong of bone and muscle. His head was massive, strongly developed. Dark hair, slightly curled, flowed in a dense mass down almost to his shoulders. Even in advanced age it was sprinkled by only about twenty grey hairs—produced by the agonies of his "Revelations." His face was oval-shaped, slightly tawny of colour. Fine, long, arched eyebrows were divided by a vein which throbbed visibly in moments of passion. Great black restless eyes shone out from under long, heavy eyelashes. His nose was large, slightly aquiline. His teeth, upon which he bestowed great care, were well set, dazzling white. A full beard framed his manly face. His skin was clear and soft, his complexion "red and white," his hands were as "silk and satin," even as those of a woman. His step was quick and elastic, yet firm, and as that of one "who steps from a high to a low place." In turning his face he would also turn his full body. His whole gait and presence were dignified and imposing. His countenance was mild and pensive. His laugh was rarely more than a smile. . . .

'In his habits he was extremely simple, though he bestowed great care on his person. His eating and drinking, his dress and his furniture, retained, even when he had reached the fulness of power, their almost primitive nature. The only luxuries he indulged in were, besides arms, which he highly prized, a pair of yellow boots, a present from the Negus of Abyssinia. Perfumes, however, he loved passionately, being most sensitive of smell. Strong drinks he abhorred.

[1] Deutsch. *Lit. Remains*, pp. 70–72.

'His constitution was extremely delicate. He was nervously afraid of bodily pain; he would sob and roar under it. Eminently unpractical in all common things of life, he was gifted with mighty powers of imagination, elevation of mind, delicacy and refinement of feeling. "He is more modest than a virgin behind her curtain." it was said of him. He was most indulgent to his inferiors, and would never allow his awkward little page to be scolded, whatever he did. "Ten years," said Anas, his servant, "was I about the Prophet, and he never said as much as 'uff' to me." He was very affectionate towards his family. One of his boys died on his breast in the smoky house of the nurse, a blacksmith's wife. He was very fond of children. He would stop them in the streets and pat their little cheeks. He never struck any one in his life. The worst expression he ever made use of in conversation was, "What has come to him?—may his forehead be darkened with mud!" When asked to curse some one he replied, "I have not been sent to curse, but to be a mercy to mankind." "He visited the sick, followed any bier he met, accepted the invitation of a slave to dinner, mended his own clothes, milked his goats, and waited upon himself," relates summarily another tradition. He never first withdrew his hand out of another man's palm, and turned not before the other had turned. . . . He was the most faithful protector of those he protected, the sweetest and most agreeable in conversation; those who saw him were suddenly filled with reverence; those who came near him loved him; they who described him would say, "I have never seen his like either before or after." He was of great taciturnity; but when he spoke it was with emphasis and deliberation, and no one could ever forget what he said. He was, however, very nervous and restless withal, often low-spirited, downcast as to heart and eyes. Yet he would at times suddenly break through these broodings, become gay, talkative, jocular, chiefly among his own. He would then delight in telling little stories, fairy tales, and the like. He would romp with the children and play with their toys.'

'He lived with his wives in a row of humble cottages, separated from one another by palm-branches, cemented together with mud. He would kindle the fire, sweep the floor, and milk the goats himself. 'Áïsheh tells us that he slept upon a leathern mat, and that he mended his clothes, and even clouted his shoes, with his own hand. For months together . . . he did not get a sufficient meal. The little food that he had was always shared with those who dropped in to partake of it. Indeed, outside the Prophet's house was a bench or gallery, on which were always to be found a number of the poor, who lived entirely on his generosity, and were hence called the "people of the bench." His ordinary food was dates and water or barley-bread; milk and honey were luxuries of which he was fond, but which he rarely allowed himself. The fare of the desert seemed most congenial to him, even when he was sovereign of Arabia.'[1]

Moḥammad was full forty before he felt himself called to be an apostle to his people. If he did not actually worship the local deities of the place, at least he made no public protest against the fetish worship of the Ḳureysh. Yet in the several phases of his life, in his contact with traders, in his association with Zeyd and other men, he had gained an insight into better things than idols and human sacrifices, divining-arrows and mountains and stars. He had heard a dim echo of some 'religion of Abraham;' he had listened to the stories of the Haggadah; he knew a very little about Jesus of Nazareth. He seems to have suffered long under the burden of doubt and self-distrust. He used to wander about the hills alone, brooding over these things; he shunned the society of men, and 'solitude became a passion to him.'

At length came the crisis. He was spending the

---

[1] R. Bosworth Smith, *Mohammed and Mohammedanism*, 2d ed. p. 131.

sacred months on Mount Ḥirá, 'a huge barren rock, torn by cleft and hollow ravine, standing out solitary in the full white glare of the desert sun, shadowless, flowerless, without well or rill.' Here in a cave Moḥammad gave himself up to prayer and fasting. Long months or even years of doubt had increased his nervous excitable disposition. He had had, they say, cataleptic fits during his childhood, and was evidently more delicately and finely constituted than those around him. Given this nervous nature, and the grim solitude of the hill where he had almost lived for long weary months, blindly feeling after some truth upon which to rest his soul, it is not difficult to believe the tradition of the cave, that Moḥammad heard a voice say, 'Cry!' 'What shall I cry?' he answers—the question that has been burning his heart during all his mental struggles—

> Cry[1]! in the name of thy Lord, who hath created;
> He hath created man from a clot of blood.
> Cry! and thy Lord is the Most Bountiful,
> Who hath taught [writing] by the pen:
> He hath taught man that which he knew not.

Moḥammad arose trembling, and went to Khadeejeh, and told her what he had seen; and she did her woman's part, and believed in him and soothed his terror, and bade him hope for the future. Yet he could not believe in himself. Was he not perhaps mad, possessed by a devil? Were these voices of a truth from God? And so he went again on his solitary wanderings, hearing strange sounds, and thinking them at one time the testimony of Heaven, at another the temptings of Satan or the ravings of madness. Doubting, wondering, hoping, he had fain put an end to a life which had become intolerable in its changings from the heaven of hope to the hell of despair, when again he heard the voice, 'Thou art the messenger of God, and I am Gabriel.' Conviction at length seized

---

[1] Or 'read,' 'recite.' These lines are the beginning of the 96th Soorah of the Ḳur-án.

hold upon him; he was indeed to bring a message of good tidings to the Arabs, the message of God through His angel Gabriel. He went back to Khadeejeh exhausted in mind and body. 'Wrap me, wrap me,' he said; and the word came unto him—

> O thou enwrapped in thy mantle
> Arise and warn!
> And thy Lord,—magnify Him!
> And thy raiment,—purify it!
> And the abomination,—flee it!
> And bestow not favours that thou mayest receive again with increase,
> And for thy Lord wait thou patiently.

There are those who see imposture in all this; for such I have no answer. Nor does it matter whether in a hysterical fit or under any physical disease soever Moḥammad saw these visions and heard these voices. We are not concerned to draw the lines of demarcation between enthusiasm and ecstasy and inspiration. It is sufficient that Moḥammad *did* see these things—the subjective creations of a tormented mind. It is sufficient that he believed them to be a message from on high, and that for years of neglect and persecution and for years of triumph and conquest he acted upon his belief.

Moḥammad now (612) came forward as the Apostle of the One God to the people of Arabia: he was at last well assured that his God was of a truth *the* God, and that He had indeed sent him with a message to his people, that they too might turn from their idols and serve the living God. He was in the minority of one, but he was no longer afraid; he had learnt that self-trust which is the condition of all true work. At first he spoke to his near kinsmen and friends; and it is impossible to overrate the importance of the fact that his closest relations and those who lived under his roof were the first to believe and the staunchest of faith. The prophet who is *with* honour in his own home need appeal to no stronger proof of his sincerity, and that Moḥammad *was* 'a hero to his own valet' is an invincible argument for his earnestness. The motherly Khadeejeh had at once, with a woman's instinct, divined her husband's heart and confirmed his fainting hope by her firm faith in him. His dearest friends, Zeyd and 'Alee, were the next converts; and though to his grief, he could never induce his lifelong protector, Aboo-Tálib, to abandon the gods of his fathers, yet the old man loved him none the less, and said, when he heard of 'Alee's conversion, 'Well, my son, he will not call thee to aught save what is good; wherefore thou art free to cleave unto him.' A priceless aid was gained in the accession of Aboo-Bekr, who succeeded Moḥammad as the first Khalif of Islám, and whose calm judgment and quick sagacity, joined to a gentle and compassionate heart, were of incalculable service to the faith. Aboo-Bekr was one of the wealthiest merchants of Mekka, and exercised no small influence among his fellow-citizens, no less by his character than his position. Like Moḥammad, he had a nickname, Eṣ-Ṣiddeeḳ, 'The True:' *The True* and *The Trusty,*—no mean augury for the future of the religion!

Five converts followed in Aboo-Bekr's steps; among them 'Othmán, the third Khalif, and Ṭalḥah, the man of war. The ranks of the faithful were swelled from humbler sources. There were many negro slaves in Mekka, and of them not a few had been predisposed by earlier teaching to join in the worship of the One God; and of those who were first converted was the Abyssinian Bilál, the original Muëddin of Islám, and ever a devoted disciple of the Prophet. These and others from the Ḳureysh raised the number of Muslims to more than thirty souls by the fourth year of Moḥammad's mission—thirty in three long years, and few of them men of influence!

This small success had been achieved with very little opposition from the idolaters. Moḥammad had not spoken much in public; and when he did speak to strangers, he restrained himself from attacking their worship, and only enjoined them to worship the One God who had created all things. The people were rather interested, and wondered whether he were a soothsayer or madman, or if indeed there were truth in his words. But now (A.D. 615) Moḥammad entered upon a more public career. He summoned the Ḳureysh to a conference at the hill of Eṣ-Ṣafá, and said, 'I am come to you as a warner, and as the forerunner of a fearful punishment. . . . I cannot protect you in this world, nor can I promise you aught in the next life, unless ye say, There is no God but Alláh.' He was laughed to scorn, and the assembly broke up; but from this time he ceased not to preach to the people of a punishment that would come upon the unbelieving city. He told them, in the fiery language of the early soorahs, how God had punished the old tribes of the Arabs who would not believe in His messengers, how the Flood had swallowed up the people who would not hearken to Noah. He swore unto them, by the wonderful sights of nature, by the noonday brightness, by the night when she spreadeth her veil, by the day when it appeareth in glory, that a like destruction would assuredly come upon them if they did not turn away from their idols and serve God alone. He enforced his message with every resource of language and metaphor, till he made it burn in the ears of the people. And then he told them of the Last Day, when a just reckoning should be taken of the deeds they had done; and he spoke of Paradise and Hell with all the glow of Eastern imagery. The people were moved, terrified; conversions increased. It was time the Ḳureysh should take some step. If the idols were destroyed, what would come to them, the keepers of the idols, and their renown throughout the land? How should they retain the allegiance of the neighbouring tribes who came to worship their several divinities at the Kaạbeh? That a few should follow the ravings of a madman or magician who preferred one god above the beautiful deities of Mekka was little matter; but that some leading men of the city should join the sect, and that the magician should terrify the people in open day with his denunciations of the worship which *they* superintended, was intolerable. The chiefs were seriously alarmed, and resolved on a more active policy. Hitherto they had merely ridiculed the professors of this new faith; they would now take stronger measures. Moḥammad himself they dared not touch; for he belonged to a noble family, which, though it was reduced and impoverished, had deserved well of the city, and which, moreover, was now headed by a man who was reverenced throughout Mekka, and was none other than the adoptive father and protector of Moḥammad himself. Nor was it safe to attack the other chief men among the Muslims, for the blood-revenge was no light risk. They were thus compelled to content themselves with the mean satisfaction of torturing the black slaves who had joined the obnoxious faction. They exposed them on the scorching sand, and withheld water till they recanted—which they did, only to profess the faith once more when they were let go. The first Muëddin alone remained steadfast: as he lay half stifled he would only answer, 'Aḥad! Aḥad!'—'One [God]! One!'—till Aboo-Bekr came and bought his freedom, as he was wont to do for many of the miserable victims. Moḥammad was very gentle with these forced renegades: he knew what stuff men are made of, and he bade them be of good cheer for their lips, so that their hearts were sound.

At last, moved by the sufferings of his lowly followers, he advised them to seek a refuge in Abyssinia—'a land of righteousness, wherein no man is wronged;' and in the fifth year of his mission (616) eleven men and four women left Mekka secretly, and were receiveḍ in Abyssinia with welcome and peace. These first emigrants were followed by more the next year, till the number reached one hundred. The Ḳureysh were very wroth at the escape of their victims, and sent ambassadors to the Nejáshee, the Christian king of Abyssinia, to demand that the refugees should be given up to them. But the Nejáshee assembled his bishops and sent for the Muslims and asked them why they had fled; and one of them answered and said—

'O king! we lived in ignorance, idolatry, and unchastity; the strong oppressed the weak; we spoke untruth; we violated the duties of hospitality. Then a prophet arose, one whom we knew from our youth, with whose descent and conduct and good faith and morality we are all well acquainted. He told us to worship one God, to speak truth, to keep good faith, to assist our relations, to fulfil the rights of hospitality, and to abstain from all things impure, ungodly, unrighteous. And he ordered us to say prayers, give alms, and to fast. We believed in him; we followed him. But our countrymen persecuted us, tortured us, and tried to cause us to forsake our religion; and now we throw ourselves upon thy protection. Wilt thou not protect us?' And he recited a chapter of the Ḳurán, which spoke of Christ; and the king and the bishops wept upon their beards. And the king dismissed the messengers and would not give up the men.

The Ḳureysh, foiled in their attempt to recapture the slaves, vented their malice on those believers who remained. Insults were heaped upon the Muslims, and persecution grew hotter each day. For a moment Moḥammad faltered in his work. Could he not spare his people these sufferings? Was it impossible to reconcile the religion of the city with the belief in one supreme God? After all, was the worship of those idols so false a thing? did it not hold the germ of a great truth? And so Moḥammad made his first and last concession. He recited a revelation to the Ḳureysh, in which he spoke respectfully of the three moon-goddesses, and asserted that their intercession with God might be hoped for: 'Wherefore bow down before God and serve Him;' and the whole audience, overjoyed at the compromise, bowed down and worshipped at the name of the God of Moḥammad—the whole city was reconciled to the double religion. But this Dreamer of the Desert was not the man to rest upon a lie. At the price of the whole city of Mekka he would not remain untrue to himself. He came forward and said he had done wrong—the devil had tempted him. He openly and frankly retracted what he had said: and 'As for their idols, they were but empty names which they and their fathers had invented.'

Western biographers have rejoiced greatly over 'Moḥammad's fall.' Yet it was a tempting compromise, and few would have withstood it. And the life of Moḥammad is not the life of a god, but of a man: from first to last it is intensely human. But if for once he was not superior to the temptation of gaining over the whole city and obtaining peace where before there was only bitter persecution, what can we say of his manfully thrusting back the rich prize he had gained, freely confessing his fault, and resolutely giving himself over again to the old indignities and insults? If he was once insincere—and who is not?—how intrepid was his after-sincerity! He was untrue to himself for a while, and he is ever referring to it in his public preaching with shame and remorse; but the false step was more than atoned for by his magnificent recantation.

Moḥammad's influence with the people at large was certainly weakened by this temporary change of front, and the opposition of the leaders of the Ḳureysh, checked for the moment by the Prophet's concession, now that he had repudiated it, broke forth into fiercer flame. They heaped insults upon him, and he could not traverse the city without the encounter of a curse. They threw unclean things at him, and vexed him in his every doing. The protection of Aboo-Ṭálib alone saved him from personal danger. This refuge the Ḳureysh determined to remove. They had attempted before, but had been turned back with a soft answer. They now went to the chief, of fourscore years, and demanded that he should either compel his nephew to hold his peace, or else that he should withdraw his protection. Having thus spoken they departed The old man sent for Moḥammad, and told him what they had said. 'Now therefore save thyself and me also, and cast not upon me a burden heavier than I can bear;' for he was grieved at the strife between his family and his wider kindred, and would fain have seen Moḥammad temporize with the Ḳureysh. But though the Prophet believed that at length his uncle was indeed about to abandon him, his courage and high resolve never faltered. 'Though they should set the sun on my right hand and the moon on my left to persuade me, yet while God commands me I will not renounce my purpose.' But to lose his uncle's love!—he burst into tears, and turned to go. But Aboo-Ṭálib called aloud, 'Son of my brother, come back.' So he came. And he said, 'Depart in peace, my nephew, and say whatsoever thou desirest; for, by the Lord, I will never deliver thee up.'

The faithfulness of Aboo-Ṭálib was soon to be tried. At first, indeed, things looked brighter. The old chief's firm bearing overawed the Ḳureysh, and they were still more cowed by two great additions that were now joined to the Muslim ranks. One was Moḥammad's uncle, Ḥamzeh, 'the Lion of God,' a mighty hunter and warrior of the true Arab mettle, whose sword was worth twenty of weaker men to the cause of Islám. The other was 'Omar, afterwards Khalif, whose fierce impulsive nature had hitherto marked him as a violent opponent of the new faith, but who afterwards proved himself one of the mainstays of Islám. The gain of two such men first frightened then maddened the Ḳureysh. The leaders met together and consulted what they should do. It was no longer a case of an enthusiast followed by a crowd of slaves and a few worthy merchants; it was a faction led by stout warriors, such as Ḥamzeh, Ṭalḥah, 'Omar,—half-a-dozen picked swordsmen; and the Muslims, emboldened by their new allies, were boldly surrounding the Kaạbeh, and performing the rites of their religion in the face of all the people. The Ḳureysh resolved on extreme measures.

They determined to shut off the obnoxious family of the Háshimees from the rest of their kindred. The chiefs drew up a document, in which they vowed that they would not marry with the Háshimees, nor buy and sell with them, nor hold with them any communication soever; and this they hung up in the Kaạbeh.

The Háshimees were not many enough to fight the whole city, so they went every man of them, save one, to the shi-b (or quarter) of Aboo-Ṭálib,—a long, narrow mountain defile on the eastern skirts of Mekka, cut off by rocks or walls from the city, except for one narrow gateway,—and there shut themselves up. For though the ban did not forbid them to go about as heretofore, they knew that no soul would speak with them, and that they would be subject to the maltreatment of any vagabond they met. So they collected their stores and waited. Every man of the family, Muslim or Pagan, cast in his lot with their common kinsman, Moḥammad, saving only his own uncle, Aboo-Lahab, a determined enemy to Islám, to whom a special denunciation is justly consecrated in the Ḳurán.

For two long years the Háshimees remained shut up in their quarter. Only at the pilgrimage-time—when the blessed institution of the sacred months made violence sacrilege—could Moḥammad come forth and speak unto the people of the things that were in his heart to say. Scarcely any converts were made during this weary time; and most of those who had previously been converted, and did not belong to the doomed clan, took refuge in Abyssinia; so that in the seventh year of Moḥammad's mission there were probably not more than twelve Muslims of any weight who remained by him. Still the Háshimees remained in their quarter. It seemed as if they must all perish: their stores were almost gone, and the cries of starving children could be heard outside. Kind-hearted neighbours would sometimes smuggle-in a camel's load of food, but it availed little. The Ḳureysh themselves were getting ashamed of their work, and were wishing for an excuse for releasing their kinsmen. The excuse came in time. It was discovered that the deed of ban was eaten up by worms, and Aboo-Ṭálib turned the discovery to his advantage. The venerable old chief went out and met the Ḳureysh at the Kaạbeh, and pointing to the crumbling leaf he bitterly reproached them with their hardness of heart towards their brethren: then he departed. And straightway there rose up five chiefs, heads of great families, and, amid the murmurs of the fiercer spirits who were still for no quarter, they put on their armour, and going to the shi-b of Aboo-Ṭálib, bade the Háshimees come forth in peace. And they came forth.

It was now the eighth year of Moḥammad's mission; and for the last two years, wasted in excommunication, Islám had almost stood still, at least externally. For though Moḥammad's patient bearing under the ban had gained over a few of his imprisoned clan to his side, he had made no converts beyond the walls of his quarter. During the sacred months he had gone forth to speak to the people,—to the caravans of strangers and the folk at the fairs,—but he had no success; for hard behind him followed Aboo-Lahab, the squinter, who mocked at him, and told the people he was only 'a liar and a sabian.' And the people answered that his own kindred must best know what he was, and they would hear nothing from him. The bold conduct of the five chiefs had indeed secured for Moḥammad a temporary respite from persecution; but this relief was utterly outweighed by the troubles that now fell upon him and fitly gave that year the name of 'The Year of Mourning.' For soon after the revoking of the ban Aboo-Ṭálib died, and five weeks later Khadeejeh. In the first Moḥammad lost his ancient protector, who, though he would never give up his old belief, had yet faithfully guarded the Prophet from his childhood upwards, and, with the true Arab sentiment of kinship, had subjected himself and his clan to years of persecution and poverty in order to defend his brother's son from his enemies. The death of Khadeejeh was even a heavier calamity to Moḥammad. She first had believed in him, and she had ever been his angel of hope and consolation. To his death he cherished a tender regret for her; and when his young bride 'Áïsheh, the favourite of his declining years, jealously abused 'that toothless old woman,' he answered with indignation, 'When I was poor, she enriched me; when they called me a liar, she alone believed in me; when all the world was against me, she alone remained true.'

Moḥammad might well feel himself alone in the world. Most of his followers were in Abyssinia; only a few tried friends remained at Mekka. All the city was against him; his protector was dead, and his faithful wife. Dejected, almost hopeless, he would try a new field. If Mekka rejected him, might not Et-Ṭáïf give him welcome? He set out on foot on his journey of seventy miles, taking only Zeyd with him; and he told the people of Et-Ṭáïf his simple message. They stoned him out of the city for three miles. Bleeding and fainting, he paused to rest in an orchard, to recover strength before he went back to the insults of his own people. The owners of the place sent him some grapes; and he gathered up his strength once more, and bent his weary feet towards Mekka. On the way, as he slept, his fancy called up a strange dream: men had rejected him, and now he thought he saw the Jinn, the spirits of the air, falling down and worshipping the One God, and bearing witness to the truth of Islám. Heartened by the vision, he pushed on; and when Zeyd asked him if he did not fear to throw himself again into the hands of the Ḳureysh, he answered, 'God will protect His religion and help His prophet.'

So this lonely man came back to dwell among his enemies. Though a brave Arab gentleman, compassionating his aloneness, gave him the Bedawee pledge of protection, yet he well knew that the power of his foes made such protection almost useless, and at any time he might be assassinated. But the Ḳureysh had not yet come to think of the last resource, and meanwhile a new prospect was opening out for Moḥammad. That same year, as he was visiting the caravans of the pilgrims who had come from all parts of Arabia to worship at the Kaạbeh, he found a group of men of Yethrib who were willing to listen to his words. He expounded to them the faith he was sent to preach, and he told them how his people had rejected him, and asked them whether Yethrib would receive him. The men were impressed with his words and professed Islám, and promised to bring news the next year; then they returned home and talked of this matter to their brethren. Now at Yethrib, besides two pagan tribes that had migrated upwards from the south, there were three clans of Jewish Arabs. Between the pagans and Jews, and then between the two pagan clans, there had been deadly wars; and now there were many parties in the city, and no one was master. The Jews, on the one hand, were expecting their Messiah; the pagans looked for a prophet. If Moḥammad were not the Messiah, the Jews thought that he might at least be their tool to subdue their pagan rivals. 'Whether he is a prophet or not,' said the pagans, 'he is our kinsman by his mother, and will help us to overawe the Jews; and if he is the coming prophet, it is our policy to recognise him before those Jews who are always threatening us with their Messiah.' The teaching of Moḥammad was so nearly Jewish, that a union of the two creeds might be hoped for; whilst to the pagan Arabs of Yethrib monotheism was no strange doctrine. All parties were therefore willing to receive Moḥammad and at least try the experiment of his influence. As a peace-maker, prophet, or messiah, he would be equally welcome in a city torn asunder by party jealousies.

When the time of pilgrimage again came round, Moḥammad waited at the appointed place in a secluded glen, and there met him men from the two pagan tribes of

Yethrib—the clans of Khazraj and Aws—ten from one and two from the other. They told him of the willingness of their people to embrace Islám, and their hope to make ready the city for his welcome. They plighted their faith with him in these words: 'We will not worship save one God; we will not steal, nor commit adultery, nor kill our children; we will in nowise slander, nor will we disobey the prophet in anything that is right.' This is the first pledge of the 'Aḳabeh.

The twelve men of Yethrib went back and preached Islám to their people. 'So prepared was the ground, so zealous the propagation, and so apt the method, that the new faith spread rapidly from house to house and from tribe to tribe. The Jews looked on in amazement at the people, whom they had in vain endeavoured for generations to convince of the errors of Polytheism and dissuade from the abominations of idolatry, suddenly and of their own accord casting away their idols and professing belief in God alone.' They asked Moḥammad to send them a teacher versed in the Ḳurán, so anxious were they to know Islám truly; and Muṣ'ab was sent, and taught them and conducted their worship; so that Islám took deep root at Yethrib.

Meanwhile Moḥammad was still among the Ḳureysh at Mekka. His is now an attitude of waiting; he is listening for news from his distant converts. Resting his hopes upon them, and despairing of influencing the Mekkans, he does not preach so much as heretofore. He holds his peace mainly, and bides his time. One hears little of this interval of quietude. Islám seems stationary at Mekka, and its followers are silent and reserved. The Ḳureysh are joyful at the ceasing of those denunciations which terrified whilst they angered them, yet they are not quite satisfied. The Muslims have a waiting look, as though there were something at hand.

It was during this year of expectation that the Prophet's celebrated 'Night Journey' took place. This Mi'ráj has been the subject of extravagant embellishments on the part of the traditionists and commentators, and the cause of much obloquy to the Prophet from his religious opponents. Moḥammad dreamed a dream, and referred to it briefly and obscurely in the Ḳurán. His followers persisted in believing it to have been a reality—an ascent to heaven in the body—till Moḥammad was sick of repeating his simple assertion that it was a dream. The traditional form of this wonderful vision may be read in any life of Moḥammad, and though it is doubtless very different from the story the Prophet himself gave, it is still a grand vision, full of glorious imagery, fraught with deep meaning.

Again the time of pilgrimage came round, and again Moḥammad repaired to the glen of the Mountain-road. Muṣ'ab had told him the good tidings of the spread of the faith at Yethrib, and he was met at the rendezvous by more than seventy men. They came by twos and threes secretly for fear of the Ḳureysh, 'waking not the sleeper, nor tarrying for the absent.' Then Moḥammad recited to them verses from the Ḳurán, and in answer to their invitation that he should come to them, and their profession that their lives were at his service, he asked them to pledge themselves to defend him as they would their own wives and children. And a murmur of eager assent rolled round about from the seventy, and an old man, one of their chiefs, stood forth and said, 'Stretch out thy hand, O Moḥammad.' And the chief struck his own hand into Moḥammad's palm in the frank Bedawee fashion, and thus pledged his fealty. Man after man the others followed, and struck their hands upon Moḥammad's. Then he chose twelve of them as leaders over the rest, saying, 'Moses chose from among his people twelve leaders. Ye shall be the sureties for the rest, even as the apostles of Jesus were; and I am the surety for my people.' A voice of some stranger was heard near by, and the assembly hastily dispersed and stole back to their camp. This is the second pledge of the 'Aḳabeh.

The Kureysh knew that some meeting had taken place, and though they could not bring home the offence to any of the Yethrib pilgrims, they kept a stricter watch on the movements of Mohammad and his friends after the pilgrims had returned homeward. It was clear that Mekka was no longer a safe place for the Muslims, and a few days after the second pledge Mohammad told his followers to betake themselves secretly to Yethrib. For two months at the beginning of the eleventh year of the mission (622) the Muslims were leaving Mekka in small companies to make the journey of 250 miles to Yethrib. One hundred families had gone, and whole quarters of the city were deserted, left with empty houses and locked doors, 'a prey to woe and wind.' There were but three believers now remaining in Mekka—these were Mohammad, Aboo-Bekr, and 'Alee. Like the captain of a sinking ship, the Prophet would not leave till all the crew were safe. But now they were all gone save his two early friends, and everything was ready for the journey; still the Prophet did not go. But the Kureysh, who had been too much taken by surprise to prevent the emigration, now prepared measures for a summary vengence on the disturber of their peace and the emptier of their city. They set a watch on his house, and, it is said, commissioned a band of armed youths of different families to assassinate him together, that the blood recompense might not fall on one household alone. But Mohammad had warning of his danger, and leaving 'Alee to deceive the enemy, he was concealed with Aboo-Bekr in a narrow-mouthed cave on Mount Thór, an hour-and-a-half's journey from Mekka, before the Kureysh knew of his escape. For three days they remained hidden there, while their enemies were searching the country for them. Once they were very near, and Abob-Bekr trembled:—'We are but two.' 'Nay,' answered Mohammad, 'we are three, for God is with us.' And a spider, they say, wove its web over the entrance of the cave, so that the Kureysh passed on, thinking that no man had entered there.

On the third night the pursuit had been almost given over, and the two fugitives took up their journey again. Mounted on camels they journeyed to Yethrib. In eight days they reached the outskirts of the city (September 622). Moḥammad was received with acclamation, and took up his residence among his kindred. The seat of Islám was transferred from Mekka to Yethrib, henceforward to be known as Medina,—*Medeenet-en-Nebee*, 'the City of the Prophet.'

This is the *Hijreh*, or Flight of the Prophet, from which the Muslims date their history. Their first year began on the 16th day of June of the Year of Grace 622.

A great change now comes over the Prophet's life. It is still the same man, but the surroundings are totally different; the work to be done is on a wider, rougher stage. Thus far we have seen a gentle, thoughtful boy tending the sheep round Mekka;—a young man of little note, of whom the people only knew that he was pure and upright and true;—then a man of forty whose solitary communion with his soul has pressed him to the last terrible questions that each man, if he will think at all, must some time ask himself—What is life? What does this world mean? What is reality, what is truth? Long months, years perhaps, we know not how long and weary, filled with the tortures of doubt and the despair of ever attaining to the truth, filled with the dreary thought of his aloneness in the relentless universe, and the longing to end it all, brought at last their fruits—sure conviction of the great secret of life, a firm belief in the Creator in whom all things live and move and have their being, whom to serve is man's highest duty and privilege, the one thing to be done. And then ten years of struggling with careless, unthinking idolators; ten years of slow results, the gaining over of a few close friends, the devoted attachment of some slaves and men of the meaner rank; finally, the conversion of half-a-dozen great citizen chiefs, ending in the flight of the whole brotherhood of believers from their native city and their welcome to a town of strangers, where the faith had forced itself home to the hearts of perhaps two hundred citizens. It was but little that was done; so many years of toil, of indomitable courage and perseverance and long-suffering, and only about three hundred converts at the end! But it was the seed of a great harvest. Moḥammad had shown men what he was; the nobility of his character, his strong friendship, his endurance and courage, above all, his earnestness and fiery enthusiasm for the truth he came to preach,—these things had revealed the hero, the master whom it was alike impossible to disobey and impossible not to love. Henceforward it is only a question of time. As the men of Medina come to know Moḥammad, they too will devote themselves to him body and soul; and the enthusiasm will catch fire and spread among the tribes till all Arabia is at the feet of the Prophet of the One God. 'No emperor with his tiaras was obeyed as this man in a cloak of His own clouting.' He had the gift of influencing men, and he had the nobility only to influence them for good.

We have now to see Moḥammad as king. Though he came as a fugitive, rejected as an impostor by his own citizens, yet it was not long before his word was supreme in his adopted city. He had to rule over a mixed and divided people, and this must have helped him to the supreme voice. There were four distinct parties at Medina. First, the 'Refugees' (Muḥájiroon), who had fled from Mekka; on these Moḥammad could always rely with implicit faith. But he attached equal importance to the early converts of Medina, who had invited him among them and given him a home when the future seemed very hopeless before him, and who were thenceforward known by the honourable title of the 'Helpers' (Anṣár). How devoted was the affection of these men is shown by the well-known scene at El-Ji'ráneh, when the Helpers were discontented with their share of the spoils, and Moḥammad answered, 'Why are ye disturbed in mind because of the things of this life wherewith I have sought to incline the hearts of these men of Mekka into Islám, whereas ye are already steadfast in the faith? Are ye not satisfied that others should obtain the flocks and the camels, while ye carry back the Prophet of the Lord unto your homes? Nay, I will not leave you for ever. If all mankind went one way, and the men of Medina went another way, verily I would go the way of the men of Medina. The Lord be favourable unto them, and bless them, and their sons, and their sons' sons, for ever!' And the 'Helpers' wept upon their beards, and cried with one voice, 'Yea, we are well satisfied, O Prophet, with our lot.' To retain the allegiance of the Refugees and the Helpers was never a trouble to Moḥammad; the only difficulty was to rein in their zeal and hold them back from doing things of blood and vengeance on the enemies of Islám. To prevent the danger of jealousy between the Refugees and the Helpers, Moḥammad assigned each Refugee to one of the Anṣár to be his brother; and this tie of gossipry superseded all nearer ties, till Moḥammad saw the time was over when it was needed. The third party in Medina was that of the 'Disaffected,' or in the language of Islám the 'Hypocrites' (Munáfiḳoon). This was composed of the large body of men who gave in their nominal allegiance to Moḥammad and his religion when they saw they could not safely withstand his power, but who were always ready to turn about if they thought there was a chance of his overthrow. Moḥammad treated these men and their leader 'Abdallah ibn Ubayy (who himself aspired to the sovranty of Medina) with patient courtesy and friendliness, and, though they actually deserted him more than once at vitally critical moments, he never retaliated, even when he was strong enough to crush them, but rather sought to win them over heartily to his cause by treating them as though they were what he would have them be. The result was that this party gradually diminished and became absorbed in the general mass of earnest Muslims, and though up to its leader's death it constantly called forth Moḥammad's powers of conciliation, after that it vanished from the history of parties.

The fourth party was the real thorn in the Prophet's side. It consisted of the Jews, of whom three tribes were settled in the suburbs of Medina. They had at first been well disposed to Moḥammad's coming. He could not indeed be the Messiah, because he was not of the lineage of David; but he would do very well to pass off upon their neighbours, the pagan Arabs, as, if not the Messiah, at least a great prophet; and by his influence the Jews might regain their old supremacy in Medina. Moḥammad's teaching was very nearly Jewish—they had taught him the fables of their Haggadah, and he believed in their prophets—why should he not be one of them and help them to the dominion? When Moḥammad came, they found out their mistake; instead of a tool they had a master. He told the people, indeed, the stories of the Midrash, and he professed to revive the religion of Abraham: but he added to this several damning articles; he taught that Jesus *was* the Messiah, and that no other Messiah was to be looked for; and, moreover, whilst reverencing and inculcating the doctrine of the Hebrew prophets and of Christ, as he knew it, he yet insisted on his own mission as in nowise inferior to theirs—as, in fact, the seal of prophecy by which all that went before was confirmed or abrogated. The illusion was over; the Jews would have nothing to say to Islám: they set themselves instead to oppose it, ridicule it, and vex its Preacher in every way that their notorious ingenuity could devise.

The step was false: the Jews missed their game, and they had to pay for it. Whether it was possible to form a coalition,—whether the Jews might have induced Moḥammad to waive certain minor points if they recognised his prophetic mission,—it is difficult to say. It seems most probable that Moḥammad would not have yielded a jot to their demands, and would have accepted nothing short of unconditional surrender to his religion. And it is at least doubtful whether Islám would have gained anything by a further infusion of Judaism. It already contained all that it could assimilate of the Hebrew faith; the rest was too narrow for the universal scope of Islám. The religion of Moḥammad lost little, we may be sure, by the standing aloof of the Arabian Jews; but the Jews themselves lost much. Moḥammad, indeed, treated them kindly so long as kindness was possible. He made a treaty with them, whereby the rights of the Muslims and the Jews were defined. They were to practise their several religions unmolested; protection and security were promised to all the parties to the treaty, irrespective of creed; each was to help the other if attacked; no alliance was to be made with the Ḳureysh; war was to be made in common, and no war could be made without the consent of Moḥammad: crime alone could do away with the protection of this treaty.

But the Jews would not content themselves with standing aloof; they must needs act on the offensive. They began by asking Moḥammad hard questions out of their law, and his answers they easily refuted from their books. They denied all knowledge of the Jewish stories in the Ḳurán—though they knew that they came from their own Haggadah, which was ever in their mouths in their own quarter,—and they showed him their Bible, where, of course, the Haggadistic legends were not to be found. Moḥammad had but one course open to him—to say they had suppressed or changed their books; and he denounced them accordingly, and said that his was the true account of the patriarchs and prophets, revealed from heaven. Not satisfied with tormenting Moḥammad with questions on that Tórah which they were always wrangling about themselves, they took hold of the every day formulas of Islám, the daily prayers and ejaculations, and, 'twisting their tongues,' mispronounced them so that they meant something absurd or blasphemous. When asked which they preferred, Islám or idolatry, they frankly avowed that they preferred idolatry. To lie about their own religion and to ridicule another religion that was doing a great and good work around them was not enough for these Jews; they must set their poets to work to lampoon the women of the believers in obscene verse, and such outrages upon common decency, not to say upon the code of Arab honour and chivalry, became a favourite occupation among the poets of the Jewish clans.

These were offences against the religion and the persons of the Muslims. They also conspired against the state. Mohammad was not only the preacher of Islám, he was also the king of Medina, and was responsible for the safety and peace of the city. As a prophet, he could afford to ignore the jibes of the Jews, though they maddened him to fury; but as the chief of the city, the general in a time of almost continual warfare, when Medina was kept in a state of military defence and under a sort of military discipline, he could not overlook treachery. He was bound by his duty to his subjects to suppress a party that might (and nearly did) lead to the sack of the city by investing armies. The measures he took for this object have furnished his European biographers with a handle for attack. It is, I believe, solely on the ground of his treatment of the Jews that Mohammad has been called 'a bloodthirsty tyrant:' it would certainly be difficult to support the epithet on other grounds.

The bloodthirstiness consists in this: some half-dozen Jews, who had distinguished themselves by their virulence against the Muslims, or by their custom of carrying information to the common enemy of Medina, were executed; two of the three Jewish clans were sent into exile, just as they had previously come into exile, and the third was exterminated—the men killed, and the women and children made slaves. The execution of the half-dozen marked Jews is generally called assassination, because a Muslim was sent secretly to kill each of the criminals. The reason is almost too obvious to need explanation. There were no police or law-courts or even courts-martial at Medina; some one of the followers of Mohammad must therefore be the executor of the sentence of death, and it was better it should be done quietly, as the executing of a man openly before his clan would have caused a brawl and more bloodshed and retaliation, till the whole city had become mixed up in the quarrel. If secret assassination is the word for such deeds, secret assassination was a necessary part of the internal government of Medina. The men must be killed, and best in that way. In saying this I assume that Moḥammad was cognisant of the deed, and that it was not merely a case of private vengeance; but in several instances the evidence that traces these executions to Moḥammad's order is either entirely wanting or is too doubtful to claim our credence.

Of the sentences upon the three whole clans, that of exile, passed upon two of them, was clement enough. They were a turbulent set, always setting the people of Medina by the ears; and finally a brawl followed by an insurrection resulted in the expulsion of one tribe; and insubordination, alliance with enemies, and a suspicion of conspiracy against the Prophet's life, ended similarly for the second. Both tribes had violated the original treaty, and had endeavoured in every way to bring Moḥammad and his religion to ridicule and destruction. The only question is whether their punishment was not too light. Of the third clan a fearful example was made, not by Moḥammad, but by an arbiter appointed by themselves. When the Ḳureysh and their allies were besieging Medina, and had well-nigh stormed the defences, this Jewish tribe entered into negotiations with the enemy, which were only circumvented by the diplomacy of the Prophet. When the besiegers had retired, Moḥammad naturally demanded an explanation of the Jews. They resisted in their dogged way, and were themselves besieged and compelled to surrender at discretion. Moḥammad, however, consented to the appointing of a chief of a tribe allied to the Jews as the judge who should pronounce sentence upon them. The man in question was a fierce soldier, who had been wounded in the attack on the Jews, and indeed died from his wound the same day. This chief gave sentence that the men, in number some six hundred, should be killed, and the women and children enslaved; and the sentence was carried out. It was a harsh, bloody sentence, worthy of the episcopal generals of the army against the Albigenses, or of the deeds of the Augustan age of Puritanism; but it must be remembered that the crime of these men was high treason against the State, during time of siege; and those who have read how Wellington's march could be traced by the bodies of deserters and pillagers hanging from the trees, need not be surprized at the summary execution of a traitorous clan.

Whilst Moḥammad's supremacy was being established and maintained among the mixed population of Mekka, a vigorous warfare was being carried on outside with his old persecutors, the Ḳureysh. On the history of this war, consisting as it did mainly of small raids and attacks upon caravans, I need not dwell; its leading features were the two battles of Bedr and Oḥud, in the first of which three hundred Muslims, though outnumbered at the odds of three to one, were completely victorious (A.D. 624, A.H. 2); whilst at Oḥud, being outnumbered in the like proportion and deserted by the 'Disaffected' party, they were almost as decisively defeated (A.H. 3). Two years later the Ḳureysh, gathering together their allies, advanced upon Medina and besieged it for fifteen days; but the foresight of Moḥammad in digging a trench, and the enthusiasm of the Muslims in defending it, resisted all assaults, and the coming of the heavy storms for which the climate of Medina is noted drove the enemy back to Mekka. The next year (A.H. 6) a ten years' truce was concluded with the Ḳureysh, in pursuance of which a strange scene took place in the following spring. It was agreed that Moḥammad and his people should perform the Lesser Pilgrimage, and that the Ḳureysh should for that purpose vacate Mekka for three days. Accordingly, in March 629, about two thousand Muslims, with Moḥammad at their head on his famous camel El-Ḳaṣwá—the same on which he had fled from Mekka—trooped down the valley and performed the rites which every Muslim to this day observes.

'It was surely a strange sight which at this time presented itself in the vale of Mekka,—a sight unique in the history of the world. The ancient city is for three days evacuated by all its inhabitants, high and low, every house deserted; and, as they retire, the exiled converts, many years banished from their birthplace, approach in a great body, accompanied by their allies, revisit the empty homes of their childhood, and within the short allotted space fulfil the rites of pilgrimage. The ousted inhabitants, climbing the heights around, take refuge under tents or other shelter among the hills and glens; and, clustering on the overhanging peak of Aboo-Ḳubeys, thence watch the movements of the visitors beneath, as with the Prophet at their head they make the circuit of the Kaạbeh and the rapid procession between Eṣ-Ṣafá and Marwah; and anxiously scan every figure if perchance they may recognise among the worshippers some long-lost friend or relative. It was a scene rendered possible only by the throes which gave birth to Islám.'[1]

When the three days were over, Moḥammad and his party peaceably returned to Medina; and the Mekkans re-entered their homes. But this pilgrimage, and the self-restraint of the Muslims therein, advanced the cause of Islám among its enemies. Converts increased daily, and

---

[1] Sir W. Muir, *Life of Mahomet*, 402.

some leading men of the Ḳureysh now went over to Moḥammad. The clans around were sending in their deputations of homage. But the final keystone was set in the eighth year of the flight (A.D. 630), when a body of Ḳureysh broke the truce by attacking an ally of the Muslims; and Moḥammad forthwith marched upon Mekka with ten thousand men, and the city, defence being hopeless, surrendered. Now was the time for the Prophet to show his bloodthirsty nature. His old persecutors are at his feet. Will he not trample on them, torture them, revenge himself after his own cruel manner? Now the man will come forward in his true colours: we may prepare our horror, and cry shame beforehand.

But what is this? Is there no blood in the streets? Where are the bodies of the thousands that have been butchered? Facts are hard things; and it is a fact that the day of Moḥammad's greatest triumph over his enemies was also the day of his grandest victory over himself. He freely forgave the Ḳureysh all the years of sorrow and cruel scorn they had inflicted on him: he gave an amnesty to the whole population of Mekka. Four criminals, whom justice condemned, made up Moḥammad's proscription list when he entered as a conqueror the city of his bitterest enemies. The army followed his example, and entered quietly and peaceably; no house was robbed, no woman insulted. One thing alone suffered destruction. Going to the Kaạbeh, Moḥammad stood before each of the three hundred and sixty idols and pointed to it with his staff, saying, 'Truth is come and lying is undone,' and at these words his attendants hewed it down; and all the idols and household gods of Mekka and round about were destroyed.

It was thus that Moḥammad entered again his native city. Through all the annals of conquest, there is no triumphant entry like unto this one.

The taking of Mekka was soon followed by the adhesion of all Arabia. Every reader knows the story of the spread of Islám. The tribes of every part of the peninsula sent embassies to do homage to the Prophet. Arabia was not enough: the Prophet had written in his bold uncompromising way to the great kings of the East, to the Persian Khusru, and the Greek Emperor; and these little knew how soon his invitation to the faith would be repeated, and how quickly Islám would be knocking at their doors with no faltering hand.

The Prophet's career was near its end. In the tenth year of the Flight, twenty years after he had first felt the Spirit move him to preach to his people, he resolved once more to leave his adopted city and go to Mekka to perform a farewell pilgrimage. And when the rites were done in the valley of Miná, the Prophet spoke unto the multitude—the forty thousand pilgrims—with solemn last words.[1]

'Ye People! Hearken to my words; for I know not whether after this year I shall ever be amongst you here again.

'Your Lives and your Property are sacred and inviolable amongst one another until the end of time.

'The Lord hath ordained to every man the share of his inheritance: a Testament is not lawful to the prejudice of heirs.

'The child belongeth to the Parent; and the violator of Wedlock shall be stoned.

'Ye people! Ye have rights demandable of your Wives, and they have rights demandable of you. Treat your women well.

'And your Slaves, see that you feed them with such food as ye eat yourselves, and clothe them with the stuff ye wear. And if they commit a fault which ye are not willing to forgive, then sell them, for they are the servants of the Lord, and are not to be tormented.

---

[1] The following is an abridgment: cp. Muir 485, and the *Seeret-er-Rasool*, tr. Weil, ii. 316, 317.

'Ye people! Hearken unto my speech and comprehend it. Know that every Muslim is the brother of every other Muslim. All of you are on the same equality: ye are one Brotherhood.'

Then, looking up to heaven, he cried, 'O Lord! I have delivered my message and fulfilled my mission.' And all the multitude answered, 'Yea, verily hast thou'!—'O Lord! I beseech Thee, bear Thou witness to it'! and, like Moses, he lifted up his hands and blessed the people.

Three months more and Moḥammad was dead.

A.H. 11. June, 632.

It is a hard thing to form a calm estimate of the Dreamer of the Desert. There is something so tender and womanly, and withal so heroic, about the man, that one is in peril of finding the judgment unconsciously blinded by the feeling of reverence and well-nigh love that such a nature inspires. He who, standing alone, braved for years the hatred of his people, is the same who was never the first to withdraw his hand from another's clasp, the beloved of children, who never passed a group of little ones without a smile from his wonderful eyes and a kind word for them, sounding all the kinder in that sweet-toned voice. The frank friendship, the noble generosity, the dauntless courage and hope of the man, all tend to melt criticism in admiration.

In telling in brief outline the story of Mohammad's life I have endeavoured to avoid controversial points. I have tried to convey in the simplest manner the view of that life which a study of the authorities must force upon every unbiassed mind. Many of the events of Moḥammad's life have been distorted and credited with ignoble motives by European biographers; but on the facts they mainly agree, and these I have narrated, without encumbering them with the ingenious adumbrations of their learned recorders. But there are some things in the Prophet's life which have given rise to charges too weighty to be dismissed without discussion. He has been accused of cruelty, sensuality, and insincerity; he has been called a 'bloodthirsty tyrant,' a voluptuary, and an impostor.

The charge of cruelty scarcely deserves consideration. I have already spoken of the punishment of the Jews, which forms the ground of the accusation. One has but to refer to Moḥammad's conduct to the prisoners after the battle of Bedr, to his patient tolerance towards his enemies at Medina, his gentleness to his people, his love of children and the dumb creatures, and above all, his bloodless entry into Mekka, and the complete amnesty he gave to those who had been his bitter enemies during eighteen years of insult and persecution and finally open war, to show that cruelty was no part of Moḥammad's nature.

To say that Moḥammad, or any other Arab, was sensual in a higher degree than an ordinary European is simply to enounce a well-worn axiom: the passions of the men of the sunland are not as those of the chill north. But to say that Moḥammad was a voluptuary is false. The simple austerity of his daily life, to the very last, his hard mat for sleeping on, his plain food, his self-imposed menial work, point him out as an ascetic rather than a voluptuary in most senses of the word. Two things he loved, perfumes and women; the first was harmless enough, and the special case of his wives has its special answer. A great deal too much has been said about these wives. It is a melancholy spectacle to see professedly Christian biographers gloating over the stories and fables of Moḥammad's domestic relations like the writers and readers of 'society' journals. It is, of course, a fact that whilst the Prophet allowed his followers only four wives he took more than a dozen himself; but be it remembered that, with his unlimited power, he need not have restricted himself to a number insignificant compared with the ḥareems of some of his successors, that he never divorced one of his wives, that all of them save one were widows, and that one of these widows was endowed with so terrific a temper that Aboo-Bekr and 'Othmán had already politely declined the honour of her alliance before the Prophet married her: the gratification of living with a vixen cannot surely be excessive. Several of these marriages must have been entered into from the feeling that those women whose husbands had fallen in battle for the faith, and who had thus been left unprotected, had a claim upon the generosity of him who prompted the fight. Other marriages were contracted from motives of policy, in order to conciliate the heads of rival factions. It was not a high motive, but one does not look for very romantic ideas about love-matches from a man who regarded women as 'crooked ribs,' and whose system certainly does its best to make marriage from love impossible; yet, on the other hand, it was not a sensual motive. Perhaps the strongest reason—one of which it is impossible to over-estimate the force—that impelled Moḥammad to take wife after wife was his desire for male offspring. It was a natural wish that he should have a son who should follow in his steps and carry on his work; but the wish was never gratified, Moḥammad's sons died young. After all, the overwhelming argument is his fidelity to his first wife. When he was little more than a boy he married Khadeejeh, who was fifteen years older than himself, with all the added age that women gain so quickly in the East. For five-and-twenty years Moḥammad remained faithful to his elderly wife, and when she was sixty-five, and they might have celebrated their 'silver wedding,' he was as devoted to her as when first he married her. During all those years there was never a breath of scandal. Thus far Moḥammad's life will bear microscopic scrutiny. Then Khadeejeh died; and though he married many women afterwards, some of them rich in youth and beauty, he never forgot his old wife, and loved her best to the end: 'when I was poor she enriched me, when they called me a liar she alone believed in me, when all the world was against me she alone remained true.' This loving, tender memory of an old wife laid in the grave belongs only to a noble nature; it is not to be looked for in a voluptuary.[1]

When, however, all has been said, when it has been shown that Moḥammad was not the rapacious voluptuary some have taken him for, and that his violation of his own marriage-law may be due to motives reasonable and just from his point of view rather than to common sensuality, there remains the fact that some of the soorahs of the Ḳurán bear unmistakable marks of self-accommodation and personal convenience; that Moḥammad justified his domestic excesses by words which he gave as from God. And hence the third and gravest charge, the charge of imposture. We must clearly understand what is meant by this accusation. It is meant that the Prophet *consciously* fabricated speeches, and palmed them off upon the people as the very word of God. The question, it will at

---

[1] An attempt has been made to explain away Moḥammad's fidelity to Khadeejeh, by adducing the motive of pecuniary prudence. Moḥammad, they say, was a poor man, Khadeejeh rich and powerfully connected; any *affaire de cœur* on the husband's part would have been followed by a divorce and the simultaneous loss of property and position. It is hardly necessary to point out that the fear of poverty —a matter of little consequence in Arabia and at that time—would not restrain a really sensual man for five-and-twenty years; especially when it is by no means certain that Khadeejeh, who loved him with all her heart in a motherly sort of way, would have procured a divorce for any cause soever. And this explanation leaves Moḥammad's loving remembrance of his old wife unaccounted for. If her money alone had curbed him for twenty-five years, one would expect him at her death to throw off the cloak, thank Heaven for the deliverance, and enter at once upon the rake's progress. He does none of those things. The story of Zeyneb, the divorced wife of Zeyd, is a favourite weapon with Moḥammad's accusers. It is not one to enter upon here; but I may say that the lady's own share in the transaction has never been sufficiently considered. In all probability Zeyd, the freed slave, was glad enough to get rid of his too well-born wife, and certainly he bore no rancour against Moḥammad. The real point of the story is the question of forged revelations, which is discussed below.

once be perceived, has nothing whatever to do with the truth or untruth of the revelations. Many an earnest enthusiast has uttered prophecies and exhortations which he firmly believed to be the promptings of the Spirit, and no man can charge such an one with imposture. He thoroughly believes what he says, and the fault is in the judgment, not the conscience. The question is clearly narrowed to this: Did Moḥammad believe he was speaking the words of God equally when he declared that permission was given him to take unto him more wives, as when he proclaimed 'There is no god but God'? It is a question that concerns the conscience of man; and each must answer it for himself. How far a man may be deluded into believing everything he says is inspired it is impossible to define. There are men to-day who would seem to claim infallibility; and in Moḥammad's time it was so much easier to believe in one's self. Now, one never wants a friend to remind him of his weakness; then, there were hundreds who would fain have made the man think himself God. It is wonderful, with his temptations, how great a humility was ever his, how little he assumed of all the god-like attributes men forced upon him. His whole life is one long argument for his loyalty to truth. He had but one answer for his worshippers, 'I am no more than a man, I am only human.' 'Do none enter Paradise save by the mercy of God?' asked 'Áïsheh. 'None, none, none,' he answered. 'Not even thou by thy own merits?' 'Neither shall I enter Paradise unless God cover me with His mercy.' He was a man like unto his brethren in all things save one, and that one difference served only to increase his humbleness, and render him the more sensitive to his shortcomings. He was sublimely confident of this single attribute, that he was the messenger of the Lord of the Daybreak, and that the words he spake came verily from Him. He was fully persuaded—and no man dare dispute his right to the belief—that God had sent him to do a great work among his people in Arabia. Nervous to the verge of madness, subject to hysteria, given to wild dreamings in solitary places, his was a temperament that easily leads itself to religious enthusiasm. He felt a subtle influence within him which he believed to be the movings of the Spirit: he thought he heard a voice; it became real and audible to him, awed and terrified him, so that he fell into frantic fits. Then he would arise and utter some noble saying; and what wonder if he thought it came straight from highest heaven? It was not without a sore struggle that he convinced himself of his own inspiration; but once admitted, the conviction grew with his years and his widening influence for good, and nothing then could shake his belief that he was the literal mouthpiece of the All-Merciful. When a man has come to this point, he cannot be expected to discriminate between this saying and that. As the instrument of God he has lost his individuality; he believes God is ever speaking through his lips; he dare not question the inspiration of the speech lest he should seem to doubt the Giver.

Yet there must surely be a limit to this delusion. There are some passages in the Ḳurán which it is difficult to think Moḥammad truly believed to be the voice of the Lord of the Worlds. Moḥammad's was a sensitive conscience in the early years of his teaching, and it is hard to think that it could have been so obscured in later times that he could really believe in the inspired source of some of his revelations. He may have thought the commands they conveyed necessary, but he could hardly have deemed them divine. In some cases he could scarcely fail to be aware that the object of the 'revelation' was his own comfort or pleasure or reputation, and not the *major Dei gloria,* nor the good of the people.

The truth would seem to be that in the latter part of his life Moḥammad was forced to enlarge the limits of his revelations as the sphere of his influence increased. From a private citizen of Mekka he had become the Emeer, the chief of the Arabs, the ruler of a factious, jealous, turbulent people; and the change must have had its effect upon his character. The man who from addressing a few devout followers in a tent in the desert finds himself the head of a nation of many tribes, king of a country twice the size of France, will find many things difficult that before seemed easy. As a statesman Moḥammad was as great as he was as a preacher of righteousness; but as his field of work enlarged, his mind had to accommodate itself to the needs of commoner minds. He learnt to see the expedient where before he knew only the right. His revelations now deal with the things of earth, when before they looked only towards the things of heaven; and petty social rules, 'general orders,' selfish permissions, are promulgated with the same authority and as from the same divine source as the command to worship one God alone. He governed the nation as a prophet and not as a king, and as a prophet his ordinances must be endorsed with the divine afflatus. He found he must regulate the meanest details of the people's life, and he believed he could only do this by using God's name for his decrees. He doubtless argued himself into the belief that even these petty, and to us sometimes immoral, regulations, being for the good of the people, as he conceived the good, were really God's ordinances; but even thus he had lowered the standard of his teaching, and alloyed with base metal the pure gold of his early ideal. It was a temptation that few men have withstood, but it was, nevertheless, a falling-off from the Moḥammad we loved at Mekka, the simple truth-loving bearer of good tidings to the Arabs.

Yet behind this engrafted character, formed by the difficulties of his position, by the invincible jealousy and treachery of the tribes he governed, the old nature still lived, and ever and anon broke forth in fervid words of faith and hope in the cause and the promises that had been the light and support of his early years of trial. In the late chapters of the Ḳurán, among complicated directions for the Muslim's guidance in all the circumstances of life, we suddenly hear an echo of the old fiery eloquence and the expression of the strong faith which never deserted him.

Surely the character of Moḥammad has been misjudged. He was not the ambitious schemer some would have him, still less the hypocrite and sham prophet others have imagined. He was an enthusiast in that noblest sense when enthusiasm becomes the salt of the earth, the one thing that keeps men from rotting whilst they live. Enthusiasm is often used despitefully, because it is joined to an unworthy cause, or falls upon barren ground and bears no fruit. So was it not with Moḥammad. He was an enthusiast when enthusiasm was the one thing needed to set the world aflame, and his enthusiasm was noble for a noble cause. He was one of those happy few who have attained the supreme joy of making one great truth their very life-spring. He was the messenger of the One God, and never to his life's end did he forget who he was, or the message which was the marrow of his being. He brought his tidings to his people with a grand dignity, sprung from the consciousness of his high office, together with a most sweet humility, whose roots lay in the knowledge of his own weakness. Well did Carlyle choose him for his prophet-hero! There have been purer lives and higher aspirations than Moḥammad's; but no man was ever more thoroughly filled with the sense of his mission or carried out that mission more heroically.

III.— ISLAM.

'Your turning your faces in prayer towards the east and the west is not piety; but the pious is he who believeth in God and the Last Day, and in the Angels, and the Scripture, and who giveth money, notwithstanding his love thereof, to relations and orphans, and to the needy and the son of the road, and to the askers, and for the freeing of slaves, and who performeth prayer and giveth the appointed alms; and those who perform their covenant when they covenant, and the patient in adversity and affliction and in the time of violence. These are they who have been true: and these are they who fear God.'—*Kur-án*, ii. 172.

WHEN it was noised abroad that the Prophet was dead, 'Omar, the fiery-hearted, the Simon Peter of Islám, rushed among the people, and fiercely told them they lied, it could not be true, Moḥammad was not dead. And Aboo-Bekr came and said, 'Ye people! he that hath worshipped Moḥammad, let him know that Moḥammad is dead; but he that hath worshipped God,—that the Lord liveth, and doth not die.'

Many have sought to answer the questions—Why was the triumph of Islám so speedy and so complete? Why have so many millions embraced the religion of Moḥammad, and scarcely a hundred ever recanted? Why do a thousand Christians become Muslims to one Muslim who adopts Christianity? Why do a hundred and fifty millions of human beings still cling to the faith of Islám? Some have attempted to explain the first overwhelming success of the Moḥammadan religion by the argument of the sword. They forget Carlyle's laconic reply, 'First get your sword.' You must win men's hearts before you can induce them to peril their lives for you, and the first conquerors of Islám must have been made Muslims before they were made 'fighters on the path of God.' Others allege the low morality of the religion and the sensual paradise it promises as a sufficient cause for the zeal of its followers; but even were these admitted to the full, to say that such reasons could win the hearts of millions of men who have the same hopes and longings after the right and the noble as we, is to libel mankind. No religion has ever gained a lasting hold upon the souls of men by the force of its sensual permissions and fleshly promises. It is urged, again, that Islám met no fair foe, that the worn-out forms of Christianity and Judaism it encountered were no test of its power as a quickening faith, and that it prevailed simply because there was nothing to prevent it; and this was undoubtedly a help to the progress of the new creed, but it could not have been the cause of its victory.

In all these reasons the religion itself is left out of the question. Decidedly Islám itself was the main cause of its triumph. By some strange intuition Moḥammad succeeded in finding the one form of Monotheism that has ever commended itself to any wide section of the Eastern world. It was only a remnant of the Jews that learned to worship the one God of the prophets after the hard lessons of the Captivity. Christianity has never gained a hold upon the East. Islám not only was at once accepted (partly in earnest, partly in name, but accepted) by Arabia, Syria, Persia, Egypt, Northern Africa, and Southern Spain at its first outburst, but, with the exception of Spain, it has never lost its vantage-ground; it has seen no country that has once embraced its doctrine turn to another faith; it has added great multitudes in India and China and Turkestan to its subjects; and in quite recent times it has been spreading in wide and swiftly—following waves over Africa, and has left but a small part of that vast continent unconverted to its creed. Admitting the mixed causes that contributed to the rapidity of the first torrent of Moḥammadan conquest, they do not account for the duration of Islám. There must be something in the religion itself to explain its persistence and increase, and to account for its present hold over so large a proportion of the dwellers on the earth.

Men trained in European ideas of religion have always found a difficulty in understanding the fascination which the Muslim faith has for so many minds in the East. 'There is no god but God, and Moḥammad is His Prophet.' There is nothing in this, they say, to move the heart. Yet this creed has stirred an enthusiasm that has never been surpassed. Islám has had its martyrs, its self-tormentors, its recluses, who have renounced all that life offered and have accepted death with a smile for the sake of the faith that was in them. It is idle to say the eternity of happiness will explain this. The truest martyrs of Islám, as well as of Christianity, did not die to gain paradise. And if they did, the belief in the promises of the creed must follow the hearty belief in the creed. Islám must have possessed a power of seizing men's belief before it could have inspired them with such a love of its paradise.

Moḥammad's conception of God has, I think, been misunderstood, and its effect upon the people consequently under-estimated. The God of Islám is commonly represented as a pitiless tyrant, who plays with humanity as on a chessboard, and works out his game without regard to the sacrifice of the pieces; and there is a certain truth in the figure. There is more in Islám of the potter who shapes the clay than of the father pitying his children. Moḥammad conceived of God as the Semitic mind has always preferred to think of Him: his God is the All-Mighty, the All-Knowing, the All-Just. Irresistible Power is the first attribute he thinks of: the Lord of the Worlds, the Author of the Heavens and the Earth, who hath created Life and Death, in whose hand is Dominion, who maketh the Dawn to appear and causeth the Night to cover the Day, the Great, All-Powerful Lord of the glorious Throne; the Thunder proclaimeth His perfection, the whole earth is His handful, and the Heavens shall be folded together in His right hand. And with the Power

He conceives the Knowledge that directs it to right ends. God is the Wise, the Just, the True, the Swift in reckoning, who knoweth every ant's weight of good and of ill that each man hath done, and who suffereth not the reward of the faithful to perish.

'God! There is no God but He, the Ever-Living, the Ever-Subsisting. Slumber seizeth Him not nor sleep. To Him belongeth whatsoever is in the Heavens and whatsoever is in the Earth. Who is he that shall intercede with Him, save by His permission? He knoweth the things that have gone before and the things that follow after, and men shall not compass aught of His knowledge, save what He willeth. His Throne comprehendeth the Heavens and the Earth, and the care of them burdeneth Him not. And He is the High, the Great.'—*Kur-án*, ii. 256.

But with this Power there is also the gentleness that belongs only to great strength. God is the Guardian over His servants, the Shelterer of the orphan, the Guider of the erring, the Deliverer from every affliction; in His hand is Good, and He is the Generous Lord, the Gracious, the Hearer, the Near-at-Hand. Every soorah of the Kurán begins with the words, 'In the Name of God, the Compassionate, the Merciful,' and Mohammed was never tired of telling the people how God was Very-Forgiving, that His love for man was more tender than the mother-bird for her young.

It is too often forgotten how much there is in the Kurán of the loving-kindness of God, but it must be allowed that these are not the main thoughts in Mohammad's teaching. It is the doctrine of the Might of God that most held his imagination, and that has impressed itself most strongly upon Muslims of all ages. The fear rather than the love of God is the spur of Islám. There can be no question which is the higher incentive to good; but it is nearly certain that the love of God is an idea absolutely foreign to most of the races that have accepted Islám, and to preach such a doctrine would have been to mistake the leaning of the Semitic mind.

The leading doctrine of Moḥammad, then, is the belief in One All-Powerful God. Islám is the self-surrender of every man to the will of God. Its danger lies in the stress laid on the power of God, which has brought about the stifling effects of fatalism. Moḥammad taught the foreknowledge of God, but he did not lay down precisely the doctrine of Predestination. He found it, as all have found it, a stumbling-block in the way of man's progress. It perplexed him, and he spoke of it, but often contradicted himself; and he would become angry if the subject were mooted in his presence: 'Sit not with a disputer about fate,' he said, 'nor begin a conversation with him.' Moḥammad vaguely recognised that little margin of Free Will which makes life not wholly mechanical.

This doctrine of one Supreme God, to whose will it is the duty of every man to surrender himself, is the kernel of Islám, the truth for which Moḥammad lived and suffered and triumphed. But it was no new teaching, as he himself was constantly saying. His was only the last of revelations. Many prophets—Abraham, Moses, and Christ—had taught the same faith before; but people had hearkened little to their words. So Moḥammad was sent, not different from them, only a messenger, yet the last and greatest of them, the 'seal of prophecy,' the 'most excellent of the creation of God.' This is the second dogma of Islám: Moḥammad is the apostle of God. It is well worthy of notice that it is not said, 'Moḥammad is the only apostle of God.' Islám is more tolerant in this matter than other religions. Its prophet is not the sole commissioner of the Most High, nor is his teaching the only true teaching the world has ever received. Many other messengers had been sent by God to guide men to the right, and these taught the same religion that was in the mouth of the preacher of Islám. Hence Muslims reverence Moses and Christ only next to Moḥammad. All they claim for their founder is that

f

he was the last and best of the messengers of the one God.*

After the belief in God and his prophets and scriptures, the Muslim must believe in angels, good and evil genii, in the resurrection and the judgment, and in future rewards and punishments. What the teaching of the Ḳurán is upon these points may be seen in the First Part of the 'Selections.' They form a very common weapon of attack on the ground of their superstition, their anthropomorphism, and their sensuality. Yet these minor beliefs have their place in all religions, and they are conceived in scarcely more absurdly realistic a manner in Islám than in any other creed. Every religion seems to need an improbable, almost a ludicrous, side, in order to provide material for the faith of the masses. Moḥammad himself was what is called a superstitious man, and the improbable side thus found its way easily into his creed. With all the fancies floating in Arabia in his time, it would have been strange if he had introduced nothing of the superstitious into Islám. The Jinn, the Afreets, and the other beings of the air and water, have not done much harm to the Mohammadan mind; and they have given so many a delightful fable to the West, that we must feel a certain grateful respect for them. The realistic pictures of paradise and hell have exercised a more serious influence. The minute details of these infernal and celestial pictures must move alternately the disgust and the contemptuous amusement of a Western reader; yet these same things were very real facts to Moḥammad, and have been of the utmost importance to generation after generation of Muslims. In the present day there are cultured

* 'The Prophet said: Whosoever shall bear witness that there is one God; and that Moḥammad is His servant and messenger; and that Jesus Christ is His servant and messenger, and that he is the son of the handmaid of God, and that he is the Word of God, the word which was sent to Mary, and Spirit from God; and [shall bear witness] that there is truth in Heaven and Hell, will enter into paradise, whatever sins he may be chargeable with.'—*Mishkát-el-Masábeeh*, i. 11.

men who receive these descriptions in the same allegorical sense as some Christians accept the Revelation of S. John—which, indeed, in some respects offers a close parallel to the pictorial parts of the Ḳurán; but the vast majority of believers (like many Christians in the parallel case) take the descriptions literally, and there can be no doubt that the belief founded on such pictures, accepted literally, must work an ill effect on the professors of the faith of which these doctrines form a minor, but a too prominent, part; and it is the aim of rational Muslims to sweep away such cobwebs from their sky.

Islám lies more in doing than in believing. That 'faith without works is dead' is a doctrine which every day's routine must bring home to the mind of the devout Muslim. The practical duties of the Mohammadan religion, beyond the actual profession of faith, are the performance of prayer, the giving of alms, the keeping of the fasts, and the accomplishing the pilgrimage. Mr. Lane has so minutely described the regular prayers used over all the Mohammadan East, that it is only necessary here to refer to his account of them in the 'Modern Egyptians.' There it will be seen that they form no light part of the religious duties of the Muslim, especially since they involve careful preparatory ablutions; for Moḥammad impressed upon his followers the salutary doctrine that cleanliness is an essential part of godliness, and the scrupulous cleanliness of the Mohammadan, which contrasts so favourably with the unsavoury state of Easterns of other creeds, is an excellent feature in the practical influence of Islám. The charge which missionaries and the like are fond of bringing against the Muslim prayers, that they are merely lifeless forms and vain repetitions, is an exaggeration. There is a vast deal of repetition in the Mohammadan ritual, just as the paternoster is repeated again and again in the principal Christian liturgies; but iteration does not necessarily kill devotion. There is plenty of real fervour in the prayers of the Mosque, and they are joined-in by the worshippers with an earnest attention which shames the listless sleepy bearing of most congregations in England. It is true the greater part of the prayers are laid down in prescribed forms; but there is an interval set apart for private supplication, and the original congregations in the mosques availed themselves of this permission more generally than is now the case, when the old fervour has become comparatively cool; and Moḥammad frequently enjoins private prayer at home, and specially praises him who 'passeth his night worshipping God.'

Almsgiving was originally compulsory, and the tax was collected by the officers of the Khalif; but now the Muslim is merely expected to give voluntarily about a fortieth part of his income in charity each year. The great fast of Ramaḍán is too well known to need more than a passing mention here; but it is not so well known that Moḥammad, ascetic as he was himself in this as in many other matters, whilst he ordained the month of fasting for the chastening of his able-bodied followers, was a determined enemy to useless mortification of the flesh, and boldly affirmed that God took no pleasure in a man's wantonly injuring himself; and so if one that was weakly and sick could not keep the fast without bodily detriment he was to omit it. And the same wise leniency was shown by the Arab prophet in respect of prayer,—which may be curtailed or omitted in certain cases,—and with regard to the pilgrimage, which no one was to perform to his hurt. This same pilgrimage is often urged as a sign of Moḥammad's tendency to superstition and even idolatry. It is asked how the destroyer of idols could have reconciled his conscience to the circuits of the Kaạbeh and the veneration of the black stone covered with adoring kisses. The rites of the pilgrimage cannot certainly be defended against the charge of superstition; but it is easy to see why Moḥammad enjoined them. They were hallowed to him by the memories of his ancestors, who had been the guardians of the sacred temple, and by the traditional reverence of all his people; and besides this tie of association, which in itself was enough to make it impossible for him to do away with the rites, Moḥammad perceived that the worship in the Kaạbeh would prove of real value to his religion. He swept away the more idolatrous and immoral part of the ceremonies, but he retained the pilgrimage to Mekka and the old veneration of the temple for reasons of which it is impossible to dispute the wisdom. He well knew the consolidating effect of forming a centre to which his followers should gather; and hence he reasserted the sanctity of the black stone that 'came down from Heaven;' he ordained that everywhere throughout the world the Muslim should pray looking towards the Kaạbeh, and he enjoined him to make the pilgrimage thither. Mekka is to the Muslim what Jerusalem is to the Jew. It bears with it all the influence of centuries of associations. It carries the Muslim back to the cradle of his faith, the childhood of his prophet; it reminds him of the struggle between the old faith and the new, of the overthrow of the idols, and the establishment of the worship of the One God. And, most of all, it bids him remember that all his brother Muslims are worshipping towards the same sacred spot; that he is one of a great company of believers, united by one faith, filled with the same hopes reverencing the same things, worshipping the same God. Moḥammad showed his knowledge of the religious emotions in man when he preserved the sanctity of the temple of Islám.

It would take too much space to look closely into the lesser duties of Islám, many of which suggest exceedingly wholesome lessons to Western civilisation. But we must not pass over one of these minor duties, for it reflects the highest credit upon the founder and the professors of Mohammadanism—I mean the humane treatment of animals.

'There is no religion which has taken a higher view in its authoritative documents of animal life, and none wherein the precept has been so much honoured by its practical observance. 'There is no beast on earth,' says the Ḳurán, 'nor bird which flieth with its wings, but the same is a people like unto you—unto the Lord shall they return;' and it is the current belief that animals will share with men the general resurrection, and be judged according to their works. At the slaughter of an animal, the Prophet ordered that the name of God should always be named; but the words, 'the Compassionate, the Merciful,' were to be omitted; for, on the one hand, such an expression seemed a mockery to the sufferer, and, on the other, he could not bring himself to believe that the destruction of any life, however necessary, could be altogether pleasing to the All-Merciful. 'In the name of God,' says a pious Musalman before he strikes the fatal blow; 'God is most great; God give thee patience to endure the affliction which He hath allotted thee!' In the East there has been no moralist like Bentham to insist in noble words on the extension of the sphere of morality to all sentient beings, and to be ridiculed for it by people who call themselves religious; there has been no naturalist like Darwin, to demonstrate by his marvellous powers of observation how large a part of the mental and moral faculties which we usually claim for ourselves alone we share with other beings; there has been no Oriental 'Society for the Prevention of Cruelty to Animals.' But one reason of this is not far to seek. What the legislation of the last few years has at length attempted to do, and, from the mere fact that it is legislation, must do ineffectually, has been long effected in the East by the moral and religious sentiment which, like almost everything that is good in that part of the world, can be traced back, in part at least, to the great Prophet of Arabia. In the East, so far as it has not been hardened by the West, there is a real sympathy between man and the domestic animals; they understand one another; and the cruelties which the most humane of our countrymen unconsciously effect in the habitual use, for instance, of the muzzle or the bearing-rein on the most docile, the most patient, the most faithful, and the most intelligent of their companions, are impossible in the East. An Arab *cannot* ill-treat his horse; and Mr. Lane bears emphatic testimony to the fact that in his long residence in Egypt he never saw an ass or a dog (though the latter is there looked upon as an unclean animal) treated with cruelty, except in those cities which were overrun by Europeans.' *

There are some very beautiful traditions of the Prophet, showing the tenderness with which he always treated animals and which he ever enjoined on his people. A man once came to him with a carpet and said, 'O Prophet, I passed through a wood and heard the voices of the young of birds, and I took and put them into my carpet, and their mother came fluttering round my head.' And the Prophet said, 'Put them down;' and when he had put them down the mother joined the young. And the Prophet said, 'Do you wonder at the affection of the mother towards her young? I swear by Him who has sent me, Verily God is more loving to his servants than the mother to these young birds. Return them to the place from which ye took them, and let their mother be with them.' 'Fear God with regard to animals,' said Moḥammad; 'ride them when they are fit to be ridden, and get off when they are tired. Verily there are rewards for our doing good to dumb animals, and giving them water to drink.'

Such, in brief outline, is the religion of Moḥammad. It is a form of pure theism, simpler and more austere than the theism of most forms of modern Christianity, lofty in its conception of the relation of man to God, and noble in its doctrine of the duty of man to man, and of man to the lower creation. There is little in it of superstition, less of complexity of dogmas; it is an exacting religion, without the repulsiveness of asceticism; severe,

* R. Bosworth Smith: *Mohammed and Mohammedanism*, 2d ed., 255–257.

but not merciless. On the other hand, it is over-rigid and formal; it leaves too little to the believer and too much to his ritual; it places a prophet and a book between man and God, and practically discourages the desire for a direct relation between the Deity and his servant; it draws the picture of that God in too harsh outlines, and leaves out too much of the tenderness and loving-kindness of the God of Christ's teaching, and hence it has been the source of more intolerance and fanatical hatred than most creeds.

This religion is Islám as understood and taught by its Prophet, so far as we can gather it from the Ḳur-án, aided by those traditions which seem to have the stamp of authenticity. It need hardly be said that it is not identical with the Islám with which the philosophers of Baghdád amused themselves, nor with the fantastic creed which the Fáṭimee Khalifs of Egypt represented, and brought in the person of El-Hákim to its limit of extravagance; nor is it the Islám with which as much as with their ferocity the Karmaṭees aroused the fear and abhorrence of all good Muslims. Neither the Soofism of Persia nor the dervish sensation-religion of Turkey conform to this ancient Islám, to which perhaps a modification of the Waḥḥábee puritanism would be the nearest approach. The original faith of Moḥammad has not gained by its development in foreign lands and alien minds, and perhaps the best we can hope for modern Islám is that it may try the experiment of retrogression, or rather seek to regain the simplicity of the old form without losing the advantages (if there be any) which it has acquired from contact with Western civilisation.

Islám is unfortunately a social system as well as a religion; and herein lies the great difficulty of fairly estimating its good and its bad influence on the world. It is but in the nature of things that the teacher who lays down the law of the relation of man to God should also endeavour to appoint the proper relation between man and his neighbour. Christianity was undoubtedly a social even more than a religious reform, but the social regulations were too indefinite, or at all events too impracticable, for any wide acceptance among the professors of the religion. Islám was less fortunate. Mohammad not only promulgated a religion; he laid down a complete social system, containing minute regulations for a man's conduct in all circumstances of life, with due rewards or penalties according to his fulfilment of these rules. As a religion Islám is great: it has taught men to worship one God with a pure worship who formerly worshipped many gods impurely. As a social system Islám is a complete failure: it has misunderstood the relations of the sexes, upon which the whole character of a nation's life hangs, and, by degrading women, has degraded each successive generation of their children down an increasing scale of infamy and corruption, until it seems almost impossible to reach a lower level of vice.

The fatal spot in Islám is the degradation of women. The true test of a nation's place in the ranks of civilisation is the position of its women. When they are held in reverence, when it is considered the most infamous of crimes to subject a woman to dishonour, and the highest distinction to protect her from wrong; when the family life is real and strong, of which the mother-wife is the heart; when each man's pulse beats loyal to womanhood, then is a nation great. When women are treated as playthings, toys, drudges, worth anything only if they have beauty to be enjoyed or strength to labour; when sex is considered the chief thing in a woman, and heart and mind are forgotten; when a man buys women for his pleasure and dismisses them when his appetite is glutted, then is a nation despicable.

And so is it in the East. Yet it would be hard to lay the blame altogether on Moḥammad. The real roots of the degradation of women lie much deeper. When Islám was instituted, polygamy was almost necessitated by the number of women and their need of support; and the facility of divorce was quite necessitated by the separation of the sexes, and the consequence that a man could not know or even see the woman he was about to marry before the marriage ceremony was accomplished. It is not Moḥammad whom we must blame for these great evils, polygamy and divorce; it is the state of society which demanded the separation of the sexes, and in which it was not safe to allow men and women freely to associate; in other words, it was the sensual constitution of the Arab that lay at the root of the matter. Moḥammad might have done better. He might boldly have swept away the traditions of Arab society, unveiled the women, intermingled the sexes, and punished by the most severe measures any license which such association might at first encourage. With his boundless influence, it is possible that he might have done this, and, the new system once fairly settled, and the people accustomed to it, the good effects of the change would have begun to show themselves. But such an idea could never have occurred to him. We must always remember that we are dealing with a social system of the seventh century, not of the nineteenth. Moḥammad's ideas about women were like those of the rest of his contemporaries. He looked upon them as charming snares to the believer, ornamental articles of furniture difficult to keep in order, pretty playthings; but that a woman should be the counsellor and companion of a man does not seem to have occurred to him. It is to be wondered that the feeling of respect he always entertained for his first wife, Khadeejeh, (which, however, is partly accounted for by the fact that she was old enough to have been his mother,) found no counterpart in his general opinion of womankind: 'Woman was made from a crooked rib, and if you try to bend it straight, it will break; therefore treat your wives kindly.' Moḥammad was not the man to make a social reform affecting women, nor was Arabia the country in which such a change should be made, nor Arab ladies perhaps the best subjects for the experiment. Still he did something towards bettering the condition of women: he limited the number of wives to four; laid his hand with the utmost severity on the incestuous marriages that were then rife in Arabia; compelled husbands to support their divorced wives during their four months of probation; made irrevocable divorce less common by adding the rough, but deterring, condition that a woman triply divorced could not return to her husband without first being married to some one else—a condition exceedingly disagreeable to the first husband; and required four witnesses to prove a charge of adultery against a wife—a merciful provision, difficult to be fulfilled. The evil permitted by Moḥammad in leaving the number of wives four instead of insisting on monogamy was not great. Without considering the sacrifice of family peace which the possession of a large harem entails, the expense of keeping several wives, each of whom must have a separate suite of apartments or a separate house, is so great that not more than one in twenty can afford it. It is not so much in the matter of wives as in that of concubines that Moḥammad made an irretrievable mistake. The condition of the female slave in the East is indeed deplorable. She is at the entire mercy of her master, who can do what he pleases with her and her companions; for the Muslim is not restricted in the number of his concubines, as he is in that of his wives. The female white slave is kept solely for the master's sensual gratification, and is sold when he is tired of her, and so she passes from master to master, a very wreck of womanhood. Her condition is a little improved if she bear a son to her tyrant; but even then he is at liberty to refuse to acknowledge the child as his own, though it must be owned he seldom does this. Kind as the Prophet was himself towards bondswomen, one cannot forget the unutterable brutalities which he suffered his followers to inflict upon conquered nations in the taking of slaves. The Muslim soldier was allowed to do as he pleased with any 'infidel' woman he might meet with on his victorious march. When one thinks of the thousands of women, mothers and daughters, who must have suffered untold shame and dishonour by this license, he cannot find words to express his horror. And this cruel indulgence has left its mark on the Muslim character, nay, on the whole character of Eastern life. Now, as at the first, young Christian girls are dragged away from their homes and given over to the unhallowed lusts of a Turkish voluptuary; and not only to Turks, but to Englishmen; for the contagion has spread, and Englishmen, even those who by their sacred order should know better, instead of uttering their protest, as men of honour and Christians, against the degradation, have followed the example of the Turk, and helped in the ruin of women. Concubinage is the black stain in Islám. With Mohammad's views of women, we could hardly expect him to do better; but, on the other hand, he could scarcely have done worse. There are, however, one or two alleviating circumstances. One is the fact that the canker has not eaten into the whole of Eastern society; it is chiefly among the rich that the evil effects of the system are felt. And another fact which shows that the Mohammadan system, bad as it is, is free from a defect which social systems better in other respects than Mohammad's are subject to is the extreme rarity of prostitution in Muslim towns. The courtesan forms a very small item in the census of a Mohammadan city, and is retained more for strangers from Europe than for the Muslim inhabitants. Instances are frequently occurring in the Indian law courts which show the strong feeling that exists on the subject among the Mohammadans of India. They consider it quite inconceivable that a Muslim should have illicit intercourse with a free Muslimeh woman, and this inconceivableness of the action is urged as evidence in trials of the legitimacy of children. But whilst admitting the importance of this remarkable feature in Islám, it must not be forgotten that the liberty allowed by their law to Muslims in the matter of concubines does not very materially differ from prostitution, and whilst the latter is directly forbidden by the dominant religion of Europe, concubinage is as directly permitted by Islám.

One would think that long intercourse with Europeans might have somewhat raised the estimation of women in the East; but either because travellers in the East are not always the best specimens of Western morality, or because the Eastern mind has an unequalled aptitude for assimilating the bad and rejecting the good in any system it meets, it is certain that women are no better off now than they were in the East. A well-known correspondent of a leading daily print writes thus of Turkish home life :—

'It is obvious that the home life of any people will depend almost entirely on the position which is assigned to women. It is not necessary to inquire what this position is according to the teaching of the sacred books of a race. Between Christianity and Islám it is enough to notice that there is apparently no country where the first is the prevailing religion in which woman is hindered by religion from obtaining a position almost, if not quite, on an equality with man, and similarly, no country where the second prevails where woman is not in a degraded position. . . . Under Christianity she is everywhere free. Under Islám she is everywhere a slave. The pious Mohammadan, like the pious Jew, thanks God that he has not been made a woman. The pious Mohammadan woman, like the pious Jewess, thanks God that she has been made according to the Creator's will. Man and woman alike recognise that to be a woman is to be, in an inferior condition. This feeling of the degradation of woman so pervades Turkey that the poorer classes of Christians have even become infected by it. When a son is born there is nothing but congratulations. When a daughter, nothing but condolences. A polite Turk, if he has occasion to mention his wife, will do so with an apology. . . . He regards it as a piece of rudeness to mention the fact to you, and it would be equally rude for him to inquire after your wife, or to hint that he knew you were guilty of anything so unmentionable as to have one. Charles the Twelfth told his queen that she had been chosen to give children, and not advice. The Turk regards woman as destined solely for the same purpose and for his pleasure. Probably polygamy is of itself sufficient to account for the way in which Mohammadans regard woman. But whether this is so or not, there is one influence which polygamy asserts which accounts for the low ideal of woman prevalent in all Muslim countries. When a man has a number of wives it is impossible that they can all become his companions and his confidantes, or that one of them can become his companion or confidante to the same extent as if the man had only one wife. Hence a man who is limited to one will not be contented with beauty alone. He must have a certain amount of intelligence and education. The Turk, on the other hand, has no reason whatever to think of anything except beauty. As he never means to see much of his wife, intelligence or education is a matter of small account. If he can afford it he will have a Circassian wife, a woman who has been reared with the intention of being sold, who has not an idea in her head, who has seen nothing, and knows nothing. Such a woman would be as objectionable as a wife to the great majority of Europeans as a South Sea Island beauty. But she satisfies the ideal of the Turk. She is beautiful, and beauty is all that he requires.'

It is this sensual and degraded view of woman that destroys to so great an extent the good influence which the better part of the teaching of Islám might exert in the East. So long as women are held in so light an esteem, they will remain ignorant, and bigoted, and sensual; and so long as mothers are what most Muslim mothers are now, their children will be ignorant and fanatical and vicious. In Turkey there are other influences at work besides the Mohammadam social system; but Turkish women may serve as an instance of the state of things which that system encourages. 'In those early years spent at home, when the child ought to have instilled into him some germ of those principles of conduct by which men must walk in the world if they are to hold up their heads among civilised nations, the Turkish child is only taught the first steps towards those vicious habits of mind and body which have made his race what it is. The root of the evil is partly found in the harem system. So long as that system keeps Turkish women in their present depressed state, so long will Turkish boys and girls be vicious and ignorant.' As I have said elsewhere,[1] 'It is quite

[1] *The People of Turkey*, by a Consul's Daughter, preface, xxii.

certain that there is no hope for the Turks so long as Turkish women remain what they are, and home-training is the initiation of vice.' If the mother is ignorant and vicious, the son cannot form a high ideal of womanhood, and thus is barred off from the chivalrous spirit wherewith alone a man may reach to the highest love :—that

> 'Subtle master under heaven,
> Not only to keep down the base in man,
> But teach high thought, and amiable words,
> And courtliness, and the desire of fame,
> And love of truth, and all that makes a man.'

The Muslin has no ideal of chivalry like this to make his life pure and honourable: his religion encourages an opposite view, and the women among whom he is brought up only confirm it.

If Islám is to be a power for good in the future, it is imperatively necessary to cut off the social system from the religion. At the beginning, among a people who had advanced but a little way on the road of civilisation, the defects of the social system were not so apparent; but now, when Easterns are endeavouring to mix on equal terms with Europeans, and are trying to adopt the manners and customs of the West, it is clear that the condition of their women must be radically changed if any good is to come of the Europeanising tendency. The difficulty lies in the close connection between the religious and social ordinances in the Ḳur-án: the two are so intermingled that it is hard to see how they can be disentangled without destroying both. The theory of revelation would have to be modified. Muslims would have to give up their doctrine of the syllabic inspiration of the Ḳur-án and exercise their moral sense in distinguishing between the particular and the general, the temporary and the permanent: they would have to recognise that there was much in Moḥammad's teaching which, though useful at the time, is inapplicable to the present conditions of life; that his knowledge was often partial, and his judgment sometimes at fault; that the moral sense is capable of education as much as the intellect, and, therefore, that what was apparently moral and wise in the seventh century may quite possibly be immoral and suicidal in a society of the nineteenth century. Moḥammad himself said, according to tradition, 'I am no more than a man: when I order you anything respecting religion, receive it; and when I order you about the affairs of the world, then I am nothing more than man.' And he seemed to foresee that the time would come when his minor regulations would call for revision: 'Ye are in an age,' he said, 'in which, if ye abandon one-tenth of what is ordered, ye will be ruined. After this, a time will come when he who shall observe one-tenth of what is now ordered will be redeemed.'[1]

If Muslims would take these warnings of their prophet to heart, there would be some hope for Islám. Some few of the higher intellects among them have already admitted the principle of moral criticism applied to the Ḳu-rán; but it is very doubtful whether 'rational Islám' will ever gain a wide following, any more than 'rational Christianity.' People in general do not care to think for themselves in matters religious. They like their creed served up to them as cooked meat, not raw flesh. They must have definite texts and hard-and-fast commandments to appeal to. They will not believe in the spirit, but prefer the letter. They will have nothing to say to tendencies, but must have facts. It is of no avail to speak to them of the spirit of a life or of a whole book; they must hang their doctrine on a solitary sentence. They will either believe every letter of their scripture, or they will believe nothing.

Such people make up the majority of the professors of Islám; and with them no reform, within Islám, seems possible. Among the upper (I will not call them the higher) classes, they are either fanatics or concealed infi-

---

[1] *Mishkát-el-Masábeeh*, i. 46, 51.

dels; and their lives are a proof of the incompatibility of ordinary Mohammadanism, real or nominal, with a high social and national life. Among the poorer classes, the social system has a more restricted field of operation, for the poor are naturally less able to avail themselves of the permissions of their Prophet. In a poor community Islám exerts an eminently salutary influence, as the condition of the Mohammadan converts in Western Africa conclusively proves. An able observer,[1] whose African birth and training qualify him in a high degree for properly understanding the true state of his countrymen, whilst his Christian profession serves as a guarantee against excessive prejudice in favour of Islám, has recorded his experience of the work of Mohammadan missionaries in Liberia and the neighbouring parts of Africa. 'All careful and candid observers,' he remarks, 'agree that the influence of Islám in Central and West Africa has been, upon the whole, of a most salutary character. . . . As an eliminatory and subversive agency it has displaced or unsettled nothing as good as itself.' It has inculcated habits of moderation and soberness over the whole of the vast region covered by its emissaries; and so great is the influence of its teaching, that where there are Muslim inhabitants, even in pagan towns, it is a very rare thing to see a person intoxicated. The Mohammadan converts drink nothing but water. 'From Senegal to Lagos, over two thousand miles, there is scarcely an important town on the seaboard where there is not at least one mosque and active representatives of Islám, side by side with the Christian teacher. And as soon as a pagan, however obscure or degraded, embraces the Muslim faith, he is at once admitted as an equal to the society. . . . The pagan village possessing a Muslim teacher is always found to be in advance of its neighbours in all the elements of civilisation. . . . The in-

[1] Dr. E. Blyden. See his article on Mohammadanism in Western Africa in *The People of Africa.* (New York, 1871.)

troduction of Islám into Central and West Africa has been the most important, if not the sole, preservative against the desolations of the slave trade. Mohammadanism furnished a protection to the tribes who embraced it, by effectually binding them together in one strong religious fraternity, and enabling them by their united efforts to baffle the attempts of powerful slave-hunters. Enjoying this comparative immunity from sudden hostile incursion, industry was stimulated among them; industry diminished their poverty; and as they increased in worldly substance, they also increased in desire for knowledge. Receiving a desire of letters by a study of the Arabic language, they acquired loftier views, wider tastes, and those energetic habits which so pleasingly distinguish them from their pagan neighbours.' Students often travel on foot from the west coast right across Africa to study at the great mosque of the Azhar in Cairo. It must be remembered that these results were observed in the very centre of African Christianity, in Sierra Leone and other coast settlements. It is said that in Sierra Leone three-fourths of the Muslim population were not born Muslims, but were converted from Christianity or paganism; and this, although 'all liberated Africans are always handed over to Christian missionaries for instruction, and their children are baptized and brought up at the public expense in Christian schools, and are thus, in a sense, ready-made Christians.'

These facts show that, even in the present day, and with the competition of Christian missionary societies, Islám may be a power for good in poor communities—that it can not only give them a pure instead of a degraded faith, but can raise them socially and intellectually. The effects of a simple form of Islám on these African converts may give one some notion of its influence on its hearers in the early days, before the theologians had corrupted it.

But this good influence is very partial and limited, even among the poorer classes. In communities where all are poor, Islám is an excellent agent for improvement; but in countries where there are many grades of wealth and rank, the poor only ape in a humble manner the vices of those whom they are taught to regard as their 'betters.' In all civilised and wealthy countries the social system of Islám exerts a ruinous influence on all classes, and if there is to be any great future for the Mohammadan world, that system of society must be done away.

> THE WOMAN'S CAUSE IS MAN'S; THEY RISE OR SINK
> TOGETHER, DWARFED OR GODLIKE, BOND OR FREE.

IV.—*THE KUR-ÁN.*

The Muslim who reads the Ḳur-án is like the orange-fruit, whose smell and taste are sweet; and the Muslim who reads not the Ḳur-án is like the date, which hath no smell, but its taste is sweet; and the Hypocrite who reads not the Ḳur-án is like the colocynth, without a smell, and with a bitter taste; and the Hypocrite who reads it is like the sweet bazil, whose smell is sweet, but its taste bitter.—*Tradition.*

It is an immense merit in the Ḳurán that there is no doubt as to its genuineness. The 'Word of the Lord' came to Moḥammad, and he uttered it, and the people wrote it down or committed it to memory; and that very word we can now read with full confidence that it has remained unchanged through nearly thirteen hundred years.

The revelations came to Moḥammad in many ways and at all times, but never 'in visions bright, transcendant, exalted. They came ghastly, weird, most horrible. After long solitary broodings, a something used to move Moḥammad, all of a sudden, with frightful vehemence. He "roared like a camel," his eyes rolled and glowed like red coals, and on the coldest day terrible perspirations would break out all over his body. When the terror ceased, it seemed to him as if he had heard bells ringing, "the sound whereof seemed to rend him to pieçes"—as if he had heard the voice of a man—as if he had seen Gabriel—or as if words *had been written in his heart.* Such was the agony he endured, that some of the verses revealed to him well-nigh made his hair turn white.'

No collection of these revelations was made during Mohammad's lifetime; at his death, the Ḳurán existed only as scattered chaotically among the believers. But about a year later, the death in battle of some of the men who had specially committed passages of the Ḳurán to memory, and the dread that the whole of Moḥammad's teaching might vanish at the end of a generation or two, induced Aboo-Bekr to make the innovation from which every one shrank, and he gave orders to the Prophet's secretary, Zeyd ibn Thábit, to collect the fragments of the Ḳurán in one book. So Zeyd gathered the Ḳurán from palm-leaves, skins, shoulder-blades, stones, and the hearts of men, arranged the chapters in a certain order, and presented Aboo-Bekr with a Ḳurán which probably differed in no essential particular from the book we have now. All scholars are agreed that Zeyd did his work faithfully, and neither inserted nor omitted anything from party motives. But he seems to have occasionally mixed up fragments of very different date in one chapter—Moḥammad himself countenanced this—and may possibly have omitted some portions that were not found till afterwards.

Some twenty years later a second recension was ordered by the Khalif 'Othmán. Slight varieties of reading, mainly dialectal, had arisen; swords were near being drawn over them; and it was evident that a serious schism would come about if a uniform authorised text of the Ḳurán were not provided. These slight dialectal differences were not sufficiently settled, it would seem, in Aboo-Bekr's edition, so this new recension was made by Zeyd and three men of the Ḳureysh, for they would best know the original dialect of the Ḳurán. The new edition followed the first one, apparently, both in order and in matter; definitely fixing, however, the true text in the dialect of the Ḳureysh, and possibly adding any verses that might have been discovered since Zeyd's first edition. This second recension was conducted with the same careful fidelity and scrupulous impartiality as the first; and it was accepted by all the different parties that were then disputing the supremacy. Copies of this edition were then distributed to the principal cities of the empire, and the old copies and fragments were called-in and burned.

This edition of 'Othmán, made about A.D. 660, is the one that has ever since been the authorised and only version of the Ḳurán throughout the Muslim world and in the studies of European linguists. The only differences that have since crept into the text are certain unimportant varieties in vocalisation and orthography and in the division of verses.

It was a singular system these early revisers went upon. They seem, indeed, to have established the authenticity of each saying satisfactorily; but in the arrangement of them they showed an extraordinary dulness. The tradition of the year when each revelation was spoken appears to have been lost even in the short time that had elapsed since it had been spoken. People remembered the words, but seldom the occasion of the words. Hence the revisers had to devise an artificial order; not according to subject, nor after the development of the style, but simply in order of length! They put the longest chapters first and the shortest last; that is to say, they inverted, roughly speaking, the true order, for the early soorahs were short and the later ones long.

Read in this order, the Ḳurán is an unintelligible jumble. Carlyle may well say that 'nothing but a sense of duty could carry any European through the Ḳurán.' You can trace no development of mind or doctrine in the present arrangement; it is indeed a confused mass of 'endless iterations, long-windedness, entanglement, most crude, incondite.' But scholars have long discovered certain signs of a true order—several kinds of evidence by which a chronological arrangement of the Ḳurán may be attempted. These are—(1.) The *references to historical events* in the Ḳurán, as identified by tradition. These, however, are but few, and occur chiefly in quite the latest soorahs; and tradition is apt to identify any reference with any event it chooses. A much more important test is (2.) the *style;* for a distinct development can be traced in the rime, in the length of verses, and in the words employed.

And then there is (3.) the *matter* test, based on what we know of Moḥammad's life, from which we can argue a certain change in his preaching at Mekka, and still more when, from addressing idolaters in his birthplace, he came to preach to Jews and Christians at Medina. The danger of this last test is that each man forms his own theory of Moḥammad's mental and religious growth, and may arrange the soorahs in accordance with that theory. Even with these three tests, used by the most accomplished critics, it is impossible to arrive at an exact order, and to determine the precise chronological position of each soorah. But whilst it is admitted that an exact chronological arrangement of each individual chapter of the Ḳur-án is impossible, it is yet no less certain that the soorahs may be roughly grouped together, and that these groups can be definitely assigned to certain periods of Moḥammad's career.

Professor Th. Nöldeke's *Geschichte des Qorâns* has established his right to the first place in this science of Ḳur-án arrangement, and his order of soorahs may fairly be accepted as authoritative. Of this order Mr. Rodwell's English version of the Ḳur-án is an example, except that a few of the earliest soorahs are transposed. Nöldeke has two great divisions of the soorahs: those revealed at Mekka, and those revealed during the Medina period. Further, he divides the Mekkan division into three groups.[1]

---

[1] It may be interesting to some readers to judge for themselves of the different characteristics of these four groups of soorahs; and though in a series of translated selections it will hardly be possible to gain a thorough appreciation of the change of style or matter, some notion may nevertheless be obtained by reading the First Part of these Selections in the following order (the numbers referring to the figures at the head of each extract):—

Mekka—First Period:—xvii., lxvi., lxv., xviii., xxxvii., xxxviii., xxxix., xl., xli., xlii., xliii., xxx., iii., i.

Second Period:—lx., xlvii., xxix., viii., xiv., lxiii., vi., li., lxii., xxxi., xliv., lxxxvi., lxxxi., xlv., xxxvi., xx.

Third Period:—lxxiii., lxiv., xxxv., liii., xlvi., xvi., lxxvi., xxxii., lix., xxi., vii., lv., xix., xii., x., lxxii., xxviii., xi.

Medina:—ii., lxxxiv., xxxiii., lxxvii., xxxiv., xxiv., xxvi., ix., lii., lxxix., lxvii., lxi., iv., lxxi., lxix., lxx., lxxv., lxxxiii., xlviii., v., lxxviii., xxii., lvi., lvii., xlix., xxvii., xxv., xiii., lviii., lxxiv., l., liv., xxiii., lxxx., xv., lxviii., lxxxv., lxxxii.

Mekka:
- I. A.D. 612–617 (Rodwell, pp. 1–64)—To the Abyssinian exile (fifth year).
- II. A.D. 617–619 (Rodwell, pp. 64–192)—Fifth and sixth years of Moḥammad's mission.
- III. A.D. 619–622 (Rodwell, pp. 193–366)—From the seventh year to the Flight.

Medina.........A.D. 622–633 (Rodwell, pp. 366–555)—At Medina.

Read in this order the Ḳurán becomes intelligible. It is still confused in its progression and strangely mixed in its contents; but the development of Moḥammad's faith can be traced in it, and we can see dimly into the workings of his mind, as it struggles with the deep things of God, wrestles with the doubts which echoed the cavils of the unbelievers, soars upwards on the wings of ecstatic faith, till at last it gains the repose of fruition. Studied thus, the Ḳurán is no longer dull reading to one who cares to look upon the working of a passionate troubled human soul, and who can enter into its trials and share in the joy of its triumphs.

In the soorahs revealed at Mekka, Moḥammad has but one theme — God; and one object — to draw his people away from their idols and bring them to the feet of that God. He tells them of Him in glowing language, that comes from the heart's white heat. He points to the glories of nature, and tells them these are God's works. With all the brilliant imagery of the Arab, he tries to show them what God is, to convince them of His power and His wisdom and His justice. The soorahs of this period are short, for they are pitched in too high a key to be long sustained. The language has the ring of poetry, though no part of the Ḳurán complies with the demands of Arab metre. The sentences are short and full of half-restrained energy, yet with a musical cadence. The thought is often only half expressed; one feels the speaker has essayed a thing beyond words, and has suddenly discovered the impotence of language, and broken off with the sentence unfinished. There is the fascination of true poetry about these earliest soorahs; as we read them we understand the enthusiasm of the Prophet's followers, though we cannot fully realise the beauty and the power, inasmuch as we cannot hear them hurled forth with Moḥammad's fiery eloquence. From first to last the Ḳur-án is essentially a book to be heard, not read, but this is especially the case with the earliest chapters.

In the soorahs of the second period of Mekka we begin to trace the decline of the Prophet's eloquence. There are still the same earnest appeals to the people, the same gorgeous pictures of the Last Day and the world to come; but the language begins to approach the quiet of prose, the sentences become longer, the same words and phrases are frequently repeated, and the wearisome stories of the Jewish prophets and patriarchs, which fill so large a place in the later portion of the Ḳur-án, now make their appearance. The fierce passion of the earliest soorahs, that could not out save in short burning verses, gives place to a calmer more argumentative style. Moḥammad appeals less to the works of God as proofs of his teaching, and more to the history of former teachers, and the punishments of the people who would not hear them. And the characteristic oaths of the first period, when Moḥammad swears by all the varied sights of nature as they mirrored themselves in his imagination, have gone, and in their place we find only the weaker oath 'by the Ḳur-án.' And this declension is carried still further in the last group of the soorahs revealed at Mekka. The style becomes more involved and the sentences longer, and though the old enthusiasm bursts forth ever and anon, it is rather an echo of former things than a new and present intoxication of faith. The fables and repetitions become more and more dreary, and but for the rich eloquence of the old Arabic tongue, which gives some charm even to inextricable sentences and dull stories, the Ḳur-án at this period would be unreadable. As it is, we feel we have fallen the whole depth from poetry to prose, and the matter of the prose is not so superlative as to give us amends for the loss of the poetic thought of the earlier time and the musical fall of the sentences.

In the soorahs of the Medina period these faults reach their climax. We read a singularly varied collection of criminal laws, social regulations, orders for battle, harangues to the Jews, first conciliatory, then denunciatory, and exhortations to spread the faith, and such-like heterogeneous matters. Happily the Jewish stories disappear in the latest soorahs, but their place is filled by scarcely more palatable materials. The chapters of this period are interesting chiefly as containing the laws which have guided every Muslim state, regulated every Muslim society, and directed in their smallest acts every Mohammadan man and woman in all parts of the world from the Prophet's time till now The Medina part of the Ḳurán is the most important part for Islám, considered as a scheme of ritual and a system of manners; the earliest Mekka revelations are those which contain what is highest in a great religion and what was purest in a great man.

The word *Ḳur-án* means the *crying, reciting, reading,* and is applied not only to the whole book, but to any chapter or section of it. The Ḳurán is also called El-Furḳán, 'the Distinguisher,' and El-Muṣḥaf, 'the Volume,' and El-Kitáb, 'the Book,' and Edh-Dhikr, 'the Admonition.' The Ḳurán contains, in its ordinary form, 114 chapters (*soorahs*), 6616 verses (*áyát,* literally 'signs' or 'wonders'), 77,934 words, and 323,671 letters, according to the estimates of laborious Muslim divines, which differ, however, in a slight manner in consequence of the various divisions of verses. After the first chapter, which is a short prayer (the Fátiḥah), the soorahs gradually decrease in length from 289 verses in the second to from three to six in the ten concluding chapters. Each chapter is headed by a title, taken from same prominent word in it (as the 'Chapter of the Striking,' 'of the Cow,' &c.); beneath which is noted whether it was promulgated (according to tradition) at Mekka or Medina, and the number of its verses. Then follow the words :—'In the Name of God, the Compassionate, the Merciful;' after which the chapter begins. To twenty-nine chapters are prefixed certain letters (*e.g.*, ch. ii. on p. 4), or a single letter, which have never been successfully interpreted. The Muslims believe them to conceal profound mysteries. In Soorah 55 a refrain is found, and traces of a like imitation in Soorahs 54 and 17. It is probable that the Ḳurán was originally *chanted* in somewhat the same manner as it is in the present day.

The Kurán is also divided in thirty sections, and these are again subdivided; and from this division rather than from chapter and verse do the Muslims generally quote.

'The Muslims absolutely deny that the Ḳurán was composed by their Prophet himself, or by any other for him; it being their general and orthodox belief that it is of divine original; nay, that it is eternal and uncreated, remaining, as some express it, in the very essence of God; that the first transcript has been from everlasting by God's throne, written on a tablet of vast size, called the Preserved Tablet, in which are also recorded the divine decrees, past and future; that a copy from this tablet, in one volume on paper, was, by the ministry of the angel Gabriel, sent down to the lowest heaven, in the month of Ramaḍán, on the Night of Power;[1] whence Gabriel revealed it to Moḥammad by parcels, some at Mekka, and some at Medina, at different times during the space of twenty-three years, as the exigency of affairs required; giving him, however, the consolation to show him the whole (which they tell us was bound in silk, and adorned with gold and precious stones of Paradise) once a year; but in the last year of his life he had the favour to see it twice. They say that few chapters were delivered entire, the most part being revealed piecemeal, and written down from time to time by the Prophet's amanuensis, in such or such

---

1 This is generally believed to be the night of (that is, preceding) the 27th day of the month.

a part of such or such a chapter, till they were completed, according to the directions of the angel. The first parcel that was revealed is generally agreed to have been the first five verses of the ninety-sixth chapter. After the new revealed passages had been from the Prophet's mouth taken down in writing by his scribe, they were published to his followers, several of whom took copies for their private use; but the far greater number got them by heart. The originals, when returned, were put promiscuously into a chest, without regard to any order of time, for which reason it is uncertain when many passages were revealed.

'The Ḳurán being the Muslims' rule of faith and practice, it is no wonder its expositors and commentators are so very numerous; and it may not be amiss to take notice of the rules they observe in expounding it.

'One of the most learned commentators distinguishes the contents of the Ḳurán into allegorical and literal. The former comprehends the more obscure, parabolical, and enigmatical passages, and such as are repealed or abrogated; the latter, those which are plain, perspicuous, liable to no doubt, and in full force.

'To explain these severally in a right manner, it is necessary, from tradition and study, to know the time when each passage was revealed, its circumstances, state, and history, and the reasons or particular emergencies for the sake of which it was revealed. Or, more explicitly, whether the passage was revealed at Mekka or at Medina; whether it be abrogated, or does itself abrogate any other passage; whether it be anticipated in order of time or postponed; whether it be distinct from the context or depend thereon; whether it be particular or general; and lastly, whether it be implicit by intention, or explicit in words.

'By what has been said, the reader may easily believe that this book is held by the Muslims in the greatest reverence and esteem. The more strict among them dare not touch it without being first washed or legally purified;

which lest they should do by inadvertence, they sometimes write these words of the book itself on the cover or label, "None shall touch it but they who are purified." They read it with great care and respect, never holding it below their girdles. They swear by it, consult it in their weighty occasions, carry it with them to war, inscribe sentences from it on their banners, sometimes adorn it with gold and precious stones, and knowingly suffer it not to be in the possession of any person of a different persuasion. It is the foundation of their education; and the children in the schools are taught to chant it, and commit the whole of it to memory.'

BOOKS.

In reading a large number of works bearing upon the subjects of this Introduction, I have remarked a curious freedom of quotation in most of the writers. I find the same sentence, or at least the same thought, repeated in several books without any reference to the author who first put it forth. Each writer seems to have studied his predecessors with such minuteness that he can quote their very words, but he does not appear to remember whence the words came. When a thought has once been perfectly expressed, it were a ridiculous vanity to seek to frame it in different words, and so far it is undoubtedly wise to make use of the best of what has preceded us; nevertheless, it is well to acknowledge our debt. Yet thoughts, and even phrases, impress themselves on the memory till one unconsciously comes to appropriate them as his own; and this, I doubt not, is the cause of much of the plagiarism I have noticed. It is extremely probable that I have been guilty of the same sin. I have crowded my pages with marks of quotation, sometimes with foot references, sometimes without (for the student of the subject will know where to look for them), but it is quite likely that I have often unconsciously used another's phrase or metaphor without rendering thanks. So I now append a list of the principal European books I have used, and beg once and for all to record my indebtedness to their writers. The original Arabic authorities will dispense with my acknowledgments, and the catalogue of them would not assist the English reader who wishes to proceed further in the study of the subject, for whom this list may prove useful.

Burckhardt, J. L. *Notes on the Bedouins and Wahábys.* 2 vols. 1831.

Deutsch, Emanuel. *Literary Remains.* 1874.

Dozy, R. *Essai sur l'Histoire de l'Islamisme,* trad. par V. Chauvin. 1879.

Fresnel, F. *Lettres sur l'Histoire des Arabes avant l'Islamisme.* 1836-38.

Hughes, Rev. T. P. *Notes on Muhammadanism.* 2d ed. 1877.

KREMER, A. VON. *Geschichte der herrschenden Ideen des Islâms.* 1868.

——— *Culturgeschichte des Orients unter den Chalifen.* 2 vols. 1876, 1877.

LANE, E. W. *The Modern Egyptians.* 5th ed. 1 vol. 1860.

——— *The Thousand and One Nights* (notes). 2d ed. 3 vols. 1859, 1860.

——— *Selections from the Kur-án.* 1st ed. 1843.

——— *Arabic-English Lexicon*, Preface, &c. 1863.

LYALL, C. J. *Translations from the Hamâseh and the Aghânî; The Mo'allaqah of Zuheyr.* (Journal As. Soc. of Bengal, 1878.)

MUIR, SIR W. *The Life of Mahomet.* 4 vols. New edition.[1] 1867.

NÖLDEKE, TH. *Geschichte des Qorâns.* 1860.

——— *Beiträge zur Kenntniss der Poesie der alten Araber.* 1864.

PALGRAVE, W. GIFFORD. *Central and Eastern Arabia.* 6th ed. 1871.

PERCEVAL, A.-P. CAUSSIN DE. *Essai sur l'Histoire des Arabes avant l'Islamisme.* 3 vols. 1847, 1848.

POOLE, R. STUART. *Pagan and Muslim Arabs.* (Fortnightly Review, October 15, 1865.)

RODWELL, J. M. *El-Korân.* 2d ed. 1876.

SALE, G. *The Koran.* 1836.

SÉDILLOT, L.-A. *Histoire Générale des Arabes.* 2d ed. 2 vols. 1877.

SMITH, R. BOSWORTH. *Mohammed and Mohammedanism.* 2d ed. 1876.

SPRENGER, A. *Das Leben und die Lehre des Mohammad.* 2d ed. 3 vols. 1869.

ST. HILAIRE, T.-BARTHÉLEMY. *Mahomet et le Coran.* 2d ed. 1865.

TIELE, C. P. *Outlines of the History of Religion*, translated by J. E. Carpenter. (Trübner's Philosophical Library. Vol. vii. 1877.)

WEIL, G. *Das Leben Mohammed's nach Ibn Ishak* bearbeitet von Ibn Hischam. 2 vols. 1864.

---

[1] In the Introduction, the references are to the new one volume edition, 1877. Since writing my chapter on the early Arabs, Sir W. Muir has published an interesting essay on old Arabic poetry in the *Journal of the Royal Asiatic Society* (xi. part i. 1879).

SELECTIONS FROM THE KURÁN.

PART THE FIRST.

NOTE.

The following extracts were all translated by Mr. Lane, with the exception of those to which an obelus (†) is prefixed, for which I alone am responsible. In the text, the words in italics are inserted from the commentary of the Jeláleyn; words in square brackets [ ] are Mr. Lane's additions, inserted where the difference between the Arabic and English idioms required them.

In the foot-notes, words in italics are from the commentary of the Jeláleyn; notes followed by the initial S., from Sale's *Koran;* the letters B., Z., and A. F., following S. in parenthesis, point to the authorities from which Sale's note was derived, the great commentaries of El-Beydáwee and Ez-Zamakhsharee, and Abu-l-Fidá's Life of Mohammad, respectively. The other notes are Mr. Lane's, either from the original edition or extracted from his *Modern Egyptians* (5th 1 vol. ed. 1860), or his notes to the *Thousand and One Nights* (2d ed. 1859); except those enclosed in square brackets, which are due to myself.

The numbers at the end of each extract refer to the chapter (soorah) and verse in Flügel's text of the Ḳur-án (Lipsiæ, 1869).

S. L. P.

PART THE FIRST.

THE OPENING PRAYER.[1]

EL-FÁTIḤAH.

I.

In the name of God, the Compassionate, the Merciful.

Praise be to God, the Lord of the Worlds,[2]
The Compassionate, the Merciful,
The King of the day of judgment.
Thee do we worship, and of Thee seek we help.[3]
Guide us in the right way,
The way of those to whom Thou hast been gracious,
Not of those with whom Thou art wroth, nor of the erring. (i.)

---

[1] The 'Lord's Prayer' of the Muslims, recited several times in each of the five daily prayers, and on many other occasions.

[2] *That is, of all creatures.*

[3] ['Do we beg assistance,' in the original ed.]

PREMONITION.

II.

A.L.M.[1] Respecting this Book there is no doubt; [2] *it is* a guidance for them that fear Him,

Who believe in the unseen,[3] and perform the prayer, and of what We have bestowed on them expend,

And who believe in that which hath been sent down to thee,[4] and what hath been sent down before thee,[5] and have firm assurance of the life to come.

Those follow a right direction from their Lord, and those are they who shall prosper.

As for those who have disbelieved, it will be equal to them whether thou admonish them or admonish them not: they will not believe.

God hath sealed their hearts and their ears, and over their eyes is a covering, and for them is [ordained] a great punishment. (ii. 1–6.)

---

1 *God knoweth best what He meaneth by these* letters.

2 *That it is from God.*

3 *In the resurrection and paradise and hell.*

4 *The Kur-án.*

5 *The Pentateuch and the Gospel and other books.*

GOD.

III.

SAY, He is God, One [God];
God, the Eternal.
He begetteth not nor is begotten,
And there is none equal unto Him. (cxii.)[1]

IV.

The Throne-Verse.[2]

God! There is no God but He, the *Ever*-Living, the Ever-Subsisting. Slumber seizeth Him not, nor sleep. To Him belongeth whatsoever is in the Heavens and whatsoever is in the Earth. Who is he that shall intercede with Him, unless by His permission? He knoweth what [hath been] before them and what [shall be] after them, and they shall not compass aught of His knowledge save what He willeth. His Throne comprehendeth the Heavens and the Earth,[3] and the care of them burdeneth Him not. And He is the High, the Great. (ii. 256.)

---

[1] This chapter is held in particular veneration by the Mohammadans, and declared, by a tradition of their prophet, to be equal in value to a third part of the whole Korân.—S.

[2] One of the most admired passages in the Ḳur-án, recited (though not by all Muslims) at the close of each of the five daily prayers, and often engraved on an ornament of gold or silver or a precious stone to be worn as an amulet.

[3] 'The seven heavens and earths in comparison with the Throne are nought but as seven dirhems [silver coins] cast into a shield.'—Trad.

V.

†SAY, O God, to whom belongeth dominion, Thou givest dominion to whom Thou wilt, and from whom Thou wilt Thou takest it away; Thou exaltest whom Thou wilt, and whom Thou wilt Thou humblest. In Thy hand is good. Verily Thou art all-powerful.

Thou causest the night to pass into the day, and Thou causest the day to pass into the night; and Thou bringest forth the living from the dead, and Thou bringest forth the dead from the living; and thou givest sustenance to whom Thou wilt without measure. (iii. 25, 26.)

VI.

Blessed be He in whose hand is the dominion and who is all-powerful;[1]

Who hath created death and life, that He may prove you, which of you [will be] best in works: and He is the Mighty, the Very-Forgiving:

Who hath created seven heavens, one above another. Thou seest not any fault in the creation of the Compassionate. But lift up the eyes again *to heaven.* Dost thou see any fissures?

Then lift up the eyes again twice; the sight shall return unto thee dull and dim. (lxvii. 1–4.)

VII.

Verily your Lord is God, who created the heavens and the earth in six days: then He ascended the throne. He causeth the night to cover the day; it followeth it swiftly: and *He created* the sun and the moon and the stars, made subject utterly to His command. Do not the *whole* creation and command belong to Him? Blessed be God, the Lord of the Worlds. (vii. 52.)

---

[1] ['Able to do everything,' orig. ed. Lit. 'potent over everything.']

VIII.

We have placed in heaven *the twelve* signs *of the Zodiac*, and adorned them for the beholders *with the constellations;*

And We have guarded them (*by means of shooting stars*) from every accursed devil,[1]

Excepting him who listeneth by stealth, whom a manifest shooting star pursueth.

We have also spread forth the earth, and thrown thereon firm *mountains*,[2] and We have caused to spring forth in it every kind [of green thing] weighed.[3]

And We have provided for you therein necessaries of life, and *for* him whom ye do not sustain;[4]

And there is not a thing but the storehouses thereof are with Us, and We send it not down save in determined quantities.

We also send the fertilizing winds,[5] and We send down water from heaven, and give you to drink thereof; and ye are not the storers of it.

And verily We give life and death, and We are the heirs *of all the creation.*

We also know those who have gone before you, and We know those who follow after [you].

And verily thy Lord will assemble them together: for He is Wise, Knowing. (xv. 16–25.)

---

1 Lit. 'driven away with stones.' This expression alludes to a tradition, that Abraham, when the devil tempted him to disobey God, in not sacrificing his son, drove the fiend away by throwing stones at him; in memory of which, the Mohammadans, at the pilgrimage of Mecca, throw a certain number of stones at the devil, with certain ceremonies, in the valley of Mina.—S. The devils, or evil jinn, it is said, had liberty to enter any of the seven heavens till the birth of Jesus, when they were excluded from three of them; on the birth of Mohammad they were forbidden the other four. They continue, however, to ascend to the confines of the lowest heaven, and there, listening to the conversation of the angels respecting things decreed by God, obtain knowledge of futurity, which they sometimes impart to men, who by means of talismans or certain invocations make them to serve the purposes of magical performances. Shooting stars are often hurled at the devils when they thus listen.

2 *That it may not move with its inhabitants.*

3 *Or determined.*

4 *Slaves and beasts and cattle: for it is God only who sustaineth them.*

5 *Which cause the clouds to fill with water.*

IX.

And your God is One God: there is no god but He, the Compassionate, the Merciful.

Verily in the creation of the heavens and the earth, and the varying of night and day, and the ships that course upon the sea *laden* with what is profitable to mankind, and the water that God hath sent down from heaven, quickening the earth thereby after its death, and scattering about it all kinds of beasts; and in the changing of the winds, and the clouds that are compelled to do service between heaven and earth, are signs unto a people who understand.

Yet among men are those who take to themselves, beside God, idols, which they love as *with* the love for God: but those who have believed are more loving towards God *than these towards their idols.* (ii. 158–160.)

X.

Verily God causeth the grain to come forth, and the date-stone: He bringeth forth the living from the dead,[1] and He bringeth forth the dead from the living:[2] This is God; then wherefore are ye turned away?

He causeth the dawn to appear, and hath ordained the night for rest, and the sun and the moon for reckoning *time:* this is the appointment of the Mighty, the Wise.

And it is He who hath ordained for you the stars, that ye may be guided by them in the darknesses of the land and of the sea: We have clearly shown the signs *of Our power* unto the people who know.[3]

And it is He who hath produced you from one soul, and *there is* a place of rest and of storing:[4] We have clearly shown the signs to the people who understand.

And it is He who hath sent down water from heaven, and We have produced thereby the germs of everything,

---

[1] *As the bird from the egg.*
[2] *As the egg from the bird.*
[3] *Or consider.*
[4] *For you previously to birth.*

and We have caused the green thing to come forth therefrom, from which We draw forth grains massed; and from the palm-tree, from its fruit-branch, clusters of dates heaped together:[1] and gardens of grapes, and the olive and the pomegranate, like one another[2] and not like.[3] Look ye at their fruits when they bear fruit, and their ripening. Verily therein are signs unto the people who believe.

Yet they have set up the Jinn[4] as partners of God, though He hath created them, and without knowledge have they falsely attributed to Him sons and daughters. Extolled be His purity, and high be He exalted above that which they attribute [to Him]!

He is the Author of the heavens and the earth. How then should He have offspring, when He hath no consort, and hath created everything and knoweth everything?

This is God your Lord. There is no God but He, the Creator of everything: therefore worship ye Him;[5] and He is guardian over everything.

The eyes see Him not, but He seeth the eyes: and He is the Gracious, the Knowing. (vi. 95–103.)

XI.

It is He who maketh the lightning to appear unto you, [causing] fear and hope *of rain*, and formeth the pregnant clouds.

And the thunder proclaimeth His perfection with His praise; and [likewise] the angels, in fear of Him. And He sendeth the thunderbolts, and striketh with them whom He pleaseth, whilst they dispute concerning God; for He is mighty in power.[6] (xiii. 13, 14.)

---

[1] ['Compacted,' orig. ed. Strictly, words such as 'come forth' should be supplied before 'clusters.']

[2] *In leaf.* [3] *In fruit.*

[4] [Genii.] *since they have obeyed them in worshipping idols.* See p. 33.

[5] *Alone.*

[6] *This was revealed with reference to a man unto whom the Prophet sent one to invite him* to the faith; *but he said, Who is the apostle of God, and what is God? Is he of gold, or silver, or brass? Whereupon a thunderbolt fell upon him, and struck off his skull.*

XII.

With Him are the keys of the hidden things: none knoweth them but He: and He knoweth whatsoever is on the land and in the sea, and there falleth not a leaf but He knoweth it, nor a grain in the dark parts of the earth, nor a moist thing nor a dry thing, but [it is noted] in a distinct writing.[1]

And it is He who taketh your souls at night, and knoweth what ye have gained in the day; then He reviveth you therein,[2] that an appointed time[3] may be fulfilled. Then unto Him shall ye return: then will He declare unto you what ye have done.

And He is the Supreme[4] over His servants, and He sendeth watchers over you,[5] until when death cometh unto any one of you, Our messengers take his soul, and they fail not.

Then are they[6] returned unto God their Lord, the True.[7] Doth not judgment belong to Him? And He is the most quick of reckoners.

SAY,[8] Who delivereth you from the darknesses of the land and of the sea, *when* ye supplicate Him humbly and in secret, *saying*, 'If Thou deliver us from these *dangers*, we will assuredly be of [the number of] the thankful'?

SAY, God delivereth you from them and from every affliction. (vi. 59–64.)

XIII.

Verily God will not forgive the associating with Him [any other being as a god], but will forgive other *sins* unto

---

1 *On the Preserved Tablet.*

2 *Restoring your souls in the day-time.*

3 *The term of life.*

4 ['Predominant,' orig. ed.]

5 *Angels who register your deeds.*

6 *The creatures.*

7 *That He may recompense them.*

8 *O Moḥammad, to the people of Mekkeh.*

whom He pleaseth; and whoso associateth [another] with God hath wrought a great wickedness. (iv. 51.)

XIV.

They[1] say, 'The Compassionate hath gotten offspring:' Ye have done an impious thing.

It wanteth little but that the heavens be rent thereat and that the earth cleave asunder, and that the mountains fall down in pieces.[2]

For that they have attributed offspring to the Compassionate, when it beseemeth not the Compassionate to get offspring.

There is none of all that are in the heavens and the earth but he shall come unto the Compassionate as a servant.[3] He hath known them and numbered them with an *exact* numbering.

And each of them shall come unto Him on the day of resurrection, alone.[4]

†Verily those who have believed and have done the things that are right, on them the Compassionate will bestow [His] love. (xix. 91–96.)

XV.

O men *of Mekkeh*, a parable is propounded, wherefore hearken unto it. Verily, those *idols* which ye invoke beside God can never create a fly, although they assembled for it: and if the fly carry off from them aught,[5] they cannot recover the same from it. Weak are the seeker and the sought! (xxii. 72.)

---

[1] *Namely, the Jews and the Christians, and those* [Arabs] *who assert that the angels are daughters of God.*

[2] ['Demolished,' orig. ed.]

[3] *On the day of resurrection.*

[4] *Without wealth or helper.*

[5] *Of the perfume and saffron with which they are overdaubed.*

XVI.

The likeness of those who take to themselves Tutelars[1] instead of God is as the likeness of the spider, which maketh for herself a dwelling; and the frailest of dwellings surely is the dwelling of the spider! If they knew[2]——!

Verily God knoweth whatever thing they invoke in His stead; and He is the Mighty, the Wise.

And these parables[3] we propound unto men; but none understand them except the wise.

God hath created the heavens and the earth in truth: verily therein is a sign unto the believers.

(xxix. 40–43.)

---

[1] *Idols.*

[2] *This they would not worship them.*

[3] ['Similitudes,' orig. ed. It is the plural of the same word as that translated 'parable' at the beginning of the preceding extract, and 'likeness' twice in this extract.]

MOHAMMAD AND THE ḲUR-ÁN.

XVII.

†O thou enwrapped *in thy mantle*,[1]
Arise and warn!
And thy Lord—magnify Him!
And thy raiment—purify it!
And the abomination[2]—flee it!
And bestow not favours that thou mayest receive again with increase.
And for thy Lord wait thou patiently.[3] (lxxiv. 1–7.)

XVIII.

†By the morning-brightness,
And by the still of night,[4]
Thy Lord hath not forsaken thee, neither hath He hated thee.
And surely the Future will be better for thee than the Present,
And thy Lord will give to thee, and thou wilt be well-pleased.
Did He not find thee an orphan, and sheltered thee?
And He found thee erring, and guided thee,
And found thee needy, and enriched thee.
Then, as to the orphan, oppress him not;
And as to him that asketh of thee, chide him not away;
And as for the bounty of thy Lord, tell it then [abroad].
(xciii.)

---

1 [It is said that Moḥammad, when a revelation came down to him, used to say, 'Cover ye me with something whereby I may become warm.' Lane: Lexicon, voce *dathara*.]

2 [Idolatry.]

3 [This rendering is Mr. Rodwell's. I do not think it can be bettered.]

4 [Lit. 'And by the night when it becometh still;' or (but this is less strongly supported) 'when it darkeneth.']

XIX.

Say, I do not say unto you, 'With me[1] are the treasures of God,' nor, 'I know what is unseen,' nor do I say unto you, 'Verily I am an angel.' I follow not [aught] but what is revealed unto me. (vi. 50.)

XX.

†Say, I am only a man like unto you. It is only revealed unto me that your God is One God. He then that hopeth to meet his Lord, let him work a righteous work, and in the worship of his Lord let him not associate any [other god]. (xviii. 110.)

XXI.

†Say, If I err, only against myself shall I err, but if I am rightly-guided, it [is] of what my Lord hath revealed to me. Verily, He is the Hearer, the Near-at-hand! (xxxiv. 49.)

XXII.

Moḥammad is nought but a Messenger.[2] The Messengers have passed away before him. If then he die or be slain, will ye turn round upon your heels?[3] But he who turneth round upon his heels will not injure God a whit;[4] and God will reward the thankful. (iii. 138.)

XXIII.

Verily We have revealed unto thee as we revealed unto Noah and the prophets after him, and *as* We revealed unto Abraham, and Ishmael, and Isaac, and Jacob, and the tribes, and Jesus, and Job, and Jonah, and Aaron, and Solomon; and We gave unto David the Psalms. (iv. 161.)

---

[1] ['In my possession,' orig. ed.]

[2] ['Apostle,' in the orig. ed.; but Christian associations have somewhat restricted the original meaning of the word, and I have therefore in this and other instances substituted 'Messenger,' which exactly represents the Arabic *rasool.*]

[3] *To unbelief.*

[4] *He will only injure himself.*

XXIV.

[1] SAY *unto them,* Do ye argue with us concerning God, when He is our Lord and your Lord,[2] and when we have our works and ye have your works, and when we are sincere towards Him?

Nay, do ye say that Abraham and Ishmael and Isaac and Jacob and the tribes were Jews or Christians? Say *unto them,* Are ye the more knowing, or is God?[3] And who is more unrighteous than they who conceal a testimony that they have from God?[4] But God is not heedless of that which ye do. (ii. 133, 134.)

XXV.

Remember, when Jesus the son of Mary said, 'O children of Israel, Verily I am the Messenger of God unto you, confirming the Law which [was] before me, and giving good tidings of a Messenger who shall come after me, whose name [shall be] Aḥmad.'[5] But when he (*Aḥmad*) came unto them with evident proofs, they said, 'This is manifest magic!'

And who is more unrighteous than he who forgeth falsehood against God, when he is invited unto El-Islám? And God directeth not the unrighteous people.

---

[1] *The Jews said unto the Muslims, We are the people of the first book* (the Pentateuch), *and our Ḳibleh* (the point to which we turn our faces in praying) *is the more ancient, and the prophets have not been of the Arabs, and if Moḥammad were a prophet, he had been of us. Therefore* the following *was revealed.*

[2] *So that He may choose of His servants whom He pleaseth.*

[3] *That is, God is; and He hath acquitted Abraham of belonging to them by His saying* [Ḳur. iii. 60], *Abraham was not a Jew nor a Christian; and the other persons above-mentioned with him were followers of him.*

[4] *They are the Jews, who have concealed the testimony of God, in the Pentateuch, of Abraham's orthodoxy.*

[5] [Moḥammad and Aḥmad are from the same root, *ḥamd*, meaning 'praise;' and both names were borne by the Prophet. The supposed prediction of Mohammad's coming arose, perhaps, from a confusion between Parakletos and Perikleitos or possibly Periklytos in Evang. S. Jo. xvi. 7, where the coming of 'the Paraclete' is promised; in some Arabic version of which the word may have been ignorantly rendered by 'Aḥmad,' and thus reported to Moḥammad.]

They desire to put out the light of God with their mouths: but God will perfect His light, though the unbelievers be loth *thereto*.

It is He who hath sent His messenger with the direction and the religion of truth, that He may exalt above every religion, though the polytheists be loth *thereto*.

(lxi. 6–9.)

XXVI.

Those to whom We have given the Scripture know him (*Moḥammad*) as they know their children.[1] But a party of them do conceal the truth[2] while they know.

(ii. 141.)

XXVII.

The Jews said unto Moḥammad, 'Verily God hath enjoined us[3] that we should not believe an apostle until he bring us a sacrifice which fire shall devour.'

SAY, Apostles have come unto you before me with manifest proofs,[4] and with that ye have mentioned:[5] then wherefore did ye slay them, if ye be speakers of truth?

(iii. 179, 180.)

XXVIII.

The unbelievers of Mekkeh have sworn by God, with the mightiest of their oaths, that if a sign come unto them they will assuredly believe therein. SAY, Signs are only with God. And what will make you to know?[6] Verily if they come they will not believe.

And We will turn away their hearts and their eyes,[7] as they believed not therein the first time; and We will leave them in their transgression, wandering about in perplexity.

---

[1] *By the description of him in their books.*

[2] *The description of him.*

[3] *In the Law.* [4] *Or miracles.*

[5] *As Zechariah and John, and ye slew them.*

[6] *Their belief, if the signs come.* The copies of the original differ in this verse, but not in an important manner.

[7] *From the truth, so that they shall not believe.*

And though We had sent down unto them the angels, and the dead had spoken unto them, and We had gathered together about them everything in tribes, they had not believed unless God had pleased; but the greater number of them know not. (vi. 109–111.)

XXIX.

And they have said, 'O thou unto whom the Admonition[1] hath been sent down, thou art certainly possessed by a Jinnee.[2]

Why dost thou not come unto us with the angels, if thou be of those that speak truth?'

We send not down the angels save with justice,[3] nor would they then be respited.

Verily, We have sent down the Admonition, and We will surely preserve it.

And We have sent *Messengers* before thee among the sects of the former generations;

And there came not unto them any Messenger but they had him in derision:

In like manner will We put it into the hearts of the sinners *of Mekkeh to do so;*

They shall not believe in him, and the punishment of the former generations hath passed.

And if We should open above them a gate in heaven, and they should pass the day mounting up to it,

They would say, 'Our eyes are only intoxicated, or rather we are a people enchanted.' (xv. 6–15.)

XXX.

†Verily, it is the excellent Kur-án,
Written in the Preserved Book.[4]
None shall touch it but they who are purified.[5]
It is a revelation from the Lord of the Worlds.
(lvi. 76–79.)

---

1 *The Kur-án.* 2 Or art mad. 3 *That is, with punishment.* 4 [The original copy kept by God.] 5 [This line is often inscribed on the covers of copies of the Kur-án.]

XXXI.

SAY, Verily if mankind and the Jinn assembled together for the purpose of producing the like of this Ḳur-án,[1] they could not produce the like thereof, although they helped one another.[2]

And We have explained unto men in this Ḳur-án every *kind of* parable,[3] but the greater number of men have refused [all else] save unbelief,

And have said, 'We will by no means believe in thee until thou cause a fountain to gush forth for us from the earth,

Or thou have a garden of palm-trees and grapes, and thou cause rivers to spring forth in the midst thereof in abundance,

Or thou cause heaven to fall down upon us, as thou hast pretended, in pieces, or thou bring God and the angels before *us*,

Or thou have a house of gold, or thou ascend into heaven, and we will not believe thy ascending until thou cause a book to descend unto us which we may read.' SAY, Extolled be the perfection of my Lord! Am I [aught] save a man, [sent] as a Messenger?

And nothing hath hindered men from believing when the direction hath come unto them, but their saying, 'Hath God sent a man as a Messenger?'[4]

SAY, If there were upon the earth angels walking at ease,[5] We had sent down unto them from heaven an angel as a Messenger.[6]

SAY, God is a sufficient witness between me and you: for He knoweth and seeth His servants. (xvii. 90–98.)

---

1 *In eloquence.*

2 [In orig. edition, and literally, 'Although some of them assisted others.']

3 *That they may be admonished.*

4 *And not sent an angel?*

5 *Instead of mankind.*

6 *For no apostle is sent unto a people but one of their own kind.*

XXXII.

And this Ḳur-án is not an invention[1] of one who is not God, but *it hath been sent down* as a confirmation of those *books which have been* before it, and an explanation of the Scripture—there is no doubt thereof—from the Lord of the Worlds.

Do they say, 'He[2] hath forged it?' SAY, Then bring ye a Soorah[3] like unto it and call whom ye can,[4] other than God, if ye speak truth.

Nay they have charged with falsehood that which they comprehend not, and the explanation thereof[5] hath not yet come unto them. In like manner did those who were before them charge *their Messengers* with falsehood; but see how was the end of the offenders! (x. 38–40.)

XXXIII.

If ye be in doubt concerning that which We have sent down unto Our servant *Moḥammad*,[6] bring ye a Soorah like unto it,[7] and invoke your witnesses,[8] other than God, if ye be speakers of truth.

But if ye do *it* not (and do *it* ye shall not), fear the fire whose fuel is men and stones: it is prepared for the unbelievers. (ii. 21, 22.)

XXXIV.

Whatsoever[9] verse We abrogate or cause *thee* to forget, We will produce one better than it or like unto it. Dost thou not know that God is all-powerful?

Dost thou not know that to God *belongeth* the dominion of the heavens and the earth, and that beside God ye have no protector or defender? (ii. 100, 101.)

---

1 Forgery. 2 *Moḥammad.*

3 Chapter. 4 *To assist you.*

5 *The result of the threat that it containeth.*

6 *As to its being from God.*

7 *In eloquence and beauty of composition and information concerning what is unseen.*

8 *Your deities whom ye worship, that they may aid you.*

9 *When the unbelievers cavilled at abrogation, and said, 'Moḥammad commandeth his companions to-day to do a thing and forbiddeth it to-morrow,'* the following *was revealed.*

XXXV.

When We substitute a verse in the stead of a verse (and God best knoweth what He revealeth), they say, 'Thou art but a forger!'—but the greater number of them know not!

SAY, The Holy Spirit *Gabriel* hath brought it down from thy Lord with truth, to stablish those who have believed, and as a direction and good tidings unto the Muslims.

And We well know that they say, 'Only a man[1] teacheth him.' The tongue of him to whom they incline is foreign, and this *is the* perspicuous Arabic tongue.

(xvi. 103–105).

XXXVI.

SAY, If the sea were ink, for *writing* the words of my Lord, the sea would be dried up or ever the words of my Lord were exhausted; and [so] if we brought its like in aid.[2] (xviii. 109).

---

[1] *Namely, a Christian slave whom the Prophet used to visit.* [The Mekkans accounted for the production of the Ḳurán by an unlearned man like Moḥammad by ascribing it to the teaching of some Christian, whom is doubtful. Moḥammad's reply is that the Christian's was a foreign tongue, whilst the Ḳurán was in Arabic.]

[2] ['As a further supply,' orig. ed.]

THE RESURRECTION, PARADISE, AND HELL.

XXXVII.

†The Striking! what is the Striking?
And what shall teach thee what the Striking is?
It is a day when mẹn shall be like scattered moths,
And the mountains like carded wool!
Then as for him whose balances are heavy, his shall be a life well-pleasing.
As for him whose balances are light, his abode shall be the Pit.
And what shall teach thee what that is?
A raging fire! (ci.)

XXXVIII.

†When the earth is shaken with her shaking,
And the earth hath cast forth her dead,[1]
And man shall say, 'What aileth her?'
On that day shall she tell out her tidings,
Because thy Lord hath inspired her.
On that day shall men come one by one to behold their works,
And whosoever shall have wrought an ant's weight of good shall behold it,
And whosoever shall have wrought an ant's weight of ill shall behold it. (xcix.)

---

[1] [Lit. 'Burdens:' explained by El-Beyḍáwee and others as *buried treasures* and as *dead.*]

XXXIX.

†When the heaven shall be cloven asunder,
And when the stars shall be scattered,
And when the seas shall be let loose,
And when the graves shall be turned upside-down,
Every soul shall know what it hath done and left undone.
O man! what hath seduced thee from thy generous Lord,
Who created thee and fashioned thee and disposed thee aright?
In the form which pleased Him hath He fashioned thee.
Nay, but ye treat the Judgment as a lie.
Verily there are watchers over you,
Worthy recorders,
Knowing what ye do.
Verily in delight shall the righteous dwell;
And verily the wicked in Hell[-Fire];
They shall be burnt at it on the day of doom,
And they shall not be hidden from it.
And what shall teach thee what the Day of Judgment is?
Again: What shall teach thee what is the Day of Judgment?
It is a day when one soul shall be powerless for another soul; and all on that day shall be in the hands of God. (lxxxii.)

XL.

When the sun shall be wrapped up,
And when the stars shall fall down,
And when the mountains shall be made to pass away,
And when the camels ten months gone with young[1] shall be neglected,
And when the wild beasts shall be gathered together,
And when the seas shall overflow,[2]
And when the souls shall be joined *to their bodies*,

---

[1] *The most highly esteemed of property.*

[2] ['Be set on fire,' orig. ed. Both these renderings, and also 'be dried up,' are supported by various authorities. See Lane: Lex. voce *sejera.*]

And when the child[1] that hath been buried alive shall be asked
For what crime she was put to death,
And when the books[2] shall be laid open,
And when the heaven shall be removed,[3]
And when Hell shall be made to burn,
And when Paradise shall be brought near,—
Then every soul shall know what it hath done.
(lxxxi. 1–14.)

XLI.

Hath the news of the Overwhelming reached thee?
Countenances on that day [shall be] abased,
Labouring, toiling:
They shall feel the heat of scorching fire,
They shall be given to drink from a fountain fiercely boiling,
There shall be no food for them but of daree',[4]—
It shall not fatten nor satisfy hunger. (lxxxviii. 1–7.)

XLII.

When one blast shall be blown on the trumpet,
And the earth shall be raised and the mountains, and be broken to dust with one breaking,
On that day the Calamity shall come to pass:
And the heaven shall cleave asunder, being frail on that day,
And the angels on the sides thereof; and over them on that day eight *of the angels*[5] shall bear the throne of thy Lord.
On that day ye shall be presented *for the reckoning;* none of your secrets shall be hidden.
And as to him who shall have his book given to him in his right hand, he shall say,[6] 'Take ye, read my book;

---

1 Woman-child.

2 *Of men's actions.*

3 *As the skin is plucked off a* slaughtered *sheep.*

4 *A kind of thorn which no beast eateth, by reason of its impurity.*

5 *Or eight ranks of them.*

6 *Unto a company, by reason of his joy thereat.*

Verily I was sure I should come to my reckoning.
And his [shall be] a pleasant life
In a lofty garden,
Whose clusters [shall be] near at hand.
[1]'Eat ye and drink with benefit on account of that which ye paid beforehand in the past days.'

But as to him who shall have his book given to him in his left hand, he shall say, 'O would that I had not had my book given to me,
Nor known what [was] my reckoning!
O would that *my death* had been the ending *of me!*
My wealth hath not profited me!
My power is passed away from me!'
'[2]Take him and chain him,
Then cast him into hell to be burnt,
Then in a chain of seventy cubits bind him:
For he believed not in God, the Great,
Nor urged to feed the poor;
Therefore he shall not have here this day a friend,
Nor any food save filth
Which none but the sinners shall eat.'

(lxix. 13–37.)

XLIII.

When the Calamity shall come to pass
There shall not be *a soul* that will deny its happening,[3]
[It will be] an abaser *of some*, an exalter *of others;*
When the earth shall be shaken with a *violent* shaking,
And the mountains shall be crumbled with a [violent] crumbling,
And shall become fine dust scattered abroad;

---

[1] *And it shall be said unto such.*
[2] *And it shall be said unto the keepers of hell.*

As it hath denied it in the present world.

And ye shall be three classes.
And the people of the right hand,[1] what [shall be] the people of the right hand![2]
And the people of the left hand, what the people of the left hand![3]
And the Preceders,[4] the Preceders!
These [shall be] the brought-nigh [unto God]
In the gardens of delight,—
A crowd of the former generations,
And a few of the latter generations,
Upon inwrought couches
Reclining thereon, face to face.
Youths ever-young[5] shall go unto them round about
With goblets and ewers and a cup of flowing wine,
Their [heads] shall ache not with it neither shall they be drunken;
And with fruits of the [sorts] which they shall choose,
And the flesh of birds of the [kinds] which they shall desire.
And damsels[6] with eyes[7] like pearls laid up
We will give them as a reward for that which they have done.
Therein shall they hear no vain discourse nor accusation of sin,
But [only] the saying, 'Peace! Peace!'

And the people of the right hand—what [shall be] the people of the right hand!
[They shall dwell] among lote-trees without thorns
And bananas loaded with fruit,[8]

---

[1] *Those who shall receive their books in their right hands.*

[2] *How honourable shall they be!*

[3] *How contemptible shall they be!*

[4] *In the way to good fortune (namely, the Prophets), how honourable shall be!*

[5] ['Destined to continue for ever *in boyhood*,' orig. ed.]

[6] [Ḥooreeyehs.]

[7] Intensely black and white, large-eyed.

[8] From bottom to top.

And a shade *ever*-spread,
And water *ever*-flowing,
And fruits abundant
Unstayed and unforbidden,
And couches raised.
Verily we have created them[1] by a [peculiar] creation,
And have made them virgins,
Beloved of their husbands, of equal age [with them],
For the people of the right hand,
A crowd of the former generations
And a crowd of the latter generations.

And the people of the left hand—what [shall be] the people of the left hand!
[They shall dwell] amidst burning wind and scalding water,
And a shade of blackest smoke,
Not cool and not grateful.
For before this they were blest with worldly goods,
And they persisted in heinous sin,[2]
And said, 'When we shall have died and become dust and bones, shall we indeed be raised to life,
And our fathers the former generations?'
SAY, Verily the former and the latter generations
Shall be gathered together for the appointed time of a known day.
Then ye, O ye erring, belying [people],
Shall surely eat of the tree of Ez-Zaḳḳoom,
And fill therewith [your] bellies,
And drink thereon boiling water,
And ye shall drink as thirsty camels drink.—
This [shall be] their entertainment on the day of retribution. (lvi. 1–56.)

---

[1] [The Ḥooreeyehs.]

[2] *Polytheism.*

XLIV.

Verily We have prepared for the offenders fire, the smoke of which shall encompass them; and if they ask relief, they shall be relieved with water like the dregs of oil, which shall scald *their* faces. Miserable shall be the drink, and evil shall be the couch.

As for those who have believed and done the things that are right, verily We will not suffer the reward of him that hath done well to perish:

For these are gardens of perpetual abode, beneath them[1] shall rivers run; they shall be adorned therein with bracelets of gold, and shall wear green garments of fine brocade and of thick brocade, reclining therein on the thrones. Excellent shall be the reward, and pleasant shall be the couch. (xviii. 28–30.)

XLV.

Call to mind the day when We will cause the mountains to pass away and thou shalt see the earth plain; and We will assemble them[2] and not leave of them any one.

And they shall be set before thy Lord in ranks: 'Now are ye come unto Us as We created you the first time.[3] Nay, ye thought that We would not perform [Our] promise to you.'[4]

And the book shall be put [in every man's hand], and thou shalt see the sinners fearful because of that which is [written] therein, and they shall say, 'O woe is us! what meaneth this book? It leaveth neither a small *sin* nor a great *sin*, but it enumerateth it!' And they shall find that which they shall have wrought present;[5] and thy Lord will not deal unjustly with any one.

(xviii. 45–47.)

---

[1] Beneath the tents thereof.

[2] *The believers and the unbelievers.*

[3] *One after another, barefooted, naked, unarmed.*

[4] *Of the resurrection.*

[5] *Written in their books.*

XLVI.

They have not esteemed God with the estimation due unto Him, since the whole earth [shall be] His handful on the day of resurrection, and the heavens [shall be] folded together by His right hand. Extolled be His perfection and high be He exalted above the [things] they associate *with Him!*

And the trumpet shall be blown, and they that are in the heavens and they that are in the earth shall die, except those whom God shall please. Then it shall be blown another time; and lo, they shall arise, waiting.

And the earth shall shine with the light of its Lord. And the book shall be placed, and the prophets shall be brought and the witnesses, and judgment shall be given between them with truth, and they shall not be treated unjustly.

And every soul shall be fully paid *the reward* of what it hath done, and He well knoweth what they do.

And those who have disbelieved shall be driven in troops unto hell, until when they come to it, its gates shall be opened, and its guardians shall say unto them, 'Did not Messengers from among you come unto you rehearsing the signs of your Lord, and warning you of the meeting of this your day?' They shall answer, 'Yea:' (But the sentence of punishment[1] hath been justly pronounced against the unbelievers:)

It shall be said, 'Enter ye the gates of hell to remain therein for ever:' and evil shall be the abode of the proud.

And those who have feared their Lord shall be urged on in troops unto paradise, until when they come unto it, its gates are already opened, and its guardians say unto them. 'Peace be on you! Ye have been good: therefore enter it to abide *therein* for ever.'

And they shall say, 'Praise be to God, who hath performed unto us His promise, and hath made us to inherit

---

[1] *I will surely fill Hell*, &c. [Ḳur. vii. 17, given below, p. 51].

the land, that we may dwell in Paradise wheresoever we please; and how excellent is the reward of the workers!'[1]

And thou shalt see the angels encompassing the throne, extolling the perfection with the praise of their Lord. And judgment shall be given between them[2] with truth: and it shall be said, 'Praise be to God, the Lord of the Worlds!'

(xxxix. 67–75.)

XLVII.

Paradise shall be brought near unto the pious, *to a place* not distant *from them, so that they shall see it.*

And it shall be said unto them, 'This is what ye have been promised, unto every one who hath earnestly turned himself unto God and kept *His laws,*

Who hath feared the Compassionate in secret, and come with a penitent heart:

Enter it in peace: this is the Day of Eternity.'

(l. 30–33.)

XLVIII.

†Fairseeming to men is the love of pleasures from women and children, and hoarded riches of gold and silver, and pastured[3] horses, and flocks, and corn-fields. Such is the enjoyment of this world's life! But God, goodly is the home with Him!

SAY, Shall I tell you of better things than these prepared in the presence of their Lord for those that fear [God]? Theirs shall be gardens beneath which rivers run, and in which they shall abide for ever, and stainless wives, and acceptance with God: for God regardeth His servants,

—Who say, 'O our Lord, verily we have believed; forgive us then our sins, and keep us from the torment of the fire,'—

The patient, and the truthful, and the lowly, and the charitable, and they who seek pardon at each daybreak.

(iii. 12–15.)

---

[1] Of righteousness. [2] *Between all creatures.*

[3] [Or 'marked' or 'goodly.']

XLIX.

†And repute not those slain in God's cause[1] to be dead: nay, alive with their Lord, they are provided for;

Joyful in what God of His bounty hath vouchsafed them, and rejoicing for those that follow after them, but have not yet overtaken them, that on them no fear shall come, neither shall they grieve;

Rejoicing at the favour of God and His bounty, and that God suffereth not the reward of the faithful to perish.

(iii. 163–165.)

L.

Whosoever doeth the things that are right, whether male or female, being a believer,—these shall enter paradise, and shall not be wronged in the least degree. (iv. 123.)

LI.

For those who have disbelieved in their Lord [is prepared] the punishment of hell; and evil [shall be] the journey.[2]

When they shall be cast into it they shall hear it braying,[3] while it boileth, well-nigh bursting with fury. (lxvii. 6–8.)

LII.

If thou shouldst see[4] those who have offended[5] when they see the punishment![6]—for power belongeth altogether unto God, and God is severe in punishing:

When those who have been followed will declare themselves clear of those who have followed [them],[7] when they have seen the punishment, and the ties [that bound them together] shall be severed from them:

And those who have followed shall say, 'O that there were for us a return *to the world!* then would we declare ourselves clear of them, like as they have *now* declared themselves clear of us!' After this manner will God show

---

1 [Fighting for the faith.]

2 [Or 'end,' 'result.']

3 "Arms on armour clashing bray'd Horrible discord."—*Par. Lost*, vi. 209.

4 *O Moḥammad.* The copies of the original differ here, but the differences are unimportant.

5 *By taking to themselves idols.*

6 *Thou wouldst see a great thing!*

7 *Denying their having led them into error.*

them their *evil* works, for which [they shall pour forth] lamentations; and they shall not come forth from the fire. (ii. 160–162.)

LIII.

And the Devil[1] shall say, when the matter shall have been determined,[2] 'Verily God promised you the promise of truth;[3] and I promised you,[4] but I deceived you: yet had I no power over you;

But I only called you and ye answered me. Therefore blame not me, but blame your own selves. I am not a helper of you, neither are ye helpers of me. Verily I renounce your having associated me *with God* heretofore.' (xiv. 26, 27).

LIV.

Verily the hypocrites shall be in the lowest abyss of the fire, and thou shalt not find for them any defender. (iv. 144.)

LV.

They[5] will ask thee respecting the Hour,[6] at what time is its coming fixed. SAY, The knowledge of it is only with my Lord: none shall manifest it in its time but He. It is grievous in the heavens and in the earth. It shall not come upon you otherwise than suddenly.

They will ask thee as though thou wert well acquainted therewith. SAY, The knowledge of it is only with God: but the greater number of men know not!

SAY, I possess not for myself *power to procure* advantage nor *to avert* mischief, save as God pleaseth: and if I knew things unseen, I should obtain abundance of good, and evil should not happen unto me. I am only a denouncer of threats *unto the unbelievers*, and an announcer of good tidings unto the people who believe. (vii. 186–188.)

---

[1] *Iblees.*

[2] *And the people of paradise are introduced into paradise, and the people of the fire into the fire, and when the latter have assembled around him.*

[3] *Respecting the resurrection and retribution.*

[4] *The contrary.*

[5] *The people of Mekkeh.*

[6] *Of the resurrection.*

PREDESTINATION.

LVI.

A soul cannot die unless by permission of God, according to a writing *of God*, definite *as to time*. (iii. 139.)

LVII.

They say [whose companions were slain at the battle of Oḥod], 'If aught of the affair had been *submitted* to us we had not been slain here.'[1] SAY, Had ye been in your houses, those *of you* who were decreed to be slain had gone forth to the places where they lie. (iii. 148.)

LVIII.

Wheresoever ye be, death will overtake you, although you be in lofty towers. If good fortune betide them,[2] they say, 'This is from God!' But if evil betide them, they say, 'This is from thee, *O Moḥammad!*' SAY, All is from God. And what aileth this people that they are not near to understanding what is said *unto them?*

Whatsoever good betideth thee, *O man, it is* from God; and whatsoever evil betideth thee, from thyself *is it*.

(iv. 80, 81.)

LIX.

† No soul can believe but by the permission of God.

(x. 100.)

LX.

† And whoso willeth taketh the way to his Lord: But ye shall not will it, unless God will it. (lxxvi. 29, 30.)

LXI.

† Expend in the way of God, and throw not yourselves into destruction.[3] (ii. 191.)

---

[1] *If the choice had been given us we had not gone forth and had not been slain.*

[2] *Namely, the Jews.*

[3] [See *Modern Egyptians*, 5th ed., p. 284.]

ANGELS AND JINN.[1]

LXII.

They say, 'The Compassionate hath gotten offspring.'[2] Extolled be His purity! Nay, *they are* honoured servants.

They prevent Him not in speech,[3] and according to His command they act.

He knoweth what is before them and what is behind them, and they shall not intercede

Save for whom He shall please, and they fear in dread of Him.

And him[4] among them who saith, 'I am a god beside Him,' that [angel] We will recompense with Hell. (xxi. 26–30.)

LXIII.

† SAY, It hath been revealed to me that a company of the Jinn listened [to me] and said, 'Verily we have heard a wonderful discourse[5]

Which guideth unto right: wherefore we believed in it, and we will by no means associate any one with our Lord. . . .

We tried the heaven, but we found it filled with a mighty garrison and darting flames;

We sat on some of its seats to listen, but whosoever listeneth now findeth a darting flame in ambush for him.

We know not whether evil be meant for them that are on the earth, or whether their Lord intendeth for them a right guidance.

There are among us the good, and among us *those who are* not so,—we are of various ways. (lxxii. 1, 2, 8–11.)

---

[1] [On the various orders of the Jinn, see Lane's *Thousand and One Nights*, Introduction, note 21. And see above, pp. 7, 9.

[2] *Consisting of the angels.*

[3] *They speak not until after He hath spoken.*

[4] *Iblees* [the devil].

[5] [In the Arabic, 'Ḳurán.']

TRUE RELIGION AND FALSE.

LXIV.

Verily God commandeth justice and the doing of good and the giving unto the relation: and He forbiddeth wickedness and iniquity and oppression. He admonisheth you that ye may reflect (xvi. 92.)[1]

LXV.

†By the Night when she spreadeth her veil,
By the Day when it appeareth in glory,
By Him who made male and female;
Verily your aims are indeed different!
As then for him who giveth [alms] and feareth [God],
And yieldeth assent to the Good,
To him will We therefore make easy the path to happiness.
But as to him who is covetous and bent on riches,
And calleth the Good a lie,
To him will We make easy the path to distress;
And what shall his wealth avail him when he goeth down
headlong?
Truly man's guidance is with Us,
And Ours the next Life and this life Present.
I warn you therefore of the flaming fire;

---

[1] *This is said to be the most comprehensive verse in the Kur-án with respect to good and evil.* [The commentators say it contains the whole duty of man, both in respect of doing and of shunning. It is needless to enumerate the various virtues and sins which they consider are implied in each of the simple words of the text.]

None shall be burned at it but the most wretched,—
Who hath called the truth a lie and turned his back.
But the greatly God-fearing shall escape it,—
Who giveth away his substance that he may become pure,
And who [offereth] not favours to any one for the sake of recompense,
But only as seeking the face of his Lord the Most High.
And assuredly in the end he shall be well content.[1]
(xcii.)

LXVI.

†What thinkest thou of him who treateth the day of judgment as a lie?
It is he who thrusteth away the orphan,
And stirreth not [others] up to feed the poor.
Woe, then, to those who pray,
Who in their prayer are careless,
Who make a show [of devotion],
But refuse help [to the needy].[1] (cvii.)

LXVII.

Your turning your faces *in prayer* towards the east and the west is not piety: but the pious is he who believeth in God and the Last Day, and in the angels, and the Scripture, and the prophets, and who giveth money, notwithstanding his love *of it*, to relations and orphans, and to the needy and the son of the road,[2] and to the askers and for *the freeing* of slaves, and who performeth prayer and giveth the [appointed] alms, and those who perform their covenant when they covenant, and the patient in adversity and affliction and in the time of violence. These are they who have been true: and these are they who fear God.
(ii. 172.)

---

[1] [Mr. Rodwell's rendering.] [2] The traveller.

LXVIII.

†He only should visit the temples of God who believeth in God and the Last Day, and observeth prayer, and payeth the [appointed] alms, and dreadeth none but God: for these are among the rightly-guided. (ix. 18.)

LXIX.

O ye who have believed, make not your alms of no effect by reproach and harm, like him who expendeth his wealth to make a vain show unto men, and believeth not in God and the Last Day. For his likeness is as the likeness of a smooth stone upon which was earth, and a violent rain hath fallen upon it, and left it smooth and hard. [Such] cannot have aught that they have gained, and God directeth not the unbelieving people.

And the likeness of those who expend their wealth from a desire of God's being pleased, and from assurance on their part,[1] is as the likeness of a garden upon a hill, on which a violent rain hath fallen, and it hath produced its fruit twofold: and if a violent rain fall not upon it, a gentle rain *falleth*. (ii. 266, 267.)

LXX.

If ye manifest alms, good will it be: but if ye conceal them and give them to the poor, it will be better for you; and it will expiate *some* of your sins. (ii. 273.)

LXXI.

A kind speech and forgiveness are better than alms which hurt[2] followeth. (ii. 265.)

LXXII.

Revile not what they invoke in preference to God,[3] lest they revile God evilly without knowledge. (vi. 108.)

---

[1] *Of being rewarded for so doing.* [2] *Or reproach.* [3] *Their idols.*

LXXIII.

Turn away *evil* by that which is better: and lo, he between whom and thyself [was] enmity [shall become] as though he were a warm friend:

But none is endowed with this[1] except those who have been patient, and none is endowed with it except he who is greatly favoured.[2] (xli. 34, 35.)

LXXIV.

†If ye are greeted with a greeting, then greet ye with a better greeting, or at least return it: verily God taketh count of all things. (iv. 88.)

LXXV.

†If there be any [debtor] under a difficulty [of paying his debt], let [his creditor] wait until it be easy: but if ye remit it as alms, it will be better for you. (ii. 280.)[3]

---

1 *Disposition.*

2 [Lit., and in orig. ed., 'hath great good fortune.']

3 [*Mod. Egypt.*, 104.]

BELIEVERS AND UNBELIEVERS.

LXXVI.

†Dispute not with the people of the Scripture[1] unless in the kindliest[2] manner, except against such of them as deal evilly [with you]; and say [unto them], We believe in that which hath been sent down unto us and [that which] hath been sent down unto you, and our God and your God is one, and to Him are we self-surrendered.[3]

(xxix. 45.)

LXXVII.

Verily those who have believed,[4] and those who have become Jews, and the Christians, and the Sabians, whosoever hath believed in God and the Last Day, and hath done that which is right,—they shall have their reward with their Lord, and *there shall come* no fear upon them, neither shall they grieve. (ii. 59.)[5]

LXVIII.

Whoso desireth any other religion than El-Islám, it shall not be accepted of him, and in the world to come he [shall be] of those that perish. (iii. 79.)

LXXIX.

The likeness of those who have disbelieved[6] is as the likeness of him who crieth out to that which heareth not [aught] save a calling and a voice. *They are* deaf, dumb, blind: therefore they do not understand. (ii. 166.)

---

1 [The Christians and Jews.]

2 [Or 'best:' so in *Mod. Egypt.*, 280.]

3 [This is Mr. Rodwell's word, and is, I think, more expressive of the original (*muslimoona*) than 'resigned.']

4 *In the prophets.*

5 [Some suppose this verse to be abrogated by the next extract: others try to explain it away.]

6 *And of him who inviteth them to the true religion.*

LXXX.

[As to] the unbelievers, their works are like a vapour[1] in a plain, which the thirsty imagineth to be water, until when he cometh to it he findeth it not aught:[2] (but he findeth God there, and He fully payeth him his account: and God is swift in reckoning:)

Or, like darknesses in a deep sea, covered by waves over waves,—over them clouds,—darknesses one over another: when [one] putteth forth his hand he is not nearly able to see it. And unto whomsoever God giveth not light, he hath no light. (xxiv. 39, 40.)

LXXXI.

Propound unto them as a parable two men, on one of whom[3] We bestowed two gardens of grape-vines, and We surrounded them with palm-trees, and put corn between them; each of the gardens brought forth its fruit, and failed not thereof at all;

And We caused a river to flow between them; and he had abundance. And he said unto his companion, disputing with him, 'I am greater than thou in wealth and more mighty in family.'

And he entered his garden, being unjust to his own soul.[4] He said, 'I do not think that this will ever perish,

And I do not think that the [Last] Hour will come; and if I should be taken back unto my Lord, I shall assuredly find a better [garden] than it in return.'

His companion said unto him, disputing with him, 'Dost thou disbelieve in Him who created thee of dust, then completely fashioned thee into a man?

God is my Lord, and I will not associate any one with my Lord.

And why when thou enteredst thy garden didst thou

---

1 Mirage (*sarâb*).

2 *In like manner the unbeliever reckoneth that his works will profit him, until, when he dieth and is brought before his Lord, he findeth not his works.*

3 *The unbeliever.*

4 *By his unbelief.*

not say, 'What God willeth[1] [cometh to pass]: there is no power but in God?' If thou seest me to be inferior to thee in amount of wealth and in number of children,

Perhaps my Lord may give me [what will be] better than thy garden; and may send upon [thine] thunderbolts from heaven, so that it shall become a smooth and slippery ground;

Or its water may become deep-sunk [in the earth], so that thou shalt not be able to draw it.'—

And his possessions were encompassed *with destruction*, and he began to turn down the palms of his hands for that which he had expended thereon; for it[s vines were] falling down upon its trellises; and he said, 'O would that I had not associated any one with my Lord!'

And there was no party for him to assist him instead of God, nor was he able to defend himself.

In that case[2] protection [belongeth] unto God, the True; He is the best rewarder and the best giver of success.

(xviii. 31–42.)

LXXXII.

Thou shalt certainly find[3] the Jews and those who have attributed partners to God[4] the most violent of men in hatred of those who have believed; and thou shalt certainly find the nearest of them to friendship to those who have believed those who say, 'We are Christians.' This is because there are among them priests and monks, and because they are not proud.[5]

And when they hear that which hath been sent down unto the Apostle, thou seest their eyes overflow with tears

---

[1] *In the tradition it is said, 'Whosoever hath any good thing given unto him, whether of family or wealth, and saith on the occasion thereof, 'What God willeth ('má-sháá-lláh)! There is no power but in God!' he will not see in it aught displeasing.'*

[2] *On the day of resurrection.*

[3] *O Moḥammad.*

[4] *Of the people of Mekkeh.*

[5] *So as to disdain receiving the truth. (This was revealed as respecting the envoys who came from the King of Abyssinia: the Prophet recited the Soorat Yá-Seen* [xxxvi.], *whereupon they wept and became Muslims, and said, 'How like is this to that which was revealed to Jesus.')*

because of the truth that they know: they say, 'O our Lord, we believe, therefore write us down among those who bear witness.' (v. 85, 86.)

LXXXIII.

The likeness of those who were charged to bear in mind the Law [of Moses], then bore it not in mind,[1] is as the likeness of the ass that beareth books. Evil is the likeness of the people who have charged the signs of God with falsehood: and God directeth not the unjust people.

(lxii. 5.)

LXXXIV.

[2]Among men are those who say, We believe in God and in the Last Day: but they are not believers.

They try to deceive God and those who have believed; but they deceive not any except themselves, and they know [it] not.

In their hearts is a disease, and God hath increased their disease, and for them [is ordained] a painful punishment, because they have charged with falsehood *the prophet of God.*

And when it is said unto them, Corrupt not in the earth, they reply, 'We are only rectifiers.'

Assuredly they are the corrupters; but they know [it] not.

And when it is said unto them, Believe ye as *other* men have believed, they say, 'Shall we believe as the fools have believed?' Assuredly they are the fools; but they know it not.

And when they meet those who have believed, they say, 'We believe:' but when they retire privately to their devils,[3] they say, 'We *hold* with you: we only mock *at them.*'

---

[1] *Not believing in Moḥammad.*

[2] *With respect to the hypocrites* the following *was revealed.*

[3] *Their chiefs.*

God will mock at them, and keep them in their exceeding wickedness, wandering about in perplexity.

These are they who have purchased error in exchange for right guidance: but their traffic hath not been profitable; and they have not been rightly guided.

Their likeness is as the likeness of those who have kindled a fire *in the dark*, and when it hath enlightened what is around them, God taketh away their light and leaveth them in darkness, seeing not.

They are deaf, dumb, blind: therefore they will not turn back.

Or *they are* like *people in* a storm of rain from heaven, wherein are darkness and thunder and lightning: they put their fingers in their ears because of the vehement sounds of the thunder, for fear of death. And God encompasseth the unbelievers.

The lightning almost snatcheth away their eyes: whenever it shineth on them they walk in *the light of* it, but when darkness cometh on them they stand still. And if God pleased He would certainly take away their ears and eyes: for God is all-powerful. (ii. 7–19.)

LXXXV.

O ye who have believed, take not the Jews and Christians as friends. They are friends one to another; and whosoever of you taketh them as his friends, verily he is *of the number* of them.

O ye who have believed, take not as friends those who have made your religion a laughing-stock and a jest, of those who have received the Scripture before you, and the unbelievers: (But fear God if ye be believers:)

And *those who* when ye call to prayer make it a laughing-stock and a jest. This *they do* because they are a people who do not understand. (v. 56, 62, 63.)

LXXXVI.

†The servants of the Merciful are they that walk upon the earth softly; and when the ignorant speak unto them, they reply 'Peace!'—

And they that pass the night worshipping their Lord, prostrate and standing;—

And that say, 'O our Lord, turn away from us the torment of Hell: verily its torment is endless; verily it is an ill abode and resting-place!'—

And those who when they spend are neither lavish nor niggard, but keep the mean;—

And those who call on no other gods with God, nor slay whom God hath forbidden to be slain, except for a just cause; nor are unchaste;—

And they who bear not witness to a lie, and when they pass by vain discourse pass it by with dignity;—

These shall be rewarded with the highest Heaven, for that they persevered, and they shall be accosted therein with 'Welcome and Peace,' to live therein for ever—a fair abode and resting-place! (xxv. 64–75.)

PART THE SECOND.

PART THE SECOND.

PROPHETS, APOSTLES, AND DIVINE BOOKS.[1]

SAY YE, We believe in God, and in that which hath been sent down unto us (*namely, the Ḳur-án*), and what hath been sent down unto Abraham (*the ten books*), and Ishmael, and Isaac, and Jacob, and the tribes, *his children*, and what

[1] The number of the prophets which have been from time to time sent by God into the world amounts to no less than 224,000, according to one Moḥammadan tradition, or to 124,000 according to another; among whom 313 were apostles, sent with special commissions to reclaim mankind from infidelity and superstition; and six of them brought new laws or dispensations, which successively abrogated the preceding: these were Adam, Noah, Abraham, Moses, Jesus, and Moḥammad. All the prophets in general the Moḥammadans believe to have been free from great sins and errors of consequence, and professors of one and the same religion, that is, El-Islám, notwithstanding the different laws and institutions which they observed. In this great number of prophets, they not only reckon divers patriarchs and persons named in Scripture but not recorded to have been prophets (wherein the Jewish and Christian writers have sometimes led the way), as Adam, Seth, Lot, Ishmael, Nun, Joshua, &c., and introduce some of them under different names, as Enoch, Heber, and Jethro, who are called in the Ḳur-án, Idrees, Hood, and Sho'eyb; but several others whose very names do not appear in Scripture (though they endeavour to find some persons there to fix them on), as Ṣáliḥ, El-Khiḍr, Dhu-l-Kifl.

As to the Scriptures, the Moḥammadans are taught by the Ḳur-án that God, in divers ages of the world, gave revelations of His will in writing to several prophets, the whole and every word of which it is absolutely necessary for a good Muslim to believe. The number of these sacred books was, according to them, 104; of which ten were given to Adam, fifty to Seth, thirty to Idrees or Enoch, ten to Abraham; and the other four, being the Pentateuch, the Psalms, the Gospel, and the Ḳur-án, were successively delivered to Moses, David, Jesus, and Moḥammad; which last being the *seal* of

Moses received (*namely, the Pentateuch*), and Jesus (*namely, the Gospel*), and what the prophets received from their Lord (*namely, books and signs*): we make no separation of any of them, *believing in some, and disbelieving in some, like the Jews and the Christians;* and we resign ourselves unto Him. (ii. 130.)

---

the prophets, those revelations are now closed and no more are to be expected. All these divine books, except the four last, they agree to be now entirely lost and their contents unknown; though the Sabians have several books which they attribute to some of the antediluvian prophets. And of those four, the Pentateuch, Psalms, and Gospel, they say, have undergone so many alterations and corruptions, that though there may possibly be some part of the true word of God therein, yet no credit is to be given to the present copies in the hands of the Jews and Christians.—S.

ADAM AND EVE.

Remember, O Moḥammad, when thy Lord said unto the angels, I am about to place in the earth a vicegerent *to act for me in the execution of my ordinances therein, namely, Adam,*—they said, Wilt Thou place in it one who will corrupt in it *by disobediences,* and will shed blood (*as did the sons of El-Jánn,*[1] *who were in it; wherefore, when they acted corruptly, God sent to them the angels, who drove them away to the islands and the mountains*), when we [on the contrary] celebrate the divine perfection, *occupying ourselves* with Thy praise, and extol Thy holiness? *Therefore we are more worthy of the vicegerency.—God* replied, Verily, I know that which ye know not, *as to the affair of appointing Adam vicegerent, and that among his posterity will be the obedient and the rebellious, and the just will be manifest among them. And He created Adam from the surface of the earth, taking a handful of every colour that it comprised, which was kneaded with various waters; and He completely formed it, and breathed into it the soul: so it became an animated sentient being.*[2] And He taught Adam the names of all things, *infusing the knowledge of them into his heart.* Then He showed them (*namely, the things*) to the angels, and said, Declare unto me the names of these *things,* if ye say truth *in your assertion that I will not create any more knowing than ye, and that ye are more worthy of the vicegerency.* They replied, [*We extol*] Thy perfection! We have

---

[1] 'El-Jánn' is here used as a name of Iblees, the father of the jinn. It also signifies the jinn themselves.

[2] According to a tradition of the Prophet, the height of Adam was equal to that of a tall palm-tree.

D

no knowledge excepting what Thou hast taught us; for Thou art the Knowing, the Wise.—*God* said, O Adam, tell them their names. And when he had told them their names, *God* said, Did I not say unto you that I know the secrets of the heavens and the earth, and know what ye reveal *of your words, saying, Wilt thou place in it*, etc., and what ye did conceal *of your words, saying, He will not create any more generous towards Him than we, nor any more knowing?* (ii. 28–31.)

We created you; *that is, your father Adam:* then we formed you; *we formed him, and you in him:* then We said unto the angels, Prostrate yourselves unto Adam, *by way of salutation;* whereupon they prostrated themselves, except Iblees, *the father of the jinn, who was amid the angels:* he was not of those who prostrated themselves. *God* said, What hath hindered thee from prostrating thyself, when I commanded thee? He answered, I am better than he: Thou hast created me of fire, and Thou hast created him of earth. [God] said, Then descend thou from it; *that is, from Paradise; or, as some say, from the heavens;* for it is not fit for thee that thou behave thyself proudly therein: so go thou forth: verily thou [shalt be] of the contemptible. He replied, Grant me respite until the day when they (*that is, mankind*) shall be raised from the dead. He said, Thou shalt be of those [who are] respited: *and, in another verse* [in xv. 38, it is said], *until the day of the known period; that is, until the period of the first blast* [of the trumpet]. [And the devil] said, Now, as Thou hast led me into error, I will surely lay wait for them (*that is, for the sons of Adam*) in Thy right way, *the way that leadeth to Thee:* then I will surely come upon them, from before them, and from behind them, and from their right hands, and from their left, *and hinder them from pursuing the way* (*but, saith Ibn-'Abbás, he cannot come upon them above, lest he should intervene between the servant and God's mercy*), and Thou shalt not find the greater number of them grateful, *or believing.* [God] said, Go forth from it, despised and driven away *from mercy.* Whosoever of them (*that is, of mankind*) shall follow thee, I will surely fill hell with you all; *with thee, and thy offspring, and with men.* (vii. 10–17.)

And we said, O Adam, dwell thou and thy wife (*Howwá* [or Eve], *whom God created from a rib of his left side*) in the garden, and eat ye therefrom plentifully, wherever ye will; but approach ye not this tree, *to eat thereof; (and it was wheat, or the grape-vine, or some other tree;)* for *if ye do so,* ye will be of *the number of* the offenders. But the devil, *Iblees,* caused them to slip from it, *that is, from the garden, by his saying unto them, Shall I show you the way to the tree of eternity? And he swore to them by God that he was one of the faithful advisers to them: so they ate of it,* and He ejected them from that *state of delight* in which they were. And We said, Descend ye[1] *to the earth, ye two with the offspring that ye comprise* [yet unborn], one of you (*that is, of your offspring*) an enemy to another; and there shall be for you, in the earth, a place of abode, and a provision, *of its vegetable produce,* for a time, *until the period of the expiration of your terms of life.* And Adam learned, from his Lord, words, *which were these:—O Lord, we have acted unjustly to our own souls, and if Thou do not forgive us, and be merciful unto us, we shall surely be of those who suffer loss.*[2] *And he prayed in these words;* and He became propitious towards him, *accepting his repentance;* for He is the Very Propitious, the Merciful. We said, Descend ye from it (*from the garden*) altogether; and if there come unto you from Me a direction (*a book and an apostle*), those

---

[1] The Moḥammadans say, that when they were cast down from Paradise [which is in the seventh heaven], Adam fell on the isle of Ceylon, or Sarandeeb, and Eve near Juddah (the port of Mekkeh) in Arabia; and that, after a separation of two hundred years, Adam was, on his repentance, conducted by the angel Gabriel to a mountain near Mekkeh, where he found and knew his wife, the mountain being thence named 'Arafát; and that he afterwards retired with her to Ceylon.—S.

[2] The prayer is inserted by the commentary from Ḳur. vii. 22.

who follow my direction, *there shall come* no fear on them, nor shall they grieve *in the world to come; for they shall enter paradise:* but they who disbelieve and accuse our signs[1] of falsehood, these shall be the companions of the fire: they shall remain therein for ever. (ii. 33–37.)

[1] This word has various significations in the Ḳurán; sometimes, as in this passage, it signifies *divine revelation*, or *scripture* in general; sometimes the *verses* of the *Ḳur-án* in particular; and at other times, *visible miracles*. But the sense is easily distinguished by the context. —S.

ABEL AND CAIN.

Recite, *O Moḥammad,* unto them (*that is, to thy people*) the history of the two sons of Adam, *namely, Abel and Cain,*[1] with truth. When they offered [their] offering *to God*[2] (*Abel's being a ram, and Cain's being produce of the earth*), and it was accepted from one of them (*that is, from Abel; for fire descended from heaven, and devoured his offering*), and it was not accepted from the other, *Cain was enraged; but he concealed his envy until Adam performed a pilgrimage, when* he said *unto his brother,* I will assuredly slay thee. *Abel said, Wherefore? Cain answered, Because of the acceptance of thine offering to the exclusion of mine. Abel* replied, God only accepteth from the pious. If thou stretch forth to me thy hand to slay me, I will not stretch forth to thee my hand to slay thee; for I fear God, the Lord of the worlds. I desire that thou shouldst bear the sin [which thou intendest to commit] against me, *by slaying me,* and thy sin *which thou hast committed before,* and

---

[1] Called in Arabic Hábeel and Ḳábeel.

[2] The occasion of their making this offering is thus related, according to the common tradition in the East. Each of them being born with a twin-sister, when they were grown up, Adam by God's direction ordered Cain to marry Abel's twin-sister, and Abel to marry Cain's; (for it being the common opinion that marriages ought not to be had in the nearest degrees of consanguinity, since they must necessarily marry their sisters, it seemed reasonable to suppose they ought to take those of the remoter degree;) but this Cain refusing to agree to, because his own sister was the handsomest, Adam ordered them to make their offerings to God, thereby referring the dispute to His determination. The commentators say Cain's offering was a sheaf of the very worst of his corn; but Abel's a fat lamb of the best of his flock.—S.

thou wilt be of the companions of the fire.—And that is the recompense of the offenders.—But his soul suffered him to slay his brother: so he slew him; and he became of [the number of] those who suffer loss. *And he knew not what to do with him; for he was the first dead person upon the face of the earth of the sons of Adam. So he carried him upon his back.* And God sent a raven, which scratched up the earth *with its bill and its talons and raised it over a dead raven that was with it until it hid it,* to show him how he should hide the corpse of his brother. He said, O my disgrace! Am I unable to be like this raven, and to hide the corpse of my brother?—And he became of [the number of] the repentant. *And he digged* [a grave] *for him, and hid him.*—On account of this *which Cain did* We commanded the children of Israel that he who should slay a soul (not for *the latter's having slain* a soul or *committed* wickedness in the earth, *such as infidelity, or adultery, or intercepting the way, and the like*) [should be regarded] as though he had slain all mankind; and he who saveth it alive, *by abstaining from slaying it,* as though he had saved alive all mankind. (v. 30–35.)

NOAH AND THE FLOOD.

We formerly sent Noah [Nooḥ] unto his people, *saying,* Verily I am unto you a plain admonisher that ye worship not [any] but God. Verily I fear for you, *if ye worship any other,* the punishment of an afflictive day *in this world and in the world to come.*—But the chiefs who disbelieved among his people replied, We see thee not to be other than a man, like unto us; and we see not any to have followed thee except the meanest of us, *as the weavers and the cobblers,* at first thought (*or rashly*), nor do we see you to have any excellence above us: nay, we imagine you to be liars *in your claim to the apostolic commission.* He said, O my people, tell me, if I have an evident proof from my Lord and He hath bestowed on me mercy (*the gift of prophecy*) from Himself which is hidden from you, shall we compel you to *receive* it when ye are averse thereto? *We cannot do so.* And, O my people, I ask not of you any riches for it; *namely, for delivering my message.* My reward is not due from any but God; and I will not drive away those who have believed *as ye have commanded me* [because they are poor people]. Verily they shall meet their Lord *at the resurrection, and He will recompense them, and will exact for them* [reparation] *from those who have treated them with injustice, and driven them away.* But I see you [to be] a people who are ignorant *of the end of your case.* And, O my people, who will defend me against God if I drive them away? Will ye not then consider? And I do not say unto you, I have the treasures of God; nor [do I say], I know the things unseen; nor do I say, Verily I am an angel; nor do I say, of those whom your eyes contemn, God will by no means bestow on them good: (God best knoweth what is in their minds:) verily I should in that case be [one] of the offenders.—They replied, O Noah, thou hast disputed with us and multiplied disputes with us: now bring upon us that *punishment* wherewith thou threatenest us, if thou be of those that speak truth. He said, Only God will bring it upon you, if He please *to hasten it unto you; for it is His affair, not mine;* and ye shall not escape *God:* nor will my counsel profit you, if I desire to counsel you, if God desire to lead you into error. He is your Lord; and unto Him shall ye be brought back. (xi. 27–36.)

And it was said by revelation unto Noah, Verily there shalt not believe of thy people [any] but they who have already believed; therefore be not grieved for that which they have done. (xi. 38.)

And he uttered an imprecation upon them, saying, O my Lord, leave not upon the earth any one of the unbelievers; for if Thou leave them, they will lead Thy servants into error, and will not beget [any] but a wicked, ungrateful [offspring]. O my Lord, forgive me and my parents (*for they were believers*), and whomsoever entereth my house (*my abode, or my place of worship*), being a believer, and the believing men, and the believing women, (*to the day of resurrection,*) and add not to the offenders [aught] save destruction. (lxxi. 27–29.)

And God answered his prayer, and said, Construct the ark in our sight and according to our revelation, and speak not unto Me concerning those who have offended, *to beg Me not to destroy them;* for they [shall be] drowned. And he constructed the ark; and whenever a company of his people passed by him, they derided him. He said, If ye deride us, we will deride you, like as ye deride, *when we are saved and ye are drowned,* and ye shall know on whom shall come a punishment which shall render him vile, and whom shall befall a lasting punishment. [Thus he was employed] until when Our decree *for their destruction* came to pass, and the *baker's* oven overflowed *with water*[1] (*for this was a signal unto Noah*), We said, Carry into it (*that is, into the ark*) of every pair, *male and female, of each of these descriptions,* two (*and it is related that God assembled for Noah the wild beasts and the birds and other creatures, and he proceeded to put his hands upon each kind, and his right hand fell always upon the male, and his left upon the female, and he carried them into the ark*), and thy family (excepting him upon whom the sentence *of destruction* hath already been pronounced, *namely, Noah's wife, and his son Canaan: but Shem and Ham and Japheth and their three wives he took*), and those who have believed; but there believed not with him save a few: *they were six men and their wives: and it is said that all who were in the ark were eighty, half of whom were men and half women.* And *Noah* said, Embark ye therein. In the name of God [be] its course and its mooring.[2] Verily my Lord is very forgiving

---

[1] Or, as the original literally signifies, boiled over [or boiled], which is consonant to what the Rabbins say, that the waters of the deluge were boiling hot.—This oven was, as some say, at El-Koofeh, in a spot whereon a mosque now stands; or, as others rather think, in a certain place in India, or else at 'Eyn-el-Wardeh in Mesopotamia. Some pretend that it was the same oven which Eve made use of to bake her bread in, being of a form different from those we use, having the mouth in the upper part, and that it descended from patriarch to patriarch till it came to Noah. It is remarkable that Moḥammad, in all probability, borrowed this circumstance from the Persian Magi, who also fancied that the first waters of the deluge gushed out of the oven of a certain old woman named Zala Cûfa.—But the word "tennoor," which is here translated "oven," also signifying "the superficies of the earth," or "a place whence waters spring forth," or "where they are collected," some suppose it means no more in this passage than the spot or fissure whence the first eruption of waters broke forth.—S.

[2] It is a custom of many Muslims to pronounce these words, 'In the name of God be its course and its mooring,' on embarking for any voyage.—L. The commentators tell us that Noah was two years in building the ark, which was framed of Indian plane-tree; that it was divided into three stories, of which the lower was designed for the beasts, the middle one for the men and women, and the upper for the birds; and the men were separated from the women by the body of Adam, which Noah had taken into the ark. This last is a tradition of the Eastern Christians.—S.

[and] merciful.—And it moved along with them amid waves like mountains; and Noah called unto his son, *Canaan*, who was apart *from the ark*, O my child, embark with us, and be not with the unbelievers! He replied, I will betake me to a mountain which will secure me from the water. [Noah] said, There is nought that will secure to-day from the decree of God [any] but him on whom He hath mercy. And the waves intervened between them; so he became [one] of the drowned. And it was said, O earth, swallow up thy water (*whereupon it drank it up, except what had descended from heaven, which became rivers and seas*), and, O heaven, cease *from raining*;—and the water abated, and the decree was fulfilled, and it (*namely, the ark*) rested on El-Joodee (*a mountain of El-Jezeereh, near El-Mósil*); and it was said, Perdition to the offending people![1] (xi. 38–46.)

And Noah called upon his Lord, and said, O my Lord, verily my son is of my family, *and Thou hast promised me to save them*, and verily Thy promise is true, and Thou art the most just of those who exercise judgment. *God* replied, O Noah, verily he is not of thy family *who should be saved, or of the people of thy religion*. Verily it (*namely, thine asking me to save him*) is not a righteous act; *for he was an unbeliever, and there is no safety for the unbelievers*; therefore ask not of me that wherein thou hast no knowledge. I admonish thee, lest thou become [one] of the ignorant.—*Noah* said, O my Lord, I beg Thee to preserve me from asking Thee that wherein I have no knowledge; and if Thou do not forgive me and have mercy upon me, I shall be of those who suffer loss.—It was said, O Noah, descend *from the ark*,[2] with peace from Us, and blessings,

---

[1] The original of this passage is considered the most sublime in the Ḳurán.

[2] The Moḥammadans say that Noah went into the ark on the tenth of Rejeb, and came out of it on the tenth of Moḥarram; which therefore became a fast: so that the whole time of Noah's being in the ark according to them was six months.—S. (B.)

upon thee and upon peoples [that shall proceed] from those who are with thee *in the ark* (*that is, their believing posterity*); but peoples [that shall proceed] *from those who are with thee* We will permit to enjoy *the provisions of this world;* then a painful punishment shall befall them from Us, *in the world to come; they being unbelievers.*

(xi. 47--50.)

'AD AND THAMOOD.

And *we sent* unto *the former* [tribe of] 'Ád [1] their brother Hood.[2] He said, O my people, worship God: *assert His unity.* Ye have no other deity than Him. Will ye not then fear *Him, and believe?*—The chiefs who disbelieved among his people answered, Verily we see thee to be in a foolish way, and verily we esteem thee one of the liars *with respect to the apostolic commission.* He replied, O my people, there is no folly in me; but I am an apostle from the Lord of the worlds. I bring unto you the messages of my Lord, and I am unto you a counsellor, intrusted *with the apostolic office.* Do ye wonder that an admonition hath come unto you from your Lord by *the tongue of* a man from among you, that he may warn you? And remember how He hath appointed you vicegerents *in the earth* after the people of Noah, and increased you in tallness of stature. (*For the tall among them was a hundred cubits, and the short among them sixty.*) Remember, then, the benefits of God, that ye may prosper. They said, Art thou come unto us that we may worship God alone, and relinquish what our fathers worshipped? Then bring upon us that *punishment* with which thou threatenest us, if thou be of those who speak truth.—He replied, Punishment and indigna-

---

[1] 'Ád was an ancient and potent tribe of Arabs, and zealous idolaters. They chiefly worshipped four deities, Sákiyeh, Háfidhah, Rázikah, and Sálimeh; the first, as they imagined, supplying them with rain, the second preserving them from all dangers abroad, the third providing food for their sustenance, and the fourth restoring them to health when afflicted with sickness; according to the signification of the several names.—S.

[2] Generally supposed to be the same person as Heber.—S.

tion from your Lord have become necessary for you. Do ye dispute with me concerning names which ye and your fathers have given *to idols which ye worship*, concerning which (*that is, the worship of which*) God hath not set down any convincing proof? Then await ye *the punishment.* I am with you, of those who await *that, for your accusing me of falsehood. And the unprofitable wind was sent upon them.* But We delivered him (*namely, Hood*) and them who were with him (*of the believers*) by Our mercy; and We cut off the uppermost part of those who charged Our signs with falsehood and who were not believers. (vii. 63–70.)

And *We sent* unto *the tribe of* Thamood[1] their brother Ṣáliḥ. He said, O my people, worship God. Ye have no other deity than Him. A *miraculous* proof *of my veracity* hath come unto you from your Lord, this she-camel of God being a sign unto you. [He had caused her, at their demand, to come forth from the heart of a rock.] Therefore let her feed in God's earth, and do her no harm, lest a painful punishment seize you. And remember how He hath appointed you vicegerents *in the earth* after [the tribe of] 'Ád, and given you a habitation in the earth: ye make yourselves, on its plains, pavilions *wherein ye dwell in summer,* and cut the mountains into houses *wherein ye dwell in winter.* Remember then the benefits of God, and do not evil in the earth, acting corruptly.—The chiefs who were elated with pride, among his people, said unto those who were esteemed weak, *namely,* to those who had believed among them, Do ye know that Ṣáliḥ hath been sent *unto you* from his Lord? They answered, *Yea:* verily we believe in that wherewith he hath been sent. Those who were elated with pride replied, Verily we disbelieve in that wherein ye have believed.—*And the she-camel had a day to water; and they had a day; and they became weary of*

---

[1] Thamood was another tribe of the ancient Arabs who fell into idolatry. They dwelt first in the country of the 'Ádites, but their numbers increasing they removed to the territory of Ḥejr.—S.

this. And they hamstrung the she-camel (*Ḳudár* [the son of Sálif] *doing so by their order and slaying her with the sword*);[1] and they impiously transgressed the command of their Lord,[2] and said, O Ṣáliḥ, bring upon us that *punishment* with which thou threatenest us *for killing her*, if thou be [one] of the apostles. And the violent convulsion (*a great earthquake, and a cry from heaven*[3]) assailed them, and in the morning they were in their dwellings prostrate *and dead.* So he turned away from them, and said, O my people, I have brought unto you the message of my Lord and given you faithful counsel; but ye loved not faithful counsellors. (vii. 71–77.)

---

1 This extraordinary camel frightening the other cattle from their pasture, a certain rich woman, named 'Oneyzeh Umm-Ghánim, having four daughters, dressed them out, and offered one Ḳudár his choice of them, if he would kill the camel. Whereupon he chose one, and with the assistance of eight other men hamstrung and killed the dam, and pursuing the young one which fled to the mountain, killed that also, and divided his flesh among them. Others tell the story somewhat differently, adding Sadaḳah Bint-El-Mukhtár as a joint-conspiratress with 'Oneyzeh, and pretending that the young one was not killed.'—S. (A.F., B.)

2 Defying the vengeance with which they were threatened; because they trusted in their strong dwellings hewn in the rocks, saying that the tribe of 'Ád perished only because their houses were not built with sufficient strength.—S.

3 'Like violent and repeated claps of thunder; which some say was no other than the voice of the angel Gabriel, which rent their hearts. It is said that after they had killed the camel, Ṣáliḥ told them that on the morrow their faces should become yellow, the next day red, and the third day black; and that on the fourth God's vengeance should light on them: and that, the first three signs happening accordingly, they sought to put him to death; but God delivered him by sending him into Palestine.—S. (A.F., B.)

DHU-L-ḲARNEYN.

They (*namely, the Jews*) will ask thee concerning Dhu-l-Ḳarneyn.[1] (*His name was El-Iskender, and he was not a prophet.*) Answer, I will recite unto you an account of him. We gave him ability in the earth, *by facilitating his journeying therein,* and gave him a way to *attain* every-thing *that he required.* And he followed a way *towards a place where the sun setteth,* until, when he came to the place where the sun setteth, he found that it set in a spring of black mud, *as it appeared to the eye; but really that spring was greater than the world;* and he found near it a people *who were unbelievers.*[2] We said, *by inspiration,* O Dhu-l-Ḳarneyn, either punish *the people by slaughter,* or proceed against them gently, *taking them captive.* He said, As to him who offendeth *by polytheism,* we will punish him *by slaughter:* then he shall be taken back to his Lord, and He will punish him with a severe punishment, *in the fire of*

---

[1] In the Mir-át-ez-Zemán it is stated that there are various opinions respecting the age in which this person lived: 1. That he lived in the first century after the Deluge, and was of the sons of Japheth, and was born in the land of the Greeks: so said 'Alee; 2. That he was after Thamood: so said El-Ḥasan; 3. That he was of the lineage of Esau, the son of Isaac: so said Muḳátil; 4. That he lived between the times of Moses and Jesus; 5. That he lived between Jesus and Mohammad; and 6. That he was of the lineage of Yoonán, son [as some say] of Noah, in the days of Abraham; and this, adds the author, is the most correct.—But some suppose him to be the same with Alexander the Great.—Respecting his surname of 'Dhu-l-Ḳarneyn,' the most obvious signification of which is 'the two-horned,' the more judicious in general are of opinion that he received it because he made expeditions to the extreme parts of the east and west, and therefore that it signifies 'Lord of the two extreme parts of the earth.'

[2] Who were clothed in the skins of wild beasts, and lived upon what the sea cast on shore.—S. (B.)

hell. But as to him who believeth, and doeth that which is right, he shall have as a reward paradise, and We will say unto him, in Our command, *that which will be* easy *unto him.*—Then he followed a way *towards the place where the sun riseth,* until, when he came to the place where the sun riseth, he found that it rose upon a people (*namely, the Zenj*) unto whom We had not given anything wherewith to shelter themselves therefrom, *neither clothing nor roof; for their land bore no building; but they had subterranean dwellings, into which they retired at sunrise, and they came forth when the sun was high.* Thus *was the case;* and We comprehended with Our knowledge what were with him (*namely, Dhu-l-Ḳarneyn*), *of weapons and forces and other things.*—Then he followed a way until, when he came between the two barriers (*or mountains, at the confines of the country of the Turks, between which is the barrier of El-Iskender, as will be related presently*), he found before them a people who could scarce understand speech. They said, O Dhu-l-Ḳarneyn, verily Yájooj and Májooj [Gog and Magog [1]] are corrupting in the earth, *by plunder and tyranny, when they came forth unto us.* Shall we therefore pay thee tribute, on the condition that thou make a barrier between us and them?—He answered, The ability which my Lord hath given me, *by wealth and other things,* is better *than your tribute, which I need not. I will make the barrier for you gratuitously:* but assist me strenuously *by doing that which I desire:* I will make between you and them a strong barrier. Bring me pieces of iron *of the size of the blocks of stone used in building.—And he built with them, and placed amid them firewood and charcoal,* until, when it [the mass]

---

[1] The Arabs call them Yájooj and Májooj, and say they are two nations or tribes descended from Japheth the son of Noah; or, as others write, Gog are a tribe of the Turks, and Magog of those of Geelán, the Geli and Gelæ of Ptolemy and Strabo.—It is said these barbarous people made their irruptions into the neighbouring countries in the spring, and destroyed and carried off all the fruits of the earth; and some pretend they were man-eaters.—S. (B.)

filled up the space between the upper parts of the two mountains, *and he had put the bellows and fire around that mass,* he said, Blow ye [with the bellows]. *So they blew* until, when he had made it (*that is, the iron*) *like* fire, he said, Bring me molten brass, that I may pour upon it. *And he poured the molten brass upon the heated iron, so that it entered between its pieces and the whole became one mass.* And they (*namely, Yájooj and Májooj*) were not able to ascend to its top *by reason of its height and smoothness;* nor were they able to perforate it *by reason of its hardness and thickness. Dhu-l-Ḳarneyn* said, This (*namely, the barrier, or the gift of the ability to construct it*) is a mercy from my Lord: but when the promise of my Lord, *as to the eruption of Yájooj and Májooj shortly before the resurrection,* shall come *to be fulfilled,* He will reduce it (*namely, the barrier*) to dust; and the promise of my Lord concerning *their eruption and other events* is true. And We will suffer some of them, on that day (*the day of their eruption*), to pour tumultuously among others: and the trumpet shall be blown *for the resurrection,* and We will gather them (*namely, all creatures*) together in a body, *in one place.* And We will set hell, on that day, *near* before the unbelievers, whose eyes have been veiled from my admonition (*the Ḳurán*), *and who, being blind, have not been directed by it,* and who could not hear *what the prophet recited unto them, by reason of their hatred of him; wherefore they believed not in him.* (xviii. 82–101.)

ABRAHAM, ISHMAEL, ISAAC.

Remember when Abraham [Ibráheem] said to his father A'zar (*this was the surname of Terah*), Dost thou take images as deities?[1] Verily I see thee and thy people to be in a manifest error.—(And thus, *as We showed him the error of his father and his people,* did We show Abraham the kingdom of the heavens and the earth, and [We did so] that he might be of [the number of] those who firmly believe.) And when the night overshadowed him, he saw a star (*it is said that it was Venus*), [and] he said *unto his people, who were astrologers,* This is my Lord, *according to your assertion.*—But when it set, he said, I like not those that set, *to take them as Lords, since it is not meet for a Lord to experience alteration and change of place, as they are of the nature of accidents. Yet this had no effect upon them.* And when he saw the moon rising, he said *unto them,* This is my Lord.—But when it set, he said, Verily if my Lord direct me not (*if He confirm me not in the right way*), I shall assuredly be of the erring people.—*This was a hint to his people that they were in error; but it had no effect upon them.* And when he saw the sun rising, he said, This is my Lord. This is greater *than the star and the moon.*—But when it set, *and the proof had been rendered more strong to them, yet they desisted not,* he said, O my

[1] The Eastern authors unanimously agree that he (Ázar) was a statuary, or carver of idols; and he is represented as the first who made images of clay, pictures only having been in use before, and taught that they were to be adored as gods. However, we are told his employment was a very honourable one, and that he was a great lord and in high favour with Nimrod, whose son-in-law he was, because he made his idols for him and was excellent in his art. Some of the Rabbins say Terah was a priest and chief of the order.—S.

people, verily I am clear of the [things] which ye associate *with God; namely, the images and the heavenly bodies. So they said unto him, What dost thou worship? He answered,* Verily I direct my face unto Him who hath created the heavens and the earth, following the right religion, and I am not of the polytheists.—And his people argued with him; [but] he said, Do ye argue with me respecting God, when He hath directed me, and I fear not what ye associate with Him, unless my Lord will *that* aught *displeasing should befall me?* My Lord comprehendeth everything by *His* knowledge. Will ye not therefore consider? And wherefore should I fear what ye have associated *with God,* when ye fear not for your having associated with God that of which He hath not sent down unto you a proof? Then which of the two parties is the more worthy of safety? *Are we, or you?* If ye know *who is the more worthy of it, follow him.—God saith,* They who have believed, and not mixed their belief with injustice (*that is, polytheism*), for these shall be safety *from punishment,* and they are rightly directed. (vi. 74–82.)

Relate *unto them,* in the book (*that is, the Ḳurán*), *the history of* Abraham. Verily he was a person of great veracity, a prophet. When he said unto his father *A'zar, who worshipped idols,* O my father, wherefore dost thou worship that which heareth not, nor seeth, nor averteth from thee aught, *whether of advantage or of injury?* O my father, verily [a degree] of knowledge hath come unto me, that hath not come unto thee: therefore follow me: I will direct thee into a right way. O my father, serve not the devil, *by obeying him in serving idols;* for the devil is very rebellious unto the Compassionate. O my father, verily I fear that a punishment will betide thee from the Compassionate, *if thou repent not,* and that thou wilt be unto the devil an aider, *and a companion in hell-fire.*—He replied, Art thou a rejector of my Gods, O Abraham, *and dost thou revile them?* If thou abstain not, I will assuredly assail thee *with stones or with ill words; therefore beware of me,* and leave me for a long time.—*Abraham* said, Peace *from me* be on thee! I will ask pardon for thee of my Lord; for He is gracious unto me: and I will separate myself from you and from what ye invoke instead of God: and I will call upon my Lord: perhaps I shall not be unsuccessful in calling upon my Lord, *as ye are in calling upon idols.*—And when he had separated himself from them, and from what they worshipped instead of God, *by going to the Holy Land,* We gave him *two sons, that he might cheer himself thereby, namely,* Isaac and Jacob; and each [of them] We made a prophet; and We bestowed upon them (*namely, the three*), of our mercy, *wealth and children;* and We caused them to receive high commendation.

(xix. 42–51.)

We gave unto Abraham his direction formerly, *before he had attained to manhood;* and We knew him *to be worthy of it.* When he said unto his father and his people, What are these images, to *the worship of* which ye are devoted? —they answered, We found our fathers worshipping them, *and we have followed their example.* He said *unto them,* Verily ye and your fathers have been in a manifest error. They said, Hast thou come unto us with truth *in saying this,* or art thou of those who jest? He answered, Nay, your Lord (*the being who deserveth to be worshipped*) is the Lord of the heavens and the earth, who created them, *not after the similitude of anything pre-existing;* and I am of those who bear witness thereof. And, by God, I will assuredly devise a plot against your idols after ye shall have retired, turning your backs.—So, *after they had gone to their place of assembly, on a day when they held a festival,* he brake them in pieces *with an axe,* except the chief of them, *upon whose neck he hung the axe;* that they might return unto it (*namely, the chief*) *and see what he had done with the others.* They said, *after they had returned and seen what he had done,* Who hath done this unto our gods? Verily he is of the unjust.—*And some of them* said, We heard a young man mention them *reproachfully:* he is called Abraham. They said, Then bring him before the eyes of the people, that they may bear witness *against him of his having done it.* They said *unto him, when he had been brought,* Hast thou done this unto our gods, O Abraham? He answered, Nay, this their chief did it: and ask ye them, if they [can] speak. And they returned unto themselves, *upon reflection,* and said *unto themselves,* Verily ye are the unjust, *in worshipping that which speaketh not.* Then they reverted to their obstinacy, *and said,* Verily thou knowest that these speak not: *then wherefore dost thou order us to ask them?* He said, Do ye then worship, instead of God, that which doth not profit you at all, nor injure you *if ye worship it not?* Fy on you, and on that which ye worship instead of God! Do ye not then understand?—They said, Burn ye him, and avenge your gods, if ye will do so. *So they collected abundance of firewood for him, and set fire to it; and they bound Abraham, and put him into an engine, and cast him into the fire. But, saith God,* We said, O fire, be thou cold, and a security unto Abraham! *So nought of him was burned save his bonds: the heat of the fire ceased, but its light remained; and by God's saying, Security,—Abraham was saved from dying, by reason of its cold.* And they intended against him a plot; but he caused them to be the sufferers.[1] And We delivered him and Lot, *the son of*

---

[1] Some tell us that Nimrod, on seeing this miraculous deliverance from his palace, cried out that he would make an offering to the God of Abraham; and that he accordingly sacrificed four thousand kine. [B.] But, if he ever relented, he soon relapsed into his former infidelity: for he built a tower that he might ascend to heaven to see Abraham's God; which being overthrown [Kur. xvi. 28], still persisting in his design, he would be carried to heaven in a chest borne by four monstrous birds; but after wandering for some time through the air, he fell down on a mountain with such force that he made it shake, whereto (as some fancy) a passage in the Kurán [xiv. 47] alludes, which may be translated, 'although their contrivances be such as to make the mountains tremble.'—Nimrod, disappointed in his design of making war with God, turned his arms against Abraham, who, being a great prince, raised forces to defend himself; but God, dividing

his brother Haran, from El-'Erák, [bringing them] unto the land which we blessed for the peoples, *by the abundance of its rivers and trees, namely, Syria. Abraham took up his abode in Palestine, and Lot in El-Mu-tekifeh, between which is a day's journey.* And *when Abraham had asked a son,* We gave unto him Isaac, and Jacob as an additional gift, *beyond what he had asked, being a son's son;* and all of them We made righteous persons *and prophets.* And We made them models of religion who directed *men* by Our command *unto Our religion;* and We commanded them by inspiration to do good works and to perform prayer and to give the appointed alms; and they served Us. And unto Lot We gave judgment and knowledge; and We delivered him from the city which committed filthy actions; for they were a people of evil, shameful doers; and We admitted him into our mercy; for he was [one] of the righteous. (xxi. 52–75.)

Hast thou not considered him who disputed with Abraham concerning his Lord, because God had given him the kingdom? *And he was Nimrod.* When Abraham said, (*upon his saying unto him, Who is thy Lord, unto whom thou invitest us?*), My Lord is He who giveth life and causeth to die,—he replied, I give life and cause to die. —*And he summoned two men, and slew one of them, and left the other. So when he saw that he understood not,* Abraham said, And verily God bringeth the sun from the east: now do thou bring it from the west.—And he who

---

Nimrod's subjects, and confounding their language, deprived him of the greater part of his people, and plagued those who adhered to him by swarms of gnats, which destroyed almost all of them; and one of those gnats having entered into the nostril, or ear, of Nimrod, penetrated to one of the membranes of his brain, where, growing bigger every day, it gave him such intolerable pain, that he was obliged to cause his head to be beaten with a mallet, in order to procure some ease, which torture he suffered four hundred years; God being willing to punish, by one of the smallest of His creatures, him who insolently boasted himself to be lord of all. A Syrian calendar places the death of Nimrod, as if the time were well known, on the eighth of Tamooz, or July.—S.

disbelieved was confounded; and God directeth not the offending people. (ii. 260.)

And Our messengers came formerly unto Abraham with good tidings *of Isaac and Jacob, who should be after him.* They said, Peace. He replied, Peace *be on you.* And he tarried not, but brought a roasted calf. And when he saw that their hands touched it not, he disliked them and conceived a fear of them. They said, Fear not: for we are sent unto the people of Lot, *that we may destroy them.* And his wife *Sarah* was standing *serving them,* and she laughed, *rejoicing at the tidings of their destruction.* And we gave her good tidings of Isaac [Is-ḥáḳ]; and after Isaac, Jacob [Yaạḳoob]. She said, Alas! shall I bear a child when I am an old woman, *of nine and ninety years,* and when this my husband is an old man, *of a hundred or a hundred and twenty years?* Verily this [would be] a wonderful thing.—They said, Dost thou wonder at the command of God? The mercy of God and His blessings be on you, O people of the house (*of Abraham*)! for He is praiseworthy, glorious.—And when the terror had departed from Abraham, and the good tidings had come unto him, he disputed with Us (*that is, with Our messengers*) respecting the people of Lot; for Abraham was gentle, compassionate, repentant. *And he said unto them, Will ye destroy a city wherein are three hundred believers? They answered, No. He said, And will ye destroy a city wherein are two hundred believers? They answered, No. He said, And will ye destroy a city wherein are forty believers? They answered, No. He said, And will ye destroy a city wherein are fourteen believers? They answered, No. He said, And tell me, if there be in it one believer? They answered, No. He said, Verily in it is Lot. They replied, We know best who is in it. And when their dispute had become tedious, they said,* O Abraham, abstain from this *disputation;* for the command of thy Lord hath come *for their destruction,* and a punishment not [to be] averted is coming upon them. (xi. 72–78.)

And when Our decree *for the destruction of the people of Lot* came [to be executed], We turned them (*that is, their cities*) upside-down; *for Gabriel raised them to heaven, and let them fall upside-down to the earth;*[1] and We rained upon them stones of baked clay, sent one after another, marked with thy Lord, *each with the name of him upon whom it should be cast:* and they [are] not far distant from the offenders; *that is, the stones are not, or the cities of the people of Lot were not, far distant from the people of Mekkeh.* (xi. 84.)

And [Abraham] said [after his escape from Nimrod], Verily I am going unto my Lord, who will direct me *unto the place whither He hath commanded me to go, namely, Syria. And when he had arrived at the Holy Land, he said,* O my Lord, give me *a son* [who shall be one] of the righteous. Whereupon We gave him the glad tidings of a mild youth. And when he had attained to the age when he could work with him (*as some say, seven years; and some, thirteen*), he said, O my child, verily I have seen in a dream that I should sacrifice thee (*and the dreams of prophets are true; and their actions, by the command of God*); therefore consider what thou seest advisable *for me to do.* He replied, O my father, do what thou art commanded: thou shalt find me, if God please, [of the number] of the patient. And when they had resigned themselves, and he had laid him down on his temple, *in* [the valley of] *Mina, and had drawn the knife across his throat (but it produced no effect, by reason of an obstacle interposed by the divine power),* We called unto him, O Abraham, thou hast verified the vision. Verily thus do We reward the well-doers. Verily this was the manifest trial. And We ransomed him *whom he had been commanded to sacrifice (and he was Ishmael* [Ismá'eel] *or Isaac; for there are two opinions*)[2] with an excellent victim,

---

[1] They tell us that Gabriel thrust his wing under them and lifted them up so high that the inhabitants of the lower heaven heard the barking of the dogs and the crowing of the cocks; and then, inverting them, threw them down to the earth.—S. (B.)

[2] It is the most received opinion among the Moḥammadans that the

a ram from Paradise, the same that Abel had offered: Gabriel (on whom be peace!) brought it, and the lord Abraham sacrificed it, saying, God is most great! And We left *this salutation* [to be bestowed] on him by the latter generations, Peace [be] on Abraham! Thus do We reward the well-doers: for he was of our believing servants.

(xxxvii. 97–111.)

Remember when Abraham said, O my Lord, show me how Thou will raise to life the dead.[1]—He said, Hast thou not believed? He answered, Yea: but *I have asked Thee* that my heart may be at ease. He replied, Then take four birds and draw them towards thee, *and cut them in pieces and mingle together their flesh and their feathers;* then place upon each mountain *of thy land* a portion of them, then call them *unto thee:* they shall come unto thee quickly: and know thou that God is mighty [and] wise.—*And he took a peacock and a vulture and a raven and a cock, and did with them as hath been described, and kept their heads with him, and called them; whereupon the portions flew about, one to another, until they became complete: then they came to their heads.* (ii. 262.)

Remember when his Lord had tried Abraham by [certain] words, *commands and prohibitions,* and he ful-

---

son whom Abraham offered was Ishmael and not Isaac; Ishmael being his only son at that time: for the promise of Isaac's birth is mentioned lower, as subsequent in time to this transaction. They also allege the testimony of their prophet, who is reported to have said, 'I am the son of the two who were offered in sacrifice;' meaning his great ancestor, Ishmael, and his own father 'Abd-Allah: for 'Abd-el-Muṭṭalib had made a vow that if God would permit him to find out and open the well Zemzem and should give him ten sons he would sacrifice one of them; accordingly, when he had obtained his desire in both respects, he cast lots on his sons, and the lot falling on 'Abd-Allah, he redeemed him by offering a hundred camels, which was therefore ordered to be the price of a man's blood in the Sunneh.—S. (B., Z.)

[1] The occasion of this request of Abraham is said to have been a doubt proposed to him by the devil in human form, how it was possible for the several parts of a corpse of a man which lay on the sea-shore and had been partly devoured by the wild beasts, the birds, and the fish, to be brought together at the resurrection.—S

filled them, *God* said *unto him,* I constitute thee a model of religion unto men. He replied, And of my offspring *constitute models of religion.* [God] said, My covenant doth not apply to the offenders, *the unbelievers among them.* —And when We appointed the house (*that is, the Kaạbeh*) to be a place for the resort of men, and a place of security (*a man would meet the slayer of his father there and he would not provoke him* [to revenge],) and [said], Take, *O men,* the station of Abraham (*the stone upon which he stood at the time of building the House*) as a place of prayer, *that ye may perform behind it the prayers of the two rek'ahs*[2] [which are ordained to be performed after the ceremony] *of the circuiting* [of the Kaạbeh].—And We commanded Abraham and Ishmael, [saying], Purify my House (*rid it of the idols*) for those who shall compass [it], and those who shall abide *there,* and those who shall bow down and prostrate themselves.—And when Abraham said, O my Lord, make this *place* a secure territory (*and God hath answered his prayer, and made it a sacred place, wherein the blood of man is not shed, nor is any one oppressed in it, nor is its game hunted* [or shot], *nor are its plants cut or pulled up*), and supply its inhabitants with fruits (*which hath been done by the transporting of Eṭ-Ṭáïf from Syria thither, when it* [that is, the territory of Mekkeh] *was desert, without sown land or water,*[3] such of them as shall believe in God and

---

[1] In the original, 'Imám,' which answers to the Latin *Antistes.* This title the Moḥammadans give to their priests [if such a title may be used, for want of one more correct] who begin the prayers in their mosques, and whom all the congregation follow.—S.

[2] The term 'rek'ah' signifies the repetition of a set form of words, chiefly from the Ḳurán, and ejaculations of 'God is most Great!' etc., accompanied by particular postures; part of the words being repeated in an erect posture, part sitting, and part in other postures: an inclination of the head and body, followed by two prostrations, distinguishing each rek'ah. Each of the five daily prayers of the Muslims consist of a certain number of rek'ahs.

[3] The city of Eṭ-Ṭáïf was so called, according to Abu-l-Fida and several other Arab authors, because it, with the adjacent fields, was separated from Syria during the Deluge, and after floating round about upon the water at length rested in its present situation, where its soil has continued to produce the fruits of Syria.

the last day.—*He mentioned them peculiarly in the prayer agreeably with the saying of God, My covenant doth not apply to the offenders.*—*God* replied, And *I will supply* him who disbelieveth: I will make him to enjoy *a supply of food in this world,* a little *while:* then I will force him, *in the world to come,* to the punishment of the fire; and evil shall be the transit. (ii. 118–120.)

And *remember* when Abraham was raising the foundations of the House[1] (*that is, building it*), together with Ishmael, *and they said,* O our Lord, accept of us *our building;* for Thou art the Hearer *of what is said,* the Knower *of what is done.* O our Lord, also make us resigned[2] unto Thee, and *make* from among our offspring a people resigned unto Thee, and show us our rites (*the ordinances of our worship, or our pilgrimage*), and be propitious towards us; for Thou art the Very Propitious, the Merciful. (*They begged Him to be propitious to them, notwithstanding their honesty, from a motive of humility, and by way of instruction to their offspring.*) O our Lord, also send unto them (*that is, the people of the House*) an apostle from among them (*and God hath answered their prayer by sending Moḥammad*), who shall recite unto them Thy signs (*the Ḳurán*), and shall teach them the book (*the Ḳurán*), and the knowledge *that it containeth,* and shall purify them *from polytheism;* for Thou art the Mighty, the Wise.—And who will be averse from the religion of Abraham but he who maketh his soul foolish, *who is ignorant that it is God's creation, and that the worship of Him is incumbent on it; or who lightly esteemeth it and applieth it to vile purposes;* when We have chosen him in this world *as an apostle and a friend,* and he shall be in the world to come one of the righteous *for whom are high ranks?*—*And*

---

1 Namely, the Kaạbeh.

2 In the original, 'Muslims,' which is the peculiar and very appropriate title of the believers in the religion taught by Moḥammad; and as he professed not to teach a religion essentially *new,* this title is given to all true believers before him.

remember when his lord said unto him, Resign thyself:—he replied, I resign myself unto the Lord of the worlds.—And Abraham commanded his children to follow it (*namely, the religion*); and Jacob, *his children; saying,* O my children, verily God hath chosen for you the religion *of El-Islám;* [1] therefore die not without your being Muslims. —*It was a prohibition from abandoning El-Islám and a command to persevere therein unto death.* (ii. 121–126.)

When the Jews said, Abraham was a Jew, and we are of his religion,—and the Christians said the like, [the following] *was revealed:*—O people of the Scripture, wherefore do ye argue respecting Abraham, *asserting that he was of your religion,* when the Pentateuch and the Gospel were not sent down but after him *a long time?* Do ye not then understand *the falsity of your saying?* So ye, O people, have argued respecting that of which ye have knowledge, *concerning Moses and Jesus, and have asserted that ye are of their religion:* then wherefore do ye argue respecting that of which ye have no knowledge, *concerning Abraham?* But God knoweth *his case,* and ye know *it* not. Abraham was not a Jew nor a Christian: but he was orthodox, a Muslim [or one resigned], *a unitarian,* and he was not of the polytheists. (iii. 58–60.)

---

[1] 'El-Islam' signifies the *resigning* oneself to God and to His service, and is the name given by Moḥammad to that religion which, he asserted, all the prophets before him had taught, and he restored; the foundation of which was the unity of God.

JACOB, JOSEPH AND HIS BRETHREN.

Remember, when Joseph [Yoosuf] said unto his father, O my father, verily I saw *in sleep* eleven stars and the sun and the moon : I saw them making obeisance unto me. He replied, O my child, relate not thy vision to thy brethren, lest they contrive a plot against thee, *knowing its interpretation to be that they are the stars and that the sun is thy mother and the moon thy father* ; for the devil is unto man a manifest enemy. And thus, *as thou sawest,* thy Lord will choose thee, and teach thee the interpretation of events, *or dreams,* and will accomplish his favour upon thee *by the gift of prophecy,* and upon the family of Jacob, as He accomplished it upon thy fathers before, Abraham and Isaac ; for thy Lord is knowing [and] wise.—Verily in *the history of* Joseph and his brethren are signs to the inquirers.—When they (*the brethren of Joseph*) said, *one to another,* Verily Joseph and his brother *Benjamin* are dearer unto our father than we, and we are a number of men ; verily our father is in a manifest error ; slay ye Joseph, or drive him away into a *distant* land ; so the face of your father shall be directed alone unto you, *regarding no other,* and ye shall be after it a just people :—a speaker among them, *namely, Judah,* said, Slay not Joseph, but throw him to the bottom of the well ; then some of the travellers may light upon him, if ye do *this. And they were satisfied therewith.* They said, O our father, wherefore dost thou not intrust us with Joseph, when verily we are faithful unto him ? Send him with us to-morrow *into the plain,* that he may divert himself and sport ; and we will surely take care of him.—He replied, Verily your taking him away will grieve me, and I fear lest the wolf devour him while ye are heedless of him. They said, Surely if the wolf devour him, when we are a number of men, we shall in that case be indeed weak. *So he sent him with them.* And when they went away with him, and agreed to put him at the bottom of the well, *they did so.*[1] *They pulled off his shirt, after they had beaten him and had treated him with contempt and had desired to slay him; and they let him down; and when he had arrived half-way down the well they let him fall, that he might die; and he fell into the water. He then betook himself to a mass of rock; and they called to him; so he answered them, imagining that they would have mercy upon him. They however desired to crush him with a piece of rock; but Judah prevented them.* And We said unto him by revelation, *while he was in the well (and he was seventeen years of age, or less), to quiet his heart,* Thou shalt assuredly declare unto them this their action, and they shall not know *thee at the time.*[2] And they came to their father at nightfall weeping. They said, O our father, we went to run races,[3] and left Joseph with our clothes, and the wolf devoured him; and thou wilt not

---

[1] This well, say some, was a certain well near Jerusalem, or not far from the river Jordan; but others call it the well of Egypt, or Midian. The commentators tell us that when the sons of Jacob had gotten Joseph with them in the field, they began to abuse and to beat him so unmercifully that they had killed him had not Judah on his crying out for help insisted on the promise they had made not to kill him but to cast him into the well. Whereupon they let him down a little way; but as he held by the sides of the well, they bound him, and took off his inner garment, designing to stain it with blood to deceive their father. Joseph begged hard to have his garment returned to him, but to no purpose, his brothers telling him, with a sneer, that the eleven stars and the sun and the moon might clothe him and keep him company.—S. (B., Z.)

[2] The commentators pretend that Gabriel also clothed him in the well with a garment of silk of Paradise. For they say that when Abraham was thrown into the fire by Nimrod, he was stripped; and that Gabriel brought him this garment and put it on him; and that from Abraham it descended to Jacob, who folded it up and put it into an amulet, which he hung about Joseph's neck, whence Gabriel drew it out.—S. (B., Z.)

[3] These races they used by way of exercise; and the commentators generally understand here that kind of race wherein they also showed their dexterity in throwing darts, which is still used in the East.—S.

believe us, though we speak truth. And they brought false blood upon his shirt. *Jacob* said *unto them*, Nay, your minds have made a thing seem pleasant unto you, *and ye have done it;*[1] but patience is seemly, and God's assistance is implored with respect to that which ye relate.

And travellers came *on their way from Midian* (*Medyen*) *to Egypt, and alighted near the well;*[2] and they sent their drawer of water,[3] and he let down his bucket *into the well: so Joseph caught hold upon it, and the man drew him forth; and when he saw him*, he said, O good news! This is a young man!—*And his brethren thereupon knew his case; wherefore they came unto him*, and they[4] concealed his case, *making him* as a piece of merchandise; *for they said, He is our slave who hath absconded. And Joseph was silent, fearing lest they should slay him.* And God knew that which they did. And they sold him for a mean price, [for] some dirhems counted down, *twenty, or two-and-twenty;* and they were indifferent to him. *The travellers then brought him to Egypt, and he who had bought him sold him for twenty deenárs and a pair of shoes and two garments.* And the Egyptian who bought him, *namely, Ḳitfeer*,[5] said unto his wife *Zeleekha*, Treat him hospitably; peradventure he may

---

[1] This Jacob had reason to suspect, because when the garment was brought to him, he observed that, though it was bloody, yet it was not torn. –S. (B.)

[2] Three days after Joseph had been thrown into it.—S.

[3] The commentators are so exact as to give us the name of this man, who as they pretend, was Málik Ibn-Doạr, of the tribe of Khuzá'ah.—S. (B.)

[4] The expositors are not agreed whether the pronoun *they* relates to Málik and his companions, or to Joseph's brethren. They who espouse the former opinion say that those who came to draw water concealed the manner of their coming by him from the rest of the caravan, that they might keep him to themselves; pretending that some people of the place had given him to them to sell for them in Egypt. And they who prefer the latter opinion tell us that Judah carried victuals to Joseph every day while he was in the well; but not finding him there on the fourth day, he acquainted his brothers with it: whereupon they all went to the caravan and claimed Joseph as their slave, he not daring to discover that he was their brother, lest something worse should befall him; and at length they agreed to sell him to them.—S. (B.)

[5] A corruption of Potiphar. He was a man of great consideration, being superintendent of the royal treasury.—S. (B.)

be advantageous to us, or we may adopt him as a son. *For he was childless.* And thus We prepared an establishment for Joseph in the land *of Egypt,* to teach him the interpretation of events, *or dreams;* for God is well able to effect His purpose; but the greater number of men, *namely, the unbelievers,* know not *this.* And when he had attained his age of strength (*thirty years, or three-and-thirty*), We bestowed on him wisdom and knowledge *in matters of religion, before he was sent as a prophet;* for thus do We recompense the well-doers. (xii. 4–22.—*Then follows an account of his temptation by his mistress, Zeleekha.*)

Then it seemed good unto them,[1] after they had seen the signs *of his innocence, to imprison him.* They will assuredly imprison him for a time, *until the talk of the people respecting him cease. So they imprisoned him.* And there entered with him into the prison two young men, *servants of the king, one of whom was his cup-bearer and the other was his victualler. And they found that he interpreted dreams; wherefore* one of them, *namely, the cup-bearer,* said, I dreamed that I was pressing grapes: and the other said, I dreamed that I was carrying upon my head some bread, whereof the birds did eat: acquaint us with the interpretation thereof; for we see thee to be [one] of the beneficent. —He replied, There shall not come unto you any food wherewith ye shall be fed *in a dream,* but I will acquaint you with the interpretation thereof *when ye are awake,* before *the interpretation of* it come unto you. This is *a part* of that which my Lord hath taught me. Verily I have abandoned the religion of a people who believe not in God and who disbelieve in the world to come; and I follow the religion of my fathers, Abraham and Isaac and Jacob. It is not *fit* for us to associate anything with God. This

---

[1] That is, to Ḳitfeer and his friends. The occasion of Joseph's imprisonment is said to be either that they suspected him to be guilty notwithstanding the proofs which had been given of his innocence, or else that Zeleekha desired it, feigning, to deceive her husband, that she wanted to have Joseph removed from her sight till she could conquer her passion by time; though her real design was to force him to compliance.—S.

knowledge of the unity [hath been given us] of the bounty of God towards us and towards mankind; but the greater number of men are not thankful. O ye two companions (*or inmates*) of the prison, are sundry lords better, or is God, the One, the Almighty? Ye worship not, beside Him, [aught] save names which ye and your fathers have given *to idols,* concerning which God hath not sent down any convincing proof. Judgment belongeth not [unto any] save unto God *alone.* He hath commanded that ye worship not [any] but Him. This is the right religion; but the greater number of men know not. O ye two companions of the prison, as to one of you, *namely, the cup-bearer,* he will serve wine unto his lord *as formerly;* and as to the other, he will be crucified, and the birds will eat from off his head.—*Upon this they said, We dreamed not aught. He replied,* The thing is decreed concerning which ye [did] ask a determination, *whether ye have spoken truth or have lied.* And he said unto him whom he judged to be the person who should escape of them two, *namely the cup-bearer,* Mention me unto thy Lord, *and say unto him, In the prison is a young man imprisoned unjustly.—And he went forth.* But the devil caused him to forget to mention *Joseph* unto his lord:[1] so he remained in the prison some years: *it is said, seven; and it is said, twelve.*

And the king *of Egypt,*[2] *Er-Reiyán the son of El-Weleed* said, Verily I saw [in a dream] seven fat kine which seven lean *kine* devoured, and seven green ears of corn and *seven* other *ears* dried up. O ye nobles, explain unto me my

---

[1] According to the explication of some who take the pronoun *him* to relate to Joseph, this passage may be rendered, 'But the devil caused him (*i.e.*, Joseph) to forget to make his application unto his lord;' and to beg the good offices of his fellow-prisoner for his deliverance, instead of relying on God alone, as it became a prophet, especially, to have done. —S. (B.)

[2] This prince, as the Oriental writers generally agree, was Er-Reiyán the son of El-Weleed the Amalekite, who was converted by Joseph to the worship of the true God, and died in the lifetime of that prophet. But some pretend that the Pharaoh of Joseph and of Moses were one and the same person, and that he lived (or rather reigned) four hundred years.—S. (B.)

dream, if ye interpret a dream.—They replied, *These are* confused dreams, and we know not the interpretation of dreams. And he who had escaped, of the two *young men, namely the cup-bearer,* said (for he remembered after a time *the condition of Joseph*), I will acquaint you with the interpretation thereof; wherefore send me. *So they sent him; and he came unto Joseph, and said,* O Joseph, O thou of great veracity, give us an explanation respecting seven fat kine which seven lean [kine] devoured, and seven green ears of corn and other [seven] dried up, that I may return unto the men (*the king and his companions*), that they may know *the interpretation thereof.* He replied, Ye shall sow seven years as usual: (*this is the interpretation of the seven fat kine:*) and what ye reap do ye leave in its ear, *lest it spoil;* except a little, whereof ye shall eat. Then there shall come, after that, seven grievous [years]: (*this is the interpretation of the seven lean kine:*) they shall consume what ye shall have provided for them, *of the grain sown in the seven years of plenty,* except a little which ye shall have kept. Then there shall come, after that, a year wherein men shall be aided *with rain,* and wherein they shall press *grapes and other fruits.*—And the king said, *when the messenger came unto him and acquainted him with the interpretation of the dream,* Bring unto me him *who hath interpreted it.* (xii. 35–50.)

And when he had spoken unto him,[1] he said *unto him,* Thou art this day firmly established with us, and intrusted *with our affairs. What then seest thou fit for us to do?— He answered, Collect provision, and sow abundant seed in*

[1] The commentators say that Joseph, being taken out of prison, after he had washed and changed his clothes, was introduced to the king, whom he saluted in the Hebrew tongue, and on the king's asking what language that was, he answered that it was the language of his fathers. This prince, they say, understood no less than seventy languages, in every one of which he discoursed with Joseph, who answered him in the same; at which the king, greatly marvelling, desired him to relate his dream, which he did, describing the most minute circumstances: whereupon the king placed Joseph by him on his throne, and made him his Wezeer, or chief minister.—S. (B.)

these plentiful years, and store up the grain in its ear: then the people will come unto thee that they may obtain provision from thee. The king said, And who will act for me in this affair? Joseph said, Set me over the granaries of the land; for I am careful [and] knowing.—Thus did We prepare an establishment for Joseph in the land, that he might take for himself a dwelling therein wherever he pleased.—*And it is related that the king crowned him, and put a ring on his finger, and instated him in the place of Kitfeer, whom he dismissed from his office; after which, Kitfeer died, and thereupon the king married him to his wife Zeleekha, and she bore him two sons.*[1] We bestow Our mercy on whom We please, and We cause not the reward of the well-doers to perish: and certainly the reward of the world to come is better for those who have believed and have feared.

And the years of scarcity began, and afflicted the land of Canaan and Syria, and the brethren of Joseph came, *except Benjamin, to procure provision, having heard that the governor of Egypt gave food for its price.*[2] And they went in unto him, and he knew them; but they knew him not;

---

[1] Namely, Ephraim and Manasses: so that according to this tradition, she was the same woman who is called Asenath by 'Moses.' This supposed marriage, which authorized their amours, probably encouraged the Mohammadan divines to make use of the loves of Joseph and Zeleekha as an allegorical emblem of the spiritual love between the Creator and the creature, God and the soul; just as the Christians apply the Song of Solomon to the same mystical purpose.—S.

[2] Joseph, being made Wezeer, governed with great wisdom; for he not only caused justice to be impartially administered and encouraged the people to industry and the improvement of agriculture during the seven years of plenty, but began and perfected several works of great benefit: the natives at this day ascribing to the patriarch Joseph almost all the ancient works of public utility throughout the kingdom; as particularly the rendering the province of El-Feiyoom, from a standing pool or marsh, the most fertile and best-cultivated land in all Egypt. When the years of famine came, the effects of which were felt not only in Egypt but in Syria and the neighbouring countries, the inhabitants were obliged to apply to Joseph for corn, which he sold to them, first for their money, jewels, and ornaments, then for their cattle and lands, and at length for their persons; so that all the Egyptians in general became slaves to the king, though Joseph by his consent soon released them and returned them their substance.—S. (B.)

and they spake unto him in the Hebrew language; whereupon he said, as one who distrusted them, What hath brought you to my country? So they answered, For corn. But he said, Perhaps ye are spies. They replied, God preserve us [from being spies]! He said, Then whence are ye? They answered, From the land of Canaan, and our father is Jacob, the prophet of God. He said, And hath he sons beside you? They answered, Yea: we were twelve; but the youngest of us went away, and perished in the desert, and he was the dearest of us unto him; and his uterine brother remained, and he retained him that he might console himself thereby for the loss of the other.[1] *And Joseph gave orders to lodge them, and to treat them generously.* And when he had furnished them with their provision, *and given them their full measure,* he said, Bring me your brother from your father, *namely, Benjamin, that I may know your veracity in that ye have said.* Do ye not see that I give full measure, and that I am the most hospitable of the receivers of guests? But if ye bring him not, there shall be no measuring *of corn* for you from me, nor shall ye approach me.—They replied, We will solicit his father for him, and we will surely perform *that.* And he said unto his young men, Put their money,[2] *which they brought as the price of the corn,* in their sacks, that they may know it when they have returned to their family: peradventure they will return *to us; for they will not deem it lawful to keep it.*—And when they returned to their father, they said, O our

---

[1] At length Joseph asked them whom they had to vouch for their veracity; but they told him they knew no man who could vouch for them in Egypt. Then, replied he, one of you shall stay behind with me as a pledge, and the others may return home with their provision; and when ye come again, ye shall bring your younger brother with you, that I may know ye have told me the truth. Whereupon, it being in vain to dispute the matter, they cast lots who should stay behind, and the lot fell upon Simeon. When they departed, Joseph gave each of them a camel, and another for their brother. —S. (B.)

[2] The original word signifying not only money but also goods bartered or given in exchange for other merchandise, some commentators tell us that they paid for their corn, not in money, but in shoes and dressed skins.—S. (B.)

father, the measuring [of corn] is denied us *if thou send not our brother unto him;* therefore send with us our brother, that we may obtain measure; and we will surely take care of him. He said, Shall I intrust you with him otherwise than as I intrusted you with his brother *Joseph* before? But God is the best guardian, and He is the most merciful of those who show mercy.—And when they opened their goods, they found their money had been returned unto them. They said, O our father, what desire we *of the generosity of the king greater than this?* This our money hath been returned unto us; and we will provide corn for our family, and will take care of our brother, and shall receive a camel-load more, *for our brother.* This is a quantity easy *unto the king, by reason of his munificence.*—He said, I will by no means send him with you until ye give me a solemn promise by God that ye will assuredly bring him back unto me unless *an inevitable and insuperable impediment* encompass you. *And they complied with this his desire.* And when they had given him their solemn promise, he said, God is witness of what we say. *And he sent him with them;* and he said, O my sons, enter not *the city of Miṣr* by one gate; but enter by different gates; *lest the* [evil] *eye fall upon you.*[1] But I shall not avert from you, *by my saying this,* anything *decreed to befall you* from God: *I only say this from a feeling of compassion.* Judgment belongeth not [unto any] save unto God *alone.* On Him do I rely, and on Him let those rely who rely.

And when they entered as their father had commanded them, *separately,* it did not avert from them anything *decreed to befall them* from God, but [only satisfied] a desire in the soul of Jacob, which he accomplished; *that is, the*

[1] The belief in the influence of the evil eye prevails among all the Muslims, even the most religious and learned; for their prophet said, 'The eye hath a complete influence; because verily, if there were a thing to overcome fate, it most certainly would be a malignant eye.' Hence he permitted charms (which he disallowed in almost every other case) to be employed for the purpose of counteracting its influence.

desire of averting the [evil] *eye, arising from a feeling of compassion:* and he was endowed with knowledge, because We had taught him: but the greater number of men, *namely the unbelievers*, know not *God's inspiration of His saints.* And when they went in unto Joseph, he received unto him (*or pressed unto him*) his brother. He said, Verily I am thy brother;[1] therefore be not sorrowful for that which they did *from envy to us. And he commanded him that he should not inform them, and agree with him that he should employ a stratagem to retain him with him.* And when he had furnished them with their provision, he put the cup, *which was a measure made of gold set with jewels,*[2] in the sack of his brother *Benjamin.* Then a crier cried, *after they had gone forth from the chamber of Joseph,* O company of travellers, ye are surely thieves. They said (and turned unto them), What is it that ye miss? They answered, We miss the king's measure; and to him who shall bring it [shall be given] a camel-load *of corn,* and I am surety for it, *namely the load.* They replied, By God! ye well know that we have not come to act corruptly in the land, and we have not been thieves. *The crier and his companions* said, Then what shall be the recompense of him *who hath stolen it,* if ye be liars *in your saying, We have not been thieves,—and it be found among you?* They answered, His recompense [shall be that] he in whose sack it shall be found *shall be made a slave:* he, *the thief,* shall be compensation for it; *namely, for the*

[1] It is related that Joseph, having invited his brethren to an entertainment, ordered them to be placed two and two together; by which means, Benjamin, the eleventh, was obliged to sit alone, and, bursting into tears, said, If my brother Joseph were alive, he would have sat with me. Whereupon Joseph ordered him to be seated at the same table with himself, and when the entertainment was over, dismissed the rest, ordering that they should be lodged two and two in a house, but kept Benjamin in his own apartment, where he passed the night. The next day, Joseph asked him whether he would accept of himself for his brother, in the room of him whom he had lost; to which Benjamin replied, 'Who can find a brother comparable unto thee? Yet thou art not the son of Jacob and Rachel.' And upon this, Joseph discovered himself to him.—S. (B.).

[2] Some, however, are of opinion that it was a drinking-cup.

thing stolen. Such was the usage of the family of Jacob. Thus do We recompense the offenders *who are guilty of theft.*—*So they turned towards Joseph, that he might search their sacks.* And he began with their sacks, *and searched them* before the sack of his brother [Benjamin], *lest he should be suspected.* Then he took it forth (*namely, the measure*) from the sack of his brother. Thus, *saith God*, did We contrive a stratagem for Joseph. It was not [lawful] for him to take his brother *as a slave for theft* by the law of the king *of Egypt* (*for his recompense by his law was beating, and a fine of twice the value of the thing stolen; not the being made a slave*), unless God had pleased, *by inspiring him to inquire of his brethren and inspiring them to reply according to their usage.* We exalt unto degrees [of knowledge and honour] whom We please, *as Joseph;* and [there is who is] knowing above every one [else] endowed with knowledge.—They said, If he steal, a brother of his hath stolen before; *namely, Joseph;*[1] *for he stole an idol of gold belonging to the father of his mother, and broke it, that he might not worship it.* And Joseph concealed it in his mind, and did not discover it to them. He said *within himself*, Ye are in a worse condition *than Joseph and his brother, by reason of your having stolen your brother from your father and your having treated him unjustly;* and God well knoweth what ye state *concerning him.*—They said, O prince, verily he hath a father, a very old man, *who loveth him more than us, and consoleth him-*

---

[1] The occasion of this suspicion, it is said, was that Joseph having been brought up by his father's sister, she became so fond of him, that when he grew up and Jacob designed to take him from her she contrived the following stratagem to keep him. Having a girdle which had once belonged to Abraham, she girt it about the child, and then pretending she had lost it, caused strict search to be made for it; and it being at length found on Joseph, he was adjudged, according to the above-mentioned law of the family, to be delivered to her as her property. Some, however, say that Joseph actually stole an idol of gold, which belonged to his mother's father, and destroyed it; a story probably taken from Rachel's stealing the images of Laban: and others tell us that he once stole a goat or a hen, to give to a poor man.—S.

self by him for the loss of his son who hath perished, and the separation of him grieveth him; therefore take one of us *as a slave* in his stead; for we see thee [to be one] of the beneficent. He replied, God preserve us from taking [any] save him in whose possession we found our property; for then (*if we took another*), we [should be] unjust.

And when they despaired of [obtaining] him, they retired to confer privately together. The chief of them *in age* (*namely, Reuben, or in judgment, namely, Judah*), said, Do ye not know that your father hath obtained of you a solemn promise in the name of God, *with respect of your brother,* and how ye formerly failed of your duty with respect to Joseph? Therefore I will by no means depart from the land *of Egypt* until my father give me permission *to return to him,* or God decide for me *by the delivery of my brother;* and He is the best, *the most just,* of those who decide. Return ye to your father, and say, O our father, verily thy son hath committed theft, and we bore not testimony *against him* save according to that which we knew *of a certainty, by our seeing the cup in his sack;* and we were not acquainted with what was unseen *by us when we gave the solemn promise: had we known that he would commit theft, we had not taken him. And send thou,* and ask *the people of* the city in which we have been (*namely, Miṣr*)[1] and the company of travellers with whom we have arrived (*who were a people of Canaan*): and we are surely speakers of truth.—*So they returned to him, and said unto him those words.* He replied, Nay, your minds have made a thing seem pleasant unto you, *and ye have done it* (*he suspected them, on account of their former conduct in the case of Joseph*); but patience is seemly: peradventure God will bring them back (*namely, Joseph and his brother*) unto me, together; for He is the Knowing *with respect to my case,* the Wise *in His*

---

[1] Miṣr is the name both of Egypt and its capital.

acts. And he turned from them, and said, O! my sorrow for Joseph! And his eyes became white in consequence of mourning, and he was oppressed with silent grief. They said, By God, thou wilt not cease to think upon Joseph until thou be at the point of death, or be of [the number of] the dead. He replied, I only complain of my great and unconcealable grief and my sorrow unto God; *not unto any beside Him; for He it is unto whom complaint is made with advantage;* and I know [by revelation] from God what ye know not; *namely, that the dream of Joseph was true, and that he is living. Then he said,* O my sons, go and seek news of Joseph and his brother; and despair not of the mercy of God; for none despaireth of the mercy of God except the unbelieving people.

So they departed towards Egypt, unto Joseph; and when they went in unto him, they said, O Prince, distress (*that is, hunger*) hath affected us and our family, and we have come with paltry money (*it was base money, or some other sort*): yet give us full measure, and be charitable to us, *by excusing the badness of our money;* for God recompenseth those who act charitably. *And he had pity upon them, and compassion affected him, and he lifted up the curtain that was between him and them: then* he said *unto them in reproach,* Do ye know what ye did unto Joseph, *in beating and selling and other actions,* and his brother, *by your injurious conduct to him after the separation of his brother,* when ye were ignorant *of what would be the result of the case of Joseph?*[1] They replied, *after they had recognised him (desiring confirmation),* Art thou indeed Joseph? He answered, I am Joseph, and this is my brother. God hath

[1] The injury they did Benjamin was the separating him from his brother, after which they kept him in so great subjection that he durst not speak to them but with the utmost submission. Some say that these words were occasioned by a letter which Joseph's brethren delivered to him from their father, requesting the releasement of Benjamin, and by their representing his extreme affliction at the loss of him and his brother. The commentators observe that Joseph, to excuse his brethren's behaviour towards him, attributes it to their ignorance and the heat of youth.—S. (B.)

been gracious unto us, *by bringing us together;* for whosoever feareth *God* and is patient [will be rewarded]: God will not suffer the reward of the well-doers to perish. They replied, By God, verily God hath preferred thee above us, and we have been indeed sinners. He said, [There shall be] no reproach [cast] on you this day: God forgive you; for He is the most merciful of those that show mercy. *And he asked them respecting his father: so they answered, His eyes are gone. And he said,* Go ye with this my shirt (*it was the shirt of Abraham, which he wore when he was cast into the fire: it was on his* [that is, Joseph's] *neck* [appended as an amulet] *in the well; and it was from paradise: Gabriel commanded him to send it, and said, In it is its odour* [that is, the odour of paradise], *and it shall not be cast upon any one afflicted* [with a disease] *but he shall be restored to health*), and cast it [said Joseph] upon the face of my father: he shall recover his sight; and bring unto me all your family.—And when the company of travellers had gone forth *from El-'Areesh*[1] *of Egypt,* their father said, *unto those who were present of his offspring,* Verily I perceive the smell of Joseph (*for the zephyr had conveyed it to him, by permission of Him whose name be exalted, from the distance of three days' journey, or eight, or more*): were it not that ye think I dote, *ye would believe me.* They replied, By God, thou art surely in thine old error. And when the messenger of good tidings (*namely, Judah*) came *with the shirt* (*and he had borne the bloody shirt; wherefore he desired to rejoice him, as he had grieved him*), he cast it upon his face, and he recovered his sight. [Thereupon Jacob] said, Did I not say unto you, I know, from God, what ye know not? They said, O our father, ask pardon of our crimes for us; for we have been sinners. He replied, I will ask pardon for you of my Lord; for He is the Very forgiving, the Merciful.—*He delayed doing so until the first appearance of the dawn,*

---

[1] The frontier town of Egypt towards Syria.

that the prayer might be more likely to be answered; or, as some say, until the night of [that is, preceding] *Friday.*

They then repaired to Egypt, and Joseph and the great men came forth to meet them; and when they went in unto Joseph, *in his pavilion or tent,* he received unto him (*or pressed unto him*) his parents (*his father and his mother and his maternal aunt*), and said unto *them,* Enter ye Miṣr, if God please, in safety.[1] *So they entered; and Joseph seated himself upon his couch,* and he caused his parents to ascend upon the seat of state, and they (*that is, his parents and his brethren*) fell down, bowing themselves unto him[2] (*bending, but not putting the forehead*) [upon the ground]: *such being their mode of obeisance in that time.* And he said, O my father, this is the interpretation of my dream of former times: my Lord hath made it true; and He hath shown favour unto me, since He took me forth from the prison (*he said not, from the well,—from a motive of generosity, that his brethren might not be abashed*), and hath brought you from the desert, after that the devil had excited discord between me and my brethren; for my Lord is gracious unto whom He pleaseth; for He is the Knowing, the Wise.—*And his father resided with him four and twenty years, or seventeen; and the period of his separation was eighteen, or forty, or eighty years. And death came unto him; and thereupon he charged Joseph that he should carry him and bury him by his fathers. So he went himself and buried him. Then he returned to Egypt and remained after him three and twenty years; and when his case was ended, and he knew that he should not last* [upon earth], *and his soul desired the lasting possession, he said,* O

---

1 El-Beyḍáwee tell us that Joseph sent carriages and provisions for his father and his family; and that he and the king of Egypt went forth to meet them. He adds that the number of the children of Israel who entered Egypt with him was seventy-two; and that when they were led out thence by Moses, they were increased to six hundred thousand five hundred and seventy men, and upwards, besides the old people and children.—S.

2 A transposition is supposed to be in these words:—he seated his father and mother after they had bowed down to him, and not before. —S. (B.)

my Lord, Thou hast given me dominion, and taught me the interpretation of events (*or dreams*): Creator of the heavens and the earth, Thou art my guardian in this world and in the world to come. Make me to die a Muslim, and join me with the righteous *among my forefathers. And he lived after that a week, or more, and died a hundred and twenty years old. And the Egyptians disputed concerning his burial: so they put him in a chest of marble, and buried him in the upper part of the Nile, that the blessing* [resulting from him] *might be general to the tracts on each side of it.*[1] *Extolled be the perfection of Him to whose dominion there is no end!* (xii. 54–102).

[1] But when Moses led the Israelites out of Egypt, he took up the coffin, and carried Joseph's bones with him into Canaan, where he buried them by his ancestors.—S. (B.)

JOB.

And remember Our servant Job [Eiyoob[1]] when he called unto his Lord, Verily the devil hath afflicted me with calamity and pain. (*The affliction is attributed to the devil, though all was from God.*) *And it was said unto him,* Strike *the earth* with thy foot. *And he did so; whereupon a fountain of water sprang forth.*[2] *And it was said,* This *is* cool *water for thee* to wash with, and to drink. *So he washed himself and drank; and every disease that he had, external and internal, quitted him.* And We gave unto him his family, and as many more with them (*that is, God raised to life for him those of his children who had died, and blest him with as many more*),[3] in Our mercy and as an admonition unto those who are endowed with faculties

---

[1] The Mohammadan writers tell us that Job was of the race of Esau, and was blessed with a numerous family and abundant riches; but that God proved him by taking away all that he had, even his children, who were killed by the fall of a house; notwithstanding which he continued to serve God and to return Him thanks as usual; that he was then struck with a filthy disease, his body being full of worms and so offensive that as he lay on the dunghill none could bear to come near him: that his wife, however (whom some call Rahmeh the daughter of Ephraim the son of Joseph, and others Makhir the daughter of Manasses), attended him with great patience, supporting him with what she earned by her labour; but that the devil appearing to her one day, after having reminded her of her past prosperity, promised her that if she would worship him, he would restore all they had lost; whereupon she asked her husband's consent, who was so angry at the proposal, that he swore, if he recovered, to give his wife a hundred stripes. —S. (B., J., A.F.)

[2] Some say there were two springs, one of hot water wherein he bathed, and the other of cold of which he drank.—S. (B.)

[3] His wife also becoming young and handsome again, and bearing him twenty-six sons. Some, to express the great riches which were bestowed on Job after his sufferings, say he had two threshing-floors, one for wheat and the other for barley, and that God sent two clouds, which rained gold on the one and silver on the other till they ran over.—(J.) The traditions differ as to the continuance of Job's calamities: one

of understanding. [And We said unto him,] Take in thy hand a handful *of dry grass, or of twigs*,[1] and strike with it *thy wife* (*for he had sworn that he would inflict upon her a hundred blows, because she had staid away from him too long one day*[2]) and break not thine oath *by abstaining from striking her.—So he took a hundred stalks of schoemanthus, or some other plant, and gave her one blow with them.* Verily We found him a patient person. How excellent a servant *was he!* For he was one who earnestly turned himself unto God. (xxxviii. 40–44.)

will have it to be eighteen years; another, thirteen; another, three; and another, exactly seven years seven months and seven hours.—S.

[1] Or 'a palm-branch having a hundred leaves.'—S.

[2] But see note 1.

SHO'EYB.

And *we sent* unto Midian [Medyen] their brother Sho'eyb.[1] He said, O my people, worship God; *assert His unity.* Ye have no other deity but Him. And give not short measure and weight. Verily I see you [to be] in a state of prosperity *that placeth you above the need of doing so;* and verily I fear for you, *if ye believe not,* the punishment of a day that will encompass *you with destruction.* And, O my people, give full measure and weight with equity; and diminish not unto men *aught* of their things nor commit injustice in the earth, acting corruptly, *by murder or other offences.* The residue of God (*His supply that remaineth to you after the completion of the measure*) will be better for you *than diminution,* if ye be believers. And I am not a guardian over you, *to recompense you for your actions: I have only been sent as an admonisher.*— They replied, *in mockery,* O Sho'eyb, do thy prayers command thee that we are to leave what our fathers worshipped, or *cease* to do with our riches what we please? Verily thou art the mild, the right director. *This they said in mockery.*—He said, O my people, tell me, if I act according to an evident proof from my Lord, and He hath supplied me with a good *lawful* provision, shall I mix it up with what is forbidden, and shall I not desire to

[1] The commentators generally suppose him to be the same person with the father-in-law of Moses, who is named in Scripture Reuel or Raguel, and Jethro. But Ahmad Ibn-'Abd-El-Haleem charges those who entertain this opinion with ignorance. They say (after the Jews) that he gave his son-in-law [Moses] that wonder-working rod with which he performed all those miracles in Egypt and the Desert, and also excellent advice and instructions; whence he had the surname of 'Khateeb-el-Ambiya,' or 'the Preacher to the Prophets.'—S.

oppose you, *and shall I betake myself* to that which I forbid you? I desire not [aught] but *your* reformation, as far as I am able [to effect it], and my help is not [in any] but in God: on Him do I rely, and unto Him do I turn me. And, O my people, let not the opposition of me procure for you the befalling you of the like of that which befell the people of Noah or the people of Hood or the people of Ṣáliḥ. And *the abodes of the* people of Lot [are] not distant from you: (*or the time of their destruction was not long ago:*) *therefore be admonished.* And ask ye forgiveness of your Lord, and turn unto Him with repentance; for my Lord is merciful *to the believers,* loving *to them.* They replied, O Sho'eyb, we understand not much of what thou sayest, and verily we see thee to be weak[1] among us; and were it not for thy family, we had stoned thee; for thou art not, in our estimation, an honourable person: *thy family only are the honourable.* He said, O my people, are my family more honourable in your estimation than God, *and do ye abstain from slaying me for their sake, and not preserve me for God,* and have ye cast Him behind you as a thing neglected? Verily my Lord comprehendeth that which ye do, *and He will recompense you.* And, O my people, act ye according to your condition: verily I will act *according to mine.* Ye shall know on whom shall come a punishment that shall render him vile, and who is a liar: and await ye *the issue of your case:* verily I await with you.—And when Our degree *for their destruction* came [to be executed], we delivered Sho'eyb and those who believed with him, in our mercy, and the cry *of Gabriel* assailed those who had offended, so that in the morning they were in their abodes prostrate *and dead,* as though they had not dwelt therein. Was not Midian removed as Thamood had been removed? (xi. 85–98.)

[1] The Arabic word 'ḍa'eef' (weak) signifying also in the Ḥimyaritic dialect 'blind,' some suppose that Sho'eyb was so, and that the Midianites objected that to him as a defect which disqualified him for the prophetic office.—S.

MOSES AND HIS PEOPLE.

We will rehearse unto thee, [O Moḥammad, somewhat] of the history of Moses [Moosá] and Pharaoh [Fir'own or Far'oon],[1] with truth, for *the sake of* people who believe. Verily Pharaoh exalted himself in the land *of Egypt*, and divided its inhabitants into parties *to serve him*. He rendered weak one class of them, *namely the children of Israel*, slaughtering their male children, and preserving alive their females, *because one of the diviners said unto him, A child will be born among the children of Israel, who will be the means of the loss of thy kingdom;*—for he was [one] of the corrupt doers. And We desired to be gracious unto those who had been deemed weak in the land, and to make them models of religion, and to make them the heirs *of the possessions of Pharaoh*, and to establish them in the land *of Egypt, and in Syria*, and to show Pharaoh and Hámán[2] and their forces what

[1] Which of the kings of Egypt this Pharaoh of Moses was is uncertain. Not to mention the opinions of the European writers, those of the East generally suppose him to have been El-Weleed, who according to some was an Arab of the tribe of 'Ád, or according to others the son of Muṣ'ab the son of Er-Reiyán the son of El-Weleed the Amalekite. There are historians, however, who suppose Ḳáboos the brother and predecessor of El-Weleed was the prince we are speaking of, and pretend he lived six hundred and twenty years and reigned four hundred. Which is more reasonable, at least, than the opinion of those who imagine it was his father Muṣ'ab or grandfather Er-Reiyán. Abu-l-Fida says that Muṣ'ab, being one hundred and seventy years old and having no child, while he kept the herds saw a cow calve, and heard her say at the same time, 'O Muṣ'ab, be not grieved, for thou shalt have a wicked son, who will be at length cast into hell.' And he accordingly had this Weleed, who afterwards coming to be king of Egypt proved an impious tyrant.—S. (A.F., Z.)

[2] This name is given to Pharaoh's chief minister; from whence it is generally inferred that Mohammad has here made Haman the favourite of Ahasuerus king of Persia, and who indisputably lived many years after Moses, to be that prophet's contemporary.—S.

they feared from them. And We said, by revelation, unto the mother of Moses, *the child above-mentioned, of whose birth none knew save his sister,* Suckle him; and when thou fearest for him cast him in the river *Nile,* and fear not *his being drowned,* nor mourn *for his separation;* for We will restore him unto thee, and will make him [one] of the apostles.[1] *So she suckled him three months, during which he wept not; and then she feared for him, wherefore she put him into an ark pitched within and furnished with a bed for him, and she closed it and cast it in the river Nile by night.* And the family (*or servants*) of Pharaoh lighted upon him *in the ark on the morrow of that night;*[2] *so they put it before him, and it was opened, and Moses was taken forth from it, sucking milk from his thumb:* [this happened] that he might be unto them *eventually* an enemy (*slaying their men*) and an affliction (*making slaves of their women*); for Pharaoh and Hámán (*his Wezeer*) and their forces were sinners; *wherefore they were punished by his hand.* And the wife of Pharaoh said, *when he and his servants had proposed to kill him, He is* delight of the eye unto me and unto thee: do not ye kill him: peradventure he may be serviceable unto us, or we may adopt him as a son. *And*

---

[1] It is related that the midwife appointed to attend the Hebrew women, terrified by a light which appeared between the eyes of Moses at his birth, and touched with an extraordinary affection for the child, did not discover him to the officers, so that his mother kept him in her house, and nursed him three months; after which it was impossible for her to conceal him any longer, the king then giving orders to make the searches more strictly.—S. (B.)

[2] The commentators say that his mother made an ark of the papyrus, and pitched it, and put in some cotton; and having laid the child therein, committed it to the river, a branch of which went into Pharaoh's garden: that the stream carried the ark thither into a fishpond, at the head of which Pharaoh was then sitting with his wife Ásiyeh the daughter of Muzáḥem; and that the king, having commanded it to be taken up and opened, and finding in it a beautiful child, took a fancy to it, and ordered it to be brought up.—Some writers mention a miraculous preservation of Moses before he was put into the ark; and tell us, that his mother having hid him from Pharaoh's officers in an oven, his sister, in her mother's absence, kindled a large fire in the oven to heat it, not knowing the child was there; but that he was afterwards taken out unhurt.—S. (B., A.F.)

they complied with her desire; and they knew not *the consequence.*

And the heart of the mother of Moses, *when she knew of his having been lighted upon,* became disquieted; and she had almost made him known *to be her son,* had We not fortified her heart with patience, that she might be [one] of the believers *in Our promise.* And she said unto his sister *Maryam* [or Mary], Trace him, *that thou mayest know his case.* And she watched him from a distance, while they knew not *that she was his sister and that she was watching him.* And We forbade him the breasts, *preventing him from taking the breast of any nurse except his mother,* before *his restoration to her:* so *his sister* said, Shall I direct you unto the people of a house who will nurse him for you, and who will be faithful unto him? *And her offer was accepted; therefore she brought his mother, and he took her breast: so she returned with him to her house, as God hath said,*—And We restored him to his mother, that her eye might be cheerful and that she might not grieve, and that she might know that the promise of God *to restore him unto her* was true: but the greater number of them (*that is, of mankind*) know not *this. And it appeared not that this was his sister and this his mother; and he remained with her until she had weaned him; and her hire was paid her, for every day a deenár, which she took* [without scruple] *because it was the wealth of a hostile person. She then brought him unto Pharaoh, and he was brought up in his abode, as God hath related of him in the Chapter of the Poets,*[1] [where Pharaoh said unto Moses,] *Have we not brought thee up among us a child, and hast thou not dwelt among us* [thirty] *years of thy life?*

And when he had attained his age of strength (*thirty years or thirty and three*), and had become of full age (*forty years*), We bestowed on him wisdom and knowledge *in religion, before he was sent as a prophet;* and thus do

---

[1] Ḳur. xxvi. 17.

We reward the well-doers. And he entered the city *of Pharaoh, which was Munf* [or Memphis], *after he had been absent from him a while,* at a time when its inhabitants were inadvertent, *at the hour of the noon-sleep,* and he found therein two men fighting; this [being] of his party (*namely an Israelite*), and this of his enemies (*an Egyptian*), *who was compelling the Israelite to carry firewood to the kitchen of Pharaoh without pay:* and he who was of his party begged him to aid him against him who was of his enemies. *So Moses said unto the latter, Let him go. And it is said that he replied to Moses, I have a mind to put the burden upon thee.* And Moses struck him with his fist, and killed him. *But he intended not to kill him; and he buried him in the sand.* He said, This is of the work of the devil, *who hath excited my anger;* for he is an enemy *unto the son of Adam,* a manifest misleader *of him.* He said, *in repentance,* O my Lord, verily I have acted injuriously unto mine own soul, *by killing him;* therefore forgive me. So He forgave him: for He is the Very Forgiving, the Merciful.—He said, O my Lord, by the *favours* with which Thou hast favoured me, *defend me,* and I will by no means be an assistant to the sinners *after this.*—And the next morning he was afraid in the city, watching *for what might happen unto him on account of the slain man;* and lo, he who had begged his assistance the day before was crying out to him for aid *against another Egyptian.* Moses said unto him, Verily thou art a person manifestly in error, *because of that which thou hast done yesterday and to-day.* But when he was about to lay violent hands upon him who was an enemy unto them both, (*namely unto Moses and him who begged his aid,*) *the latter* said, *imagining that he would lay violent hands upon him, because of that which he had said unto him,* O Moses, dost thou desire to kill me, as thou killedst a soul yesterday? Thou desirest not [aught] but to be an oppressor in the land, and thou desirest not to be [one] of the reconcilers.—*And the Egyptian heard that: so he knew that the killer was Moses; wherefore he departed unto Pharaoh and acquainted him therewith, and Pharaoh commanded the executioners to slay Moses, and they betook themselves to seek him.* But a man *who was a believer of the family of Pharaoh* [1] came from the furthest part of the city, running *by a way that was nearer than the way by which they had come:* he said, O Moses, verily the chiefs *of the people of Pharaoh* are consulting respecting thee, to slay thee; therefore go forth *from the city:* verily I am unto thee [one] of the admonishers. So he went forth from it in fear, watching *in fear of pursuer, or for the aid of God.* He said, O my Lord, deliver me from the unjust people *of Pharaoh!* [2]

And when he was journeying towards Medyen, *which was the city of Sho'eyb, eight days' journey from Miṣr (named after Medyen the son of Abraham), and he knew not the way unto it,* he said, Peradventure my Lord will direct me unto the right way, *or the middle way. And God sent unto him an angel, having in his hand a short spear; and he went with him thither.*[3] And when he came unto the water (*or well*) of Medyen, he found at it a company of men watering *their animals;* and he found besides them two women keeping away *their sheep from the water.* He said *unto them (namely the two women),* What is the matter with you *that ye water not?* They answered, We shall not water until the pastors shall have driven away *their animals;* and our father is a very old man, *who cannot water the sheep.* And he watered for them *from another well near unto them, from which he lifted a stone that none*

---

[1] This person, says the tradition, was an Egyptian and Pharaoh's uncle's son.—S.

[2] The Jews pretend he was actually imprisoned for the fact, and condemned to be beheaded; but that when he should have suffered his neck became as hard as ivory, and the sword rebounded on the executioner.—S.

[3] According to El-Beyḍáwee, Moses knew not the way, and, coming to a place where three roads met, committed himself to the guidance of God, and took the middle road, which was the right; Providence likewise so ordering it that his pursuers took the other two roads, and missed him.—S.

could lift but ten persons. Then he retired to the shade *of an Egyptian thorn-tree on account of the violence of the heat of the sun; and he was hungry,* and he said, O my Lord, verily I am in need of the good *provision* which Thou shalt send down unto me. *And the two women returned unto their father in less time than they were accustomed to do: so he asked them the reason thereof; and they informed him of the person who had watered for them; whereupon he said unto one of them, Call him unto me.*

And one of them[1] came unto him, walking bashfully, *with the sleeve of her shift over her face, by reason of her abashment at him:* she said, My father calleth thee, that he may recompense thee with the reward of thy having watered for us. *And he assented to her call, disliking in his mind the receiving of the reward: but it seemeth that she intended the compensation if he were of such as desired it. And she walked before him; and the wind blew her garment, and her legs were discovered: so he said unto her, Walk behind me and direct me in the way. And she did so, until she came unto her father, who was Sho'eyb, on whom be peace! and with him was* [prepared] *a supper. He said unto him, Sit and sup. But he replied, I fear lest it be a compensation for my having watered for them, and we are a family who seek not a compensation for doing good. He said, Nay, it is my custom and hath been the custom of my fathers to entertain the guest and to give food. So he ate; and acquainted him with his case.* And when he had come unto him, and had related to him the story *of his having killed the Egyptian and their intention to kill him and his fear of Pharaoh,* he replied, Fear not: thou hast escaped from the unjust people. (*For Pharaoh had no dominion over Medyen.*) One of them [namely of the women] said (*and she was the one who had been sent*), O my father, hire him *to tend our sheep in our stead;* for the best whom

[1] This was Ṣafoora [also called Ṣafoorah and Ṣafooriya], or Zipporah, the elder, or as others suppose the younger, daughter of Sho'eyb, whom Moses afterwards married.—S.

thou canst hire is the strong, the trustworthy. *So he asked her respecting him, and she acquainted him with what hath been above related, his lifting up the stone of the well, and his saying unto her, Walk behind me;—and moreover, that when she had come unto him, and he knew of her presence, he hung down his head and raised it not.* He *therefore* said, Verily I desire to marry thee unto one of these my two daughters, on the condition that thou shalt be a hired servant to me, *to tend my sheep,* eight years; and if thou fulfil ten *years,* it shall be of thine own will; and I desire not to lay a difficulty upon thee *by imposing as a condition the ten years:* thou shalt find me, if God please, [one] of the just, *who are faithful to their covenants.* He replied, This [be the covenant] between me and thee: whichever of the two terms I fulfil, there shall be no injustice against me *by demanding an addition thereto;* and God is witness of what we say. *And the marriage-contract was concluded according to this; and Sho'eyb ordered his daughter to give unto Moses a rod wherewith to drive away the wild beasts from his sheep: and the rods of the prophets were in his possession; and the rod of Adam, of the myrtle of paradise, fell into her hand; and Moses took it, with the knowledge of Sho'eyb.* (xxviii. 21–28.)

Hath the history of Moses been related to thee? when he saw fire,[1] *during his journey from Medyen, on his way to Egypt,* and said unto his family, *or his wife,* Tarry ye *here;* for I have seen fire: perhaps I may bring you a brand from it, or find at the fire a guide *to direct me in the way. For he had missed the way in consequence of the darkness of the night.* And when he came unto it (*and it*

[1] The commentators say, that Moses, having obtained leave of Sho'eyb or Jethro, his father-in-law, to visit his mother, departed with his family from Midian towards Egypt; but coming to the valley of Ṭuwa, wherein Mount Sinai stands, his wife fell in labour and was delivered of a son in a very dark and snowy night: he had also lost his way, and his cattle were scattered from him, when on a sudden he saw a fire by the side of a mountain, which on his nearer approach he found burning in a green bush.—S. (B.)

was a bramble-bush), he was called to [by a voice saying], O Moses, verily I am thy Lord; therefore pull off thy shoes;[1] for thou art in the holy valley of Ṭuwa. And I have chosen thee *from among thy people;* wherefore hearken attentively unto that which is revealed *unto thee by Me.* Verily I am God: there is no Deity except Me; therefore worship Me, and perform prayer in remembrance of Me. Verily the hour is coming: I will manifest it *unto mankind, and its nearness shall appear unto them by its signs,* that every soul may be recompensed *therein* for its *good and evil* work: therefore let not him who believeth not in it, and followeth his lust, hinder thee from *believing in* it, lest thou perish. And what is that in thy right hand, O Moses?—He answered, It is my rod, whereon I lean and wherewith I beat down leaves for my sheep *that they may eat them;* and I have other uses for it, *as the carrying of provision and the water-skin, and the driving away of reptiles.* He said, Cast it down, O Moses. So he cast it down; and lo, it was a serpent,[2] running along. *God* said, Take it, and fear *it* not:[3] we will restore it to its former state. *And he put his hand into its mouth; whereupon it became again a rod.* [And God said,] And put thy *right* hand to thy *left* arm-pit, *and take it forth:* it shall come forth white, without evil, (*that is, without leprosy; shining like the rays of the sun, dazzling the sight,*) as another sign, that We may show thee the greatest of our signs *of thine apostleship.* (*And when he desired to restore his hand to its first state, he put it as before described, and drew it forth.*) Go *as an apostle* unto Pharaoh *and those*

---

[1] This was a mark of humility and respect: though some fancy there was some uncleanness in the shoes themselves, because they were made of the skin of an ass not dressed.—S. (B.)

[2] Which was at first no bigger than the rod, but afterwards swelled to a prodigious size.—S. (B.)

[3] When Moses saw the serpent move about with great nimbleness and swallow stones and trees, he was greatly terrified, and fled from it; but recovering his courage at these words of God, he had the boldness to take the serpent by the jaws.—S. (B.)

who are with him; for he hath acted with exceeding impiety *by arrogating to himself divinity.*—*Moses* said, O my Lord, dilate my bosom, *that it may bear the message,* and make my affair easy unto me, and loose the knot of my tongue (*this had arisen from his having been burned in his mouth by a live coal when he was a child*),[1] that they may understand my speech *when I deliver the message.* And appoint unto me a Wezeer of my family, *namely* Aaron [Hároon] my brother. Strengthen my back by him, and make him a colleague in my affair, that we may glorify Thee much, and remember Thee much; for Thou knowest us.

God replied, Thou hast obtained thy petition, O Moses, and We have been gracious unto thee another time: forasmuch as We revealed unto thy mother what was revealed, *when she gave birth to thee and feared that Pharaoh would kill thee among the others that were born,* [saying,] Cast him into the ark, and then cast him, *in the ark,* into the river *Nile,* and the river shall throw him on the shore; then an enemy unto Me and an enemy unto him (*namely Pharaoh*) shall take him. And I bestowed on thee, *after he had taken thee,* love from Me, *that thou mightest be loved by men, so that Pharaoh and all that saw thee loved thee;* and that thou mightest be bred up in Mine eye. [Also] forasmuch as thy sister *Maryam* went *that she might learn what became of thee, after they had brought nurses and thou hadst refused to take the breast of any one of them,* and she said, Shall I direct you unto one who will nurse him? (*whereupon her proposal was*

---

[1] **Moses had an impediment in his speech, which was occasioned by the following accident. Pharaoh one day carrying him in his arms when a child, he suddenly laid hold of his beard and plucked it in a very rough manner, which put Pharaoh into such a passion that he ordered him to be put to death: but Ásiyeh his wife representing to him that he was but a child, who could not distinguish between a burning coal and a ruby, he ordered the experiment to be made; and a live coal and a ruby being set before Moses, he took the coal and put it into his mouth, and burnt his tongue: and thereupon he was pardoned.—This is a Jewish story a little altered.—S.**

accepted, and she brought his mother): so We restored thee to thy mother, that her eye might become cheerful and that she might not grieve. And thou slewest a soul, *namely the Copt in Egypt, and wast sorry for his slaughter, on account of Pharaoh,* and We delivered thee from sorrow; and We tried thee with *other* trial, *and delivered thee from it.*[1] And thou stayedst *ten* years among the people of Medyen, *after thou hadst come thither from Egypt, at the abode of Sho'eyb the prophet, and he married thee to his daughter.* Then thou camest according to *My* decree, *as to the time of thy mission, when thou hadst attained the age of forty years,* O Moses; and I have chosen thee for Myself. Go thou and thy brother [2] *unto the people,* with My *nine* signs, and cease ye not to remember Me. Go ye unto Pharaoh; for he hath acted with exceeding impiety, *by arrogating to himself divinity,* and speak unto him with gentle speech, *exhorting him to relinquish that conduct:* peradventure he will consider, or will fear *God, and repent.* (*The* [mere] *hope with respect to the two* [results is expressed] *because of God's knowledge that he would not repent.*)—They replied, O our Lord, verily we fear that he may be precipitately violent against us, *hastening to punish us,* or that he may act with exceeding injustice *towards us.* He said, Fear ye not; for I am with you: I will hear and will see. Therefore go ye unto him, and say, Verily we are the apostles of thy Lord: therefore send with us the children of Israel *unto Syria,* and do not afflict them, *but cease to employ them in thy difficult works, such as digging and building and carrying the heavy burden.* We have come unto thee with a sign from thy Lord, *attesting our veracity in asserting ourselves apostles:*

---

[1] For he was obliged to abandon his country and his friends, and to travel several days in great terror and want of necessary provisions to seek a refuge among strangers; and was afterwards forced to serve for hire to gain a livelihood.—S.

[2] Aaron being by this time come out to meet his brother, either by divine inspiration, or having notice of his design to return to Egypt.—S. (B.)

and peace be on him who followeth the right direction:—*that is, he shall be secure from punishment.* Verily it hath been revealed unto us that punishment [shall be inflicted] upon him who chargeth with falsehood *that wherewith we have come,* and turneth away *from it.* (xx. 8–50.)

Then We sent after them, *namely the apostles before mentioned* [who were Sho'eyb and his predecessors], Moses, with Our signs unto Pharaoh and his nobles, and they acted unjustly with respect to them, *disbelieving in the signs:* but see what was the end of the corrupt doers. And Moses said, O Pharaoh, verily I am an apostle from the Lord of the worlds *unto thee. But he charged him with falsehood: so he said, I am* right not to say of God aught but the truth. I have come unto you with a proof from your Lord: therefore send with me *to Syria* the children of Israel.—*Pharaoh* said *unto him,* If thou hast come with a sign *confirmatory of thy pretension,* produce it, if thou be of those who speak truth, So he cast down his rod; and lo, it was a manifest serpent.[1] And he drew forth his hand *from his bosom;* and lo, it was white *and radiant* unto the beholders.[2] The nobles of the people of Pharaoh said, Verily this is a knowing enchanter: he desireth to expel you from your land. What then do ye command? —They answered, Put off for a time him and his brother, and send unto the cities collectors [of the inhabitants],

---

1 The Arab writers tell enormous fables of this serpent or dragon. For they say that he was hairy and of so prodigious a size that when he opened his mouth his jaws were fourscore cubits asunder and when he laid his lower jaw on the ground his upper reached to the top of the palace [or rather, I believe, the *throne* of Pharaoh]: that Pharaoh, seeing this monster make towards him, fled from it; and that the whole assembly also betaking themselves to their heels, no less than twenty-five thousand of them lost their lives in the press. They add that Pharaoh upon this abjured Moses by God who had sent him to take away the serpent, and promised he would believe on Him and let the Israelites go; but when Moses had done what he requested, he relapsed and grew as hardened as before.—S. (B.)

2 There is a tradition that Moses was a very swarthy man; and that when he put his hand into his bosom, and drew it out again, it became extremely white and splendid, surpassing the brightness of the sun.—S. (B.)

that they may bring unto thee every knowing enchanter. And the enchanters came unto Pharaoh. They said, Shall we surely have a reward if we be the party who overcome? He answered, Yea; and verily ye shall be of those who are admitted near [unto my person]. They said, O Moses, either do thou cast down *thy rod,* or we will cast down *what we have with us.* He replied, Cast ye. And when they cast down *their cords and their rods,* they enchanted the eyes of the men, *diverting them from the true perception of them;* and they terrified them; *for they imagined them to be serpents running;* and they performed a great enchantment.[1] And We spake by revelation unto Moses, [saying,] Cast down thy rod. And lo, it swallowed up what they had caused to appear changed.[2] So the truth was confirmed, and that which they had wrought became vain; and they were overcome there, and were rendered contemptible. And the enchanters cast themselves down prostrate:[3] they said, We believe in the Lord of the worlds, the Lord of Moses and Aaron. Pharaoh said,

---

[1] They provided themselves with a great number of thick ropes and long pieces of wood, which they contrived by some means to move and make them twist themselves one over the other; and so imposed on the beholders, who at a distance took them to be true serpents. It is also said that they rubbed them over with quicksilver, which being wrought upon by the heat of the sun caused them to move.—S. (B.)

[2] The expositors add that when this serpent had swallowed up all the rods and cords he made directly towards the assembly and put them into so great a terror that they fled and a considerable number were killed in the crowd: then Moses took it up and it became a rod in his hand as before. Whereupon the magicians declared that it could be no enchantment, because in such case their rods and cords would not have disappeared.—S. (B.)

[3] Sale observes that some writers introduce only two of the enchanters as acknowledging Moses' miracle to be wrought by the power of God. These two, they say, were brothers, and the sons of a famous magician then dead; but on their being sent for to court on this occasion, their mother persuaded them to go to their father's tomb and ask his advice. Being come to the tomb, the father answered their call, and when they had acquainted him with the affair, he told them that they should inform themselves whether the rod of which they spoke became a serpent while its masters slept, or only when they were awake; for, said he, enchantments have no effect while the enchanter is asleep, and therefore if it be otherwise in this

Have ye believed in Him before I have given you permission? Verily this is a plot that ye have contrived in the city, that ye may cause its inhabitants to go forth from it. But ye shall know *what shall happen unto you at my hand.* I will assuredly cut off your hands and your feet on the opposite sides—*the right hand of each and his left foot:* then I will crucify you all.—They replied. Verily unto our Lord shall we return, *after our death, of whatever kind it be;* and thou dost not take vengeance on us but because we believed in the signs of our Lord when they came unto us. O our Lord, pour upon us patience, and cause us to die Muslims![1] (vii. 101–123.)

And Pharaoh said, Let me alone, that I may kill Moses, (*for they had diverted him from killing him,*) and let him call upon his Lord *to defend him from me.* Verily I fear lest he change your religion, *and prevent your worshipping me,* or that he may cause corruption to appear in the earth (*that is, slaughter, and other offences*).—And Moses said *unto his people, having heard this,* Verily I have recourse for defence unto my Lord and your Lord from every proud person who believeth not in the day of account. And a man [who was] a believer, of the family of Pharaoh (*it is said that he was the son of his paternal uncle,*)[2] who concealed his faith, said, Will ye kill a man because he saith, My Lord is God,—when he hath come unto you with evident proofs from your Lord? And if he be a liar, on him [will be] *the evil consequence of* his lie; but if he be a speaker of truth, somewhat of that *punishment with* which he threateneth you will befall you *speedily.* Verily God directeth not him who is a trans-

case, you may be assured that they act by a divine power. These two magicians then, arriving at the capital of Egypt, on inquiry found to their great astonishment that when Moses and Aaron went to rest their rod became a serpent and guarded them while they slept. And this was the first step towards their conversion.—S.

[1] Some think these converted magicians were executed accordingly: but others deny it, and say that the king was not able to put them to death; insisting on these words of the Ḳur-án [xxviii. 35], 'Ye two, and they who follow you, shall overcome.'—S.

[2] See p. 101, l. 5, n. 1.

gressor, *or polytheist,* [and] a liar. O my people, ye have the dominion to-day, being overcomers in the land *of Egypt;* but who will defend us from the punishment of God *if ye kill his favourite servants,* if it come unto us?[1] —Pharaoh said, I will not advise you to do [aught] save what I see to be advisable, *which is, to kill Moses;* and I will not direct you save into the right way. And he who had believed said, O my people, verily I fear for you the like of the day of the confederates,[2] the like of the condition of the people of Noah and 'Ád and Thamood and those who [have lived] after them: and God willeth not injustice unto [His] servants. And, O my people, verily I fear for you the day of calling (*that is, the day of resurrection, when the people of Paradise and those of Hell shall often call one to another*). On the day when ye shall turn back *from the place of reckoning unto hell,* ye shall have no protector against God. And he whom God shall cause to err shall have no director. Moreover, Joseph (*who was Joseph the son of Jacob according to one opinion, and who lived unto the time of Moses; and Joseph the son of Abraham the son of Joseph the son of Jacob, according to another opinion*) came unto you before *Moses,* with evident *miraculous* proofs; but ye ceased not to be in doubt respecting that wherewith he came unto you, until, when he died, ye said *without proof* God will by no means send an apostle after him. Thus God causeth to err him who is a transgressor, *or polytheist,* [and] a sceptic. They who dispute respecting the signs of God, without any convincing proof having come unto them, *their disputing* is very hateful with God and with those who have believed. Thus God sealeth every heart (*or the whole heart*) of a proud contumacious person.

And Pharaoh said, O Hámán, build for me a tower, that I may reach the avenues, the avenues of the heavens,

---

[1] Cp. Act. Apost. v. 38, 39.

[2] 'The people of Noah and of 'Ád and of Thamood, and those whom God destroyed after them.' So explained in the Ḳámoos.

and ascend unto the God of Moses;[1] but verily I think him, *namely Moses*, a liar *in his assertion that he hath any god but myself.* And thus the wickedness of his deed was made to seem comely unto Pharaoh, and he was turned away from the path *of rectitude;* and the artifice of Pharaoh [ended] not save in loss. And he who had believed said, O my people, follow me: I will direct you into the right way. O my people, this present life is only a temporary enjoyment; but the world to come is the mansion of firm continuance. Whosoever doeth evil, he shall not be recompensed save with the like of it; and whosoever doeth good, whether male or female, and is a believer, these shall enter Paradise; they shall be provided for therein without reckoning. And, O my people, how is it that I invite you unto salvation, and ye invite me unto the Fire? Ye invite me to deny God, and to associate with Him that of which I have no knowledge; but I invite you unto the Mighty, the Very Forgiving. [There is] no doubt but that the [false gods] to *the worship of* which ye invite me are not to be invoked in this world, nor in the world to come, and that our return [shall be] unto God, and that the transgressors [shall be] the companions of the Fire. And ye shall remember, *when ye see the punishment*, what I say unto you; and I commit my case unto God; for God seeth [His] servants.—*This he said when they threatened him for his opposing their religion.* Therefore God preserved him from the evils which they had artfully devised (*namely slaughter*), and a most evil punishment encompassed the people of Pharaoh,[2] *with*

---

[1] It is said that Hámán having prepared bricks and other materials employed no less than fifty thousand men besides labourers in the building, which they carried to so immense a height that the workmen could no longer stand on it: that Pharaoh ascending this tower threw a javelin towards heaven, which fell back again stained with blood, whereupon he impiously boasted that he had killed the god of Moses; but at sunset God sent the angel Gabriel, who with one stroke of his wing demolished the tower, a part whereof falling on the king's army destroyed a million of men.—S. (Z.)

[2] Some are of opinion that those who were sent by Pharaoh to seize the true believer, his kinsman, are

Pharaoh himself (*namely the drowning*); *then* they shall be exposed to the Fire morning and evening;[1] and on the day when the hour [of judgment] shall come, *it shall be said unto the angels,* Introduce the people of Pharaoh into the most severe punishment. (xl. 27–49.)

And the nobles of the people of Pharaoh said *unto him,* Wilt thou let Moses and his people go that they may act corruptly in the earth, *by inviting to disobey thee,* and leave thee and thy gods? (*For he had made for them little idols for them to worship, and he said, I am your Lord and their Lord;—and therefore he said, I am your Lord the Most High.*) He answered, We will slaughter their male children and will suffer their females to live: and verily we shall prevail over them. *And thus they did unto them; wherefore the children of Israel complained, and* Moses said unto his people, Seek aid of God, and be patient; for the earth belongeth unto God: He causeth whomsoever He will of His servants to inherit it; and the *prosperous* end is for those who fear *God.* They replied, We have been afflicted before thou camest unto us and since thou hast come unto us. He said, Perhaps your Lord will destroy your enemy and cause you to succeed [him] in the earth, and He will see how ye will act *therein.*—And We had punished the family of Pharaoh with dearth and with scarcity of fruits, that they might be admonished *and might believe.* But when good betided them, they said, This is ours:—*that is, we deserve it;—and they were not grateful for it;* and if evil befell them,

---

the persons more particularly meant in this place: for they tell us that the said believer fled to a mountain, where they found him at prayers, guarded by the wild beasts, which ranged themselves in order about him; and that his pursuers thereupon returned in a great fright to their master, who put them to death for not performing his command.—S. (B.)

[1] Some expound these words of the previous punishment they are doomed to suffer, according to a tradition of Ibn-Mes'ood, which informs us that their souls are in the crops of black birds which are exposed to hell-fire every morning and evening until the Day of Judgment.—S. (B.)

they ascribed it to the ill luck of Moses and those *believers* who were with him. Nay, their ill luck was only with God: *He brought it upon them:* but the greater number of them know not *this.* And they said *unto Moses,* Whatsoever sign thou bring unto us, to enchant us therewith, we will not believe in thee. *So he uttered an imprecation upon them,* and We sent upon them the flood, *which entered their houses and reached to the throats of the persons sitting, seven days,*[1] and the locusts, *which ate their corn and their fruits,* and the ḳummal, *or grubs, or a kind of tick, which sought after what the locusts had left,* and the frogs, *which filled their houses and their food,* and the blood *in their waters;* distinct signs: but they were proud, *refusing to believe in them,* and were a wicked people. And when the punishment fell upon them, they said, O Moses, supplicate for us thy Lord, according to that which He hath covenanted with thee, *namely that He will withdraw from us the punishment if we believe:* verily, if thou remove from us the punishment, we will assuredly believe thee, and we will assuredly send with thee the children of Israel. But when We removed from them the punishment until a period at which they should arrive, lo, they brake their promise. Wherefore We took vengeance on them, and drowned them in the sea, because they charged our signs with falsehood and were heedless of them. And We caused the people who had been rendered weak, *by being enslaved,* to inherit the eastern parts of the earth and its western parts,[2] which we blessed *with water and trees, (namely Syria)*; and the gracious word of thy Lord was

---

[1] As there is no mention of any such miraculous inundation in the [so-called] Mosaic writings, some have imagined this plague to have been either a pestilence, or the small-pox, or some other epidemical distemper. (B.) For the word 'ṭoofán,' which is used in this place, and is generally rendered a 'deluge,' may also signify any other universal destruction or mortality.—S.

[2] That is, the land of Syria, of which the Eastern geographers reckon Palestine a part, and wherein the commentators say the children of Israel succeeded the kings of Egypt and the Amalekites.—S. (B.)

fulfilled on the children of Israel, because they had been patient; and We destroyed the *structures* which Pharaoh and his people had built and what they had erected.[1] (vii. 124–133.)

We brought the children of Israel across the sea, and Pharaoh and his troops pursued them with violence and hostility, until, when drowning overtook him, he said, I believe that there is no deity but He in whom the children of Israel believe, and I am [one] of the Muslims. *But Gabriel thrust into his mouth some of the mire of the sea, lest mercy should be granted him, and said,* Now *thou believest,* and thou hast been rebellious hitherto, and wast [one] of the corrupters. But to-day we will raise thee with thy lifeless body *from the sea,* that thou mayest be a sign unto those [who shall come] after thee. (*It is related, on the authority of Ibn-'Abbás, that some of the children of Israel doubted his death; wherefore he was brought forth to them that they might see him.*)[2] But verily many men are heedless of Our signs. (x. 90–92.)

And We brought the children of Israel across the sea; and they came unto a people who gave themselves up to *the worship of* idols belonging to them;[3] [whereupon] they said, O Moses, make for us a god (*an idol for us to worship*), like as they have gods. He replied, Verily ye are a people who are ignorant, *since ye have requited God's favour towards you with that which ye have said;* for that [religion] in which these are [occupied shall be] destroyed, and vain is that which they do. He said, Shall I seek for you any other deity than God, when He hath preferred you above the peoples *of your time?* (vii. 134–136.)

---

[1] Particularly the lofty tower [before mentioned] which Pharaoh caused to be built, that he might attack the God of Moses.—S.

[2] The word here translated 'body' signifying also a 'coat of mail,' some imagine the meaning to be that his corpse floated armed with his coat of mail, which they tell us was of gold, by which they knew that it was he.—S.

[3] These people some will have to be of the tribe of Amalek, whom Moses was commanded to destroy, and others of the tribe of Lakhm. Their idols, it is said, were images of oxen, which gave the first hint to the making of the golden calf.—S. (B.)

And We caused the thin clouds to shade you *from the heat of the sun in the desert,* and caused the manna and the quails[1] to descend upon you, *and said,* Eat of the good things which We have given you for food, *and store not up.—But they were ungrateful for the benefit, and stored up; wherefore it was cut off from them.* And they injured not Us *thereby;* but they did injure their own souls. (ii. 54.)

[Remember, O children of Israel,] when ye said, O Moses, we will not bear patiently the having one *kind of* food, *the manna and the quails;* therefore supplicate for us thy Lord, that He may produce for us *somewhat* of that which the earth bringeth forth, of its herbs and its cucumbers and its wheat and its lentils and its onions:—he said *unto them,* Will ye take in exchange that which is worse for that which is better?—*But they refused to recede; therefore he supplicated God, and He said,* Get ye down into a great city;[2] for ye shall have *therein* what ye have asked.—And *the marks of* abjection and poverty were stamped upon them: *so these characteristics necessarily belong to them, even if they are rich, as necessarily as the stamped coin belongeth to its die;* and they returned with indignation from God. This was because they did disbelieve in the signs of God, and slay the prophets (*as Zechariah and John*) unjustly: this was because they rebelled and did transgress. (ii. 58.)

And *remember* when Moses asked drink for his people, *who had become thirsty in the desert,* and We said, Strike with thy rod the stone. (*It was the stone that fled away*

---

[1] The Eastern writers say these quails were of a peculiar kind to be found nowhere but in El-Yemen, from whence they were brought by a south wind in great numbers to the Israelites' camp in the desert. The Arabs call these birds 'selwa,' which is plainly the same with the Hebrew 'salwim,' and say they have no bones, but are eaten whole.—S.

[2] The word here rendered 'a great city,' namely 'miṣran,' is rendered by Marracci and Sale 'Egypt,' and is so understood by many learned Arabs; but according to a general rule, to have this signification it should be 'miṣra:' in some copies of the Ḳur-án, however, it *is* thus written.

with his garment:[1] *it was light, square, like the head of a man, marble or kedhdhán.*[2]) *Accordingly he struck it;* and there gushed out from it twelve fountains, *according to the number of the tribes,* all men (*each tribe of them*) knowing their drinking-place. *And We said unto them,* Eat ye and drink of the supply of God, and commit not evil in the earth, acting corruptly. (ii. 57.)

Remember also when We obtained your bond *that ye would do according to that which is contained in the Law,* and *had* lifted up over you the mountain [namely Mount Sinai], *pulled it up by the roots and raised it over you when ye had refused to accept the Law, and We said,* Receive that which We have given you, with resolution, and remember that which is contained in it, *to do according thereto:* peradventure ye will fear *the Fire, or acts of disobedience.*— Then ye turned back after that; and had it not been for the grace of God towards you and His mercy, ye had certainly been of those who perish. And ye know those of you who transgressed on the Sabbath, *by catching fish, when We had forbidden them to do so* (*and they were the people of Eyleh*[3],) and We said unto them, Be ye apes,

---

[1] See Sale's note *in loc.*

[2] A kind of soft stone, like dry mud.

[3] The story here alluded to, though it occurs among passages respecting Moses and his people, is said to relate to a different age and to be as follows:—In the days of David, some Israelites dwelt at Eyleh, or Elath, on the Red Sea, where, on the night of the Sabbath, the fish used to come in great numbers to the shore, and stay there all the Sabbath, to tempt them; but the night following they returned into the sea again. At length, some of the inhabitants, neglecting God's commandment, catched fish on the Sabbath, and dressed and ate them; and afterwards cut canals from the sea, for the fish to enter, with sluices, which they shut on the Sabbath, to prevent their return to the sea. The other part of the inhabitants, who strictly observed the Sabbath, used both persuasion and force to stop this impiety, but to no purpose, the offenders growing only more and more obstinate; whereupon David cursed the Sabbath-breakers, and God transformed them into apes. It is said, that one going to see a friend of his that was among them found him in the shape of an ape moving his eyes about wildly; and asking him whether he was not such a one, the ape made a sign with his head that it was he; whereupon the friend said to him, Did not I advise you to desist? at which the ape wept. They add, that these unhappy people remained three days in this condition, and were afterwards destroyed by a wind which swept them all into the sea.—S. (A. F.)

driven away from the society of men.—*Thereupon they became such, and they perished after three days.*—And We made it (*namely that punishment*) an example unto those who were contemporary with them and those who came after them, and a warning to the pious. (ii. 60–62.)

And We appointed unto Moses thirty nights, *at the expiration of which We would speak to him, on the condition of his fasting during them; and they were* [the nights of the month of] *Dhu-l-Ḳaạdeh; and he fasted during them: but when they were ended, he disliked the smell of his breath; so he used a tooth-stick; whereupon God commanded him to fast ten other nights, that He might speak to Him with the odour of his breath,*[1] *as He whose name be exalted hath said,*—and We completed them by [adding] ten *nights of Dhu-l-Ḥijjeh:* so the stated time of his Lord was completed, forty nights. And Moses said unto his brother Aaron, *at his departure to the mountain for the private collocution,* Be thou my deputy among my people, and act rightly, and follow not the way of the corrupt doers *by agreeing with them in acts of disobedience.* And when Moses came at Our appointed time, and his Lord spake unto him *without an intermediary,* he said, O my Lord, show me *Thyself,* that I may see Thee. He replied, Thou shalt not see Me: but look at the mountain, *which is stronger than thou;* and if it remain firm in its place, then shalt thou see Me. And when his Lord displayed Himself to the mountain (*that is, when there appeared, of His light, half of the tip of His little finger, as related in a tradition which El-Ḥákim hath verified*), He reduced it to powder, *levelling it even with the ground around it;* and Moses fell down in a swoon. And when he recovered, he said, Extolled be Thy perfection! I turn unto Thee repenting, and I am the first of the believers *in my time.*—*God* said *unto him,* O Moses, I have chosen thee above the people *of thy time*

---

[1] His breath before [he used the tooth-stick] had the odour of musk.—S. (B.)

[by honouring thee] by My commissions and by My speaking *unto thee:* therefore receive what I have given thee, and be of those who are grateful. And We wrote for him upon the tables *of the Law*[1] (*which were of the lote-tree of Paradise, or of chrysolite, or of emerald; in number seven, or ten*) an admonition concerning every *requisite matter of religion,* and a distinct explanation of every-thing; *and said,* Therefore receive it with resolution, and command thy people to act according to the most excellent [precepts] thereof. (vii. 138–142.)

And the people of Moses, after it (*that is, after his departure for the private collocution*), made, of their ornaments (*which they had borrowed of the people of Pharaoh*), a corporeal calf[2] *which Es-Sámiree cast for them,*[3] *and* which lowed; *for he had the faculty of doing so in consequence of their having put into its mouth some dust taken from* [beneath] *the hoof of the horse of Gabriel; and they took it as a god.* Did they not see that it spake not to them, nor directed them in the way? They took it *as a god,* and were offenders. But when they repented, and saw that they had erred, *which was after the return of Moses,* they said, Verily if our Lord do not have mercy upon us and forgive us, we shall assuredly be of those who perish. (vii. 146–148.)

---

[1] It is said that not only the ten commandments, but the whole law was written thereon.—S.

[2] That is, as some understand it, consisting of flesh and blood; or, as others, being a mere body or mass of metal, without a soul.—S. (B.)

[3] The person who cast this calf, the Mohammadans say, was not Aaron but Es-Sámiree, one of the principal men among the children of Israel, some of whose descendants, it is pretended, still inhabit an island of that name in the Arabian Gulf. It was made of the rings and bracelets of gold, silver, and other materials, which the Israelites had borrowed of the Egyptians; for Aaron, who commanded in his brother's absence, having ordered Es-Sámiree to collect those ornaments from the people, who carried on a wicked commerce with them, and to keep them together till the return of Moses, Es-Sámiree, understanding the founder's art, put them altogether into a furnace, to melt them down into one mass, which came out in the form of a calf. One writer says, that all the Israelites adored this calf, except only twelve thousand.—S. (A. F.)

And Moses returned unto his people[1] enraged *against them,* exceedingly sorrowful. He said, O my people, did not your Lord promise you a good *true* promise, *that He would give you the Law?* But did the time *of my absence* seem tedious to you, or did ye desire that indignation from your Lord should befall you, and therefore did ye break your promise to me, *and abstain from coming after me?*—They answered, We did not break our promise to thee of our own authority; but we were made to carry loads of the ornaments of the people *of Pharaoh* (*which the children of Israel had borrowed of them under pretence of* [requiring them for] *a wedding, and which remained in their possession*), and we cast them *into the fire, by order of Es-Sámiree.* And in like manner also Es-Sámiree cast *their ornaments which he had, and some of the dust which he had taken from the traces of the hoofs of the horse of Gabriel;* and he produced unto them a corporeal calf, *of flesh and blood,* which lowed, *by reason of the dust, the property of which is to give life to that into which it is put; and he had put it, after he had moulded the calf, into its mouth.* And they (*namely, Es-Sámiree and his followers*) said, This is your god, and the god of Moses; but he hath forgotten *his lord here, and gone to seek him. God saith,* But did they not see that it returned them not an answer, nor was able to cause them hurt or profit? And Aaron had said unto them, before *the return of Moses,* O my people, ye are only tried by it; and verily your Lord is the Compassionate; therefore follow me, *by worshipping Him,* and obey my command. They replied, We will by no means cease to be devoted to *the worship of* it until Moses return unto us. *Moses* said *after his return,* O Aaron, what hindered thee, when thou sawest that they had gone astray, from following me? Hast thou then been disobedient to my command, *by remaining among them who worshipped another than God?*

---

[1] After he had completed his forty days' stay in the mount, and had received the Law.—S. (B.)

—He answered, O son of my mother, seize me not by my beard (*for he had taken hold of his beard with his left hand*), nor by [the hair of] my head (*for he had taken hold of his hair with his right hand, in anger*). Verily I feared lest *if I followed thee* (*for a company of those who worshipped the calf would inevitably have followed me*) thou shouldst say, Thou hast made a division among the children of Israel, and hast not waited for my sentence. *Moses* said, And what was thy motive *for doing as thou hast*, O Sámiree? He answered, I saw that which they saw not;[1] therefore I took a handful *of dust* from the foot-marks *of the horse* of the apostle *Gabriel*, and cast it *into the molten calf;* and thus my soul allured me *to take a handful of the dust above-mentioned, and to cast it upon that which had no life, that it might have life; and I saw that thy people had demanded of thee that thou wouldst make them a god; so my soul suggested to me that this calf should be their god. Moses* said *unto him*, Then get thee gone *from among us*, and [the punishment] for thee during *the period of thy* life [shall be], that thou shalt say *unto whomsoever thou shalt see*, Touch *me* not:—(*so he used to wander about the desert, and when he touched any one, or any one touched him, they both became affected with a burning fever:*) and verily for thee is a threat which thou shalt by no means find to be false. And look at thy god, to *the worship of* which thou hast continued devoted. We will assuredly burn it: then we will assuredly reduce it to powder and scatter it in the sea. (*And Moses, after he had slaughtered it, did this.*) Your deity is God only, except whom there is no deity. He comprehendeth all things by *His* knowledge.—Thus, *O Moḥammad*, do We relate unto thee accounts of

[1] Or, I know that which they knew not—that the messenger sent to thee from God was a pure spirit, and that his footsteps gave life to whatever they touched; being no other than the angel Gabriel, mounted on the horse of life: and therefore I made use of the dust of his feet to animate the molten calf. It is said, Es-Sámiree knew the angel because he had saved and taken care of him when a child and exposed by his mother for fear of Pharaoh.—S. (B., Jelál.)

what hath happened heretofore; and We have given thee, from Us, an admonition; *namely the Ḳur-án.* (xx. 88–99.)

And they were made to drink down the calf into their hearts,[1] (*that is, the love of it mingled with their hearts as drink mingleth,*) because of their unbelief. (ii. 87.)

[Remember, O children of Israel,] when Moses said unto his people *who worshipped the calf*, O my people, verily ye have injured your own souls by your taking to yourselves the calf *as a god;* therefore turn with repentance unto your Creator *from the worship of it*, and slay one another: (*that is, let the innocent among you slay the criminal:*) this will be best for you in the estimation of your Creator. *And He aided you to do that, sending upon you a black cloud, lest one of you should see another and have compassion on him, until there were slain of you about seventy thousand.* And *thereupon* He became propitious towards you, *accepting your repentance;* for He is the Very Propitious, the Merciful. (ii. 51.)

[Remember also, O children of Israel,] when ye said, *having gone forth with Moses to beg pardon of God for your worship of the calf, and having heard his words,* O Moses, we will not believe thee until we see God manifestly:—whereupon the vehement sound assailed you, *and ye died,* while ye beheld *what happened to you.* Then We raised you to life after ye had been dead, that peradventure ye might give thanks.[2] (ii. 52, 53.)

And Moses chose *from* his people seventy men, *of those who had not worshipped the calf, by the command of God,* at the time appointed by Us *for their coming to ask pardon*

---

[1] The word here rendered 'hearts' often signifies stomachs; and if this be its meaning here, the narrative agrees with the [so-called] Mosaic account: for Moses 'took the calf which they had made, and burnt it in the fire, and ground it to powder, and strawed it upon the water, and made the children of Israel to drink of it.'—Exod. xxxii. 20.

[2] The persons here meant are said to have been seventy men, who were made choice of by Moses, and heard the voice of God talking with him. But not being satisfied with that, they demanded to see God; whereupon they were all struck dead by lightning, and on Moses' intercession restored to life.—S.

for their companions' worship of the calf; and he went forth with them; and when the convulsion (*the violent earthquake*) took them away (*because, saith Ibn-'Abbás, they did not separate themselves from their people when the latter worshipped the calf*), *Moses* said, O my Lord, if Thou hadst pleased, Thou hadst destroyed them before *my going forth with them, that the children of Israel might have beheld it and might not suspect me;* and me [also]. Wilt Thou destroy us for that which the foolish among us have done? It is naught but Thy trial: Thou wilt cause to err thereby whom Thou pleasest, and Thou wilt rightly guide whom Thou pleasest. Thou art our guardian; and do Thou forgive us and have mercy upon us; for Thou art the best of those who forgive: and appoint for us in this world what is good, and in the world to come; for unto Thee have we turned with repentance.—*God* replied, I will afflict with My punishment whom I please, and My mercy extendeth over everything *in the world;* and I will appoint it, *in the world to come,* for those who fear and give the legal alms, and those who believe on Our signs, who shall follow the apostle, the illiterate prophet, *Moḥammad,* whom they shall find written down with them in the Pentateuch and the Gospel, *by his name and his description.* He will command them that which is right, and forbid them that which is evil; and will allow them as lawful the good things *among those forbidden in their law,* and prohibit them the impure, *as carrion and other things,* and will take off from them their burden and the yokes that were upon them, *as the slaying of a soul* [for an atonement] *in repentance, and the cutting off of the mark left by impurity.* And those who shall believe in him and honour him and assist him and follow the light which shall be sent down with him, *namely the Ḳur-án,* these shall be the prosperous. (vii. 154–156).

And *remember* when Moses said unto his people, O my people, remember the favour of God towards you, since He hath appointed prophets from among you, and made you princes (*masters of servants and other attendants*), and given you what He hath not given any [other] of the peoples (*as the manna and the quails and other things*). O my people, enter the Holy Land which God hath decreed for you (*namely Syria*), and turn not back, lest ye turn losers.—They replied, O Moses, verily there is in it a gigantic people, *of the remains of the tribe of 'Ád*, and we will not enter it until they go forth from it; but if they go forth from it, then we will enter.—[Thereupon] two men, of those who feared *to disobey God, namely Joshua and Caleb, of the chiefs whom Moses sent to discover the circumstances of the giants, and* upon whom God had conferred favour, *and who had concealed what they had seen of the state of the giants, excepting from Moses, wherefore the other chiefs became cowardly*, said *unto them*, Enter ye upon them through the gate *of the city, and fear them not; for they are bodies without hearts;* and when ye enter it, ye overcome; and upon God place your dependence, if ye be believers.—[But] they said, O Moses, we will never enter it while they remain therein. Therefore go thou and thy Lord, and fight: for we remain here.—*Then Moses* said, O my Lord, verily I am not master of any but myself and my brother: therefore distinguish between us and the unrighteous people.—*God* replied, Verily it (*namely the Holy Land*) shall be forbidden them forty years; they shall wander in perplexity in the land: and be not thou solicitous for the unrighteous people.—*The land* [through which they wandered] *was* [only] *nine leagues* [in extent]. *They used to journey during the night with diligence; but in the morning they found themselves in the place whence they had set forth; and they journeyed during the day in like manner. Thus they did until all of them had become extinct, excepting those who had not attained the age of twenty years; and it is said that they were six hundred thousand. Aaron and Moses died in the desert; and mercy was their lot: but punishment was the lot of those. And Moses begged his Lord, when he was about to die, that He would bring him as near as a stone's throw to the Holy Land: wherefore He did so. And Joshua was made a prophet after the forty* [years], *and he gave orders to fight against the giants. So he went with those who were with him, and fought against them: and it was Friday; and the sun stood still for him awhile, until he had made an end of fighting against them.* (v. 23–29).

Ḳároon [1] [or Korah] was of the people of Moses (*he was the son of his paternal uncle, and the son of his maternal aunt, and he believed in him*); but he behaved insolently towards them; for We had bestowed upon him such treasures that their keys were heavy burdens for a company of men endowed with strength, *in number, as some say, seventy; and some, forty; and some, ten; and some, another number. Remember* when his people (*the believers among the children of Israel*) said unto him, Rejoice not *exultingly in the abundance of thy wealth;* for God loveth not those who *so* rejoice; but seek to attain, by means of the *wealth* which God hath given thee, the latter abode [of Paradise], *by expending thy wealth in the service of God;* and neglect not thy part in this world, *to work therein for the world to come;* but be beneficent *unto mankind, by bestowing alms,* as God hath been beneficent unto thee; and seek not to act corruptly in the earth; for God loveth not the corrupt doers. He replied, I have only been given it on account of the knowledge that I possess. *For he was the most learned of the children of Israel in the Law, after Moses and Aaron. God saith,* Did he not know that God had destroyed before him, of the generations, those that were mightier than he in strength and who had amassed more abundance *of wealth?* And the wicked shall not be asked respecting their sins, *because God knoweth them: therefore they shall be sent into the Fire without a reckoning.* And *Ḳároon* went forth unto his people

---

[1] This person is represented by the commentators as the most beautiful of the Israelites, and so far surpassing them all in opulence that the riches of Ḳároon have become a proverb.—S.

in his pomp, *with his many dependants mounted, adorned with garments of gold and silk, upon decked horses and mules.* Those who desired the present life said, O would that we had the like of that which hath been bestowed on Ḳároon *in this world!* Verily he is possessed of great good fortune!—But those unto whom knowledge *of what God hath promised in the world to come* had been given, said *unto them,* Woe to you! The reward of God *in the world to come* (*which is Paradise*) is better for him who believeth and worketh righteousness *than that which hath been bestowed on Ḳároon in the present world;* and none shall receive it but the patient *in the service of God.* And We caused the earth to cleave asunder and swallow up him and his mansion,[1] and he had no forces to defend him, in the place of God, nor was he of the [number of the] saved. And the next morning, those who had wished for his place the day before said, Aha! God enlargeth provision unto whom He pleaseth of His servants, and is sparing *of it unto whom He pleaseth!* Had not God been gracious unto us, He had caused [the earth] to cleave asunder and swallow up us! Aha! the ungrateful *for His benefits* do not prosper! (xxviii. 76–82.)

Remember, [O children of Israel,] when Moses said unto his people (*when one of them had been slain, whose murderer was not known, and they asked him to beg God that He would discover him to them, wherefore he supplicated Him*), Verily God commandeth you to sacrifice a cow. They said, Dost

[1] Moses, as some say, having complained to God of a false accusation brought against him by Ḳároon, He directed him to command the earth what he pleased, and it should obey him; whereupon he said, 'O earth, swallow them up;' and immediately the earth opened under Ḳároon and his confederates, and swallowed them up, with his palace and all his riches. —There goes a tradition that as Ḳároon sank gradually into the ground, first to his knees, then to his waist, then to his neck, he cried out four several times, 'O Moses, have mercy on me!' but that Moses continued to say, 'O earth, swallow them up!' till at last he wholly disappeared: upon which God said to Moses, 'Thou hadst no mercy on Ḳároon, though he asked pardon of thee four times; but I would have had compassion on him if he had asked pardon of me but once.'—S. (B.)

thou make a jest of us? He said, I beg God to preserve me from being *one* of the foolish. *So when they knew that he decidedly intended* [what he had ordered], they said, Supplicate for us thy Lord, that He may manifest to us what she is; *that is, what is her age. Moses* replied, He saith, She is a cow neither old nor young; *but* of a middle age, between those *two:* therefore do as ye are commanded. They said, Supplicate for us thy Lord, that He may manifest to us what is her colour. He replied, He saith, She is a red[1] cow: her colour is very bright: she rejoiceth the beholders. They said, Supplicate for us thy Lord, that He may manifest to us what she is, *whether she be a pasturing or a working cow;* for cows *of the description mentioned* are to us like one another; and we, if God please, shall indeed be rightly directed *to her.* (*In a tradition it is said, Had they not said, 'If God please,'—she had not ever been manifested to them.*) He replied, He saith, She is a cow not subdued *by work* that plougheth the ground, nor doth she water the field: [she is] free *from defects and the marks of work;* there is no colour in her different from the rest of her colour. They said, Now thou hast brought the truth. *And they sought her, and found her in the possession of the young man who acted piously towards his mother, and they bought her for as much gold as her hide would contain.*[2]

---

[1] Or rather, fawn-coloured; as are most of the cows of Arabia. The word in the original properly signifies yellow.

[2] The story of this young man is thus related:—A certain man at his death left his son, then a child, a cow-calf, which wandered in the desert till he came to age; at which time his mother told him the heifer was his, and bid him fetch her and sell her for three pieces of gold. When the young man came to the market with his heifer, an angel in the shape of a man accosted him and bid him six pieces of gold for her; but he would not take the money till he had asked his mother's consent; which when he had obtained, he returned to the market-place, and met the angel, who now offered him twice as much for the heifer, provided he would say nothing of it to his mother; but the young man, refusing, went and acquainted her with the additional offer. The woman, perceiving it was an angel, bid her son go back and ask him what must be done with the heifer; whereupon the angel told the young man that in a little time the children of Israel would buy that heifer of him at any price.—S. (A.F.)

Then they sacrificed her; but they were near to leaving it undone, *on account of the greatness of her price.* (*And in a tradition it is said, Had they sacrificed any cow whatever, He had satisfied them: but they acted hardly towards themselves; so God acted hardly towards them.*) And when ye slew a soul, and contended together respecting it, (and God brought forth [to light] that which ye did conceal—*this is the beginning of the story* [and was the occasion of the order to sacrifice this particular cow,]) We said, Strike him (*that is, the slain person*) with part of her. *So he was struck with her tongue, or the root of her tail, or, as some say, with her right thigh; whereupon he came to life, and said, Such-a-one and such-a-one slew me,—to the two sons of his uncle. And he died. They two* [the murderers] *were therefore deprived of the inheritance, and were slain.*[1] Thus God raiseth to life the dead, and showeth you His signs (*the proof of His power*), that peradventure ye may understand, *and know that He who is able to raise to life one soul is able to raise to life many souls.* Then your hearts became hard, *O ye Jews, so as not to accept the truth,* after that, and they [were] as stones, or more hard: for of stones there are indeed some from which rivers gush forth; and of them there are indeed some that cleave asunder and water issueth from them; and of them there are indeed some that fall down through fear of God; *whereas your hearts are not impressed, nor do they grow soft, nor do they become humble.* But God is not heedless of that which ye do: *He only reserveth you unto your time.* (ii. 63–69.)

Remember when Moses said to his young man *Joshua the son of Nun, who served him and acquired knowledge from him,* I will not cease *to go forward* until I reach the place where the two seas (*the Sea of Greece and the Sea of Persia*) meet, or travel for a long space of time. And when they reached the place where they (*the two seas*) met they for-

[1] The more common tradition seems to be that the man was murdered by *one* person, the son of his brother, who desired to obtain his property (as his inheritance), or his daughter, or both. (Mir-át-ez-Zemán).

got their fish: *Joshua forgot to take it up, on their departure; and Moses forgot to remind him;* and it made its way in the sea by a hollow passage, *God withholding the water from it.* And when they had passed beyond *that place, and proceeded until the time of the morning-meal on the following day,* [Moses] said unto his young man, Bring us our morning-meal: we have experienced fatigue from this our journey. He replied, What thinkest thou? When we repaired to the rock to rest *at that place,* I forgot the fish, and none made me forget to mention it but the devil; and it made its way in the sea in a wonderful manner.—*Moses* said, That (*namely our loss of the fish*) is what we were desiring; *for it is a sign unto us of our finding him whom we seek.* And they returned by the way that they had come, following the footsteps, *and came to the rock.* And they found one of Our servants (*namely El-Khiḍr*[1]) unto whom We had granted mercy from Us (*that is the gift of prophecy in the opinion of some, and the rank of a saint according to another opinion which most of the learned hold*), and whom We had taught knowledge from Us *respecting things unseen.—El-Bukháree hath related a tradition stating that Moses performed the office of a preacher among the children of Israel, and was asked who was the most knowing of men; to which he answered, I:—whereupon God blamed him for this, because he did not refer the*

---

[1] Also called El-Khaḍir. This mysterious person, whom the vulgar and some others regard as a prophet, and identify with Ilyás (Elias or Elijah), and whom some confound with St. George, was, according to the more approved opinion of the learned, a just man or saint, the Wezeer and counsellor of that equally doubtful personage Dhu-l-Ḳarneyn, whose story has already been related in this volume. El-Khiḍr is said to have drunk of the Fountain of Life, by virtue of which he still lives, and will live till the day of judgment. He is also said to appear frequently to Muslims in perplexity, and to be generally clad in green garments; whence, according to some, his name.—Sale states, in a note on this passage, that the Muslims usually confound El-Khiḍr with Phineas, as well as Elias and St. George, saying that his soul passed by a metempsychosis successively through all three; and he adds, that part of these fictions they took from the Jews, some of whom also fancy Phineas was Elias.

knowledge thereof to Him. And God said unto him by revelation, Verily I have a servant at the place where the two seas meet, and he is more knowing than thou. Moses said, O my Lord, and how shall I meet with him? He answered, Thou shalt take with thee a fish, and put it into a measuring-vessel, and where thou shalt lose the fish, there is he. So he took a fish, and put it into a vessel. Then he departed, and Joshua the son of Nun departed with him, until they came to the rock, where they laid down their heads and slept. And the fish became agitated in the vessel, and escaped from it, and fell into the sea, and it made its way in the sea by a hollow passage, God withholding the water from the fish so that it became like a vault over it: and when Moses' companion awoke, he forgot to inform him of the fish.

Moses said unto him [namely El-Khiḍr], Shall I follow thee, that thou mayest teach me [part] of that which thou hast been taught, for a direction *unto me?* He answered, Verily thou canst not have patience with me. For how canst thou be patient with respect to that whereof thou comprehendest not the knowledge?—He replied, Thou shalt find me, if God please, patient; and I will not disobey any command of thine. He said, Then if thou follow me, ask me not respecting anything: *but be patient* until I give thee an account thereof. *And Moses assented to his condition.* And they departed, *walking along the shore of the sea,* until, when they embarked in the ship *that passed by them,* he (*El-Khiḍr*) made a hole in it, *by pulling out a plank or two planks from it on the outside by means of an axe when it reached the middle of the sea. Moses* said *unto him,* Hast thou made a hole in it that thou mayest drown its people? Thou hast done a grievous thing.—(*But it is related that the water entered not the hole.*) He replied, Did I not say that thou couldst not have patience with me? [Moses] said, Chastise me not for my forgetfulness, nor impose on me a difficulty in my case.—And they departed, *after they had gone forth from the vessel, walking on,* until, when they found a boy *who had not attained the age of knowing right and wrong, playing with other children, and he was the most beautiful of them in countenance,* and he (*El-Khiḍr*) slew him, *Moses* said *unto him,* Hast thou slain an innocent soul, without *his having slain* a soul? Thou hast done an iniquitous thing. —He replied, Did I not say that thou couldst not have patience with me? [Moses] said, If I ask thee concerning anything after this *time*, suffer me not to accompany thee. Now hast thou received from me an excuse *for thy separating thyself from me.*—And they departed [and proceeded] until, when they came to the people of a city (*which was Antioch* [1]), they asked food of its people; but they refused to entertain them: and they found therein a wall, *the height whereof was a hundred cubits,* which was about to fall down; whereupon he (*El-Khiḍr*) set it upright *with his hand. Moses* said *unto him,* If thou wouldst, thou mightest have obtained pay for it, *since they did not entertain us, notwithstanding our want of food. El-Khiḍr* said *unto him,* This shall be a separation between me and thee; *but before my separation from thee,* I will declare unto thee the interpretation of that which thou couldst not bear with patience.

As to the vessel, it belonged to *ten* poor men,[2] who pursued their business on the sea; and I desired to render it unsound; for there was behind them a king, *an unbeliever,* who took every *sound* vessel by force. And as to the boy, his parents were believers, and we feared that he would transgress against them rebelliously and impiously: *for, according to a tradition related by Muslim, he was constituted by nature an unbeliever, and had he lived he had so acted;* wherefore we desired that their Lord should create for them a better than he in virtue, and [one] more disposed than he to filial piety. *And God created for them a daughter, who married a prophet, and gave birth to*

---

[1] Or, as some rather think, El-Ubulleh, near El-Basrah, or else Bájarwán in Armenia.—S. (B.)

[2] They were ten brothers, five of whom were past their labour by reason of their age.—S. (B.)

a prophet, by means of whom God directed a people to the right way. And as to the wall, it belonged to two orphan youths in the city, and beneath it was a treasure *buried, of gold and silver,* belonging to them; and their father was a righteous man; and thy Lord desired that they should attain their age of strength and take forth their treasure through the mercy of thy Lord. And I did it not (*namely what hath been mentioned*) of mine own will, *but by direction of God.* This is the interpretation of that which thou couldst not bear with patience. (Chap. xviii. 59–81.)

SAUL, DAVID, SOLOMON.

HAST thou not considered the assembly of the children of Israel after *the death of* Moses, when they said unto a prophet of theirs, *namely Samuel,* Set up for us a king, *under whom* we will fight in the way of God? He said *unto them,* If fighting be prescribed as incumbent on you, will ye, peradventure, abstain from fighting? They replied, And wherefore should we not fight in the way of God, since we have been expelled from our habitations and our children *by their having been taken prisoners and slain?—The people of Goliath* [Jáloot] *had done thus unto them.*—But when fighting was commanded them, they turned back, excepting a few of them, *who crossed the river with Saul* [Ṭáloot], *as will be related.* And God knoweth the offenders. *And the prophet begged his Lord to send a king; whereupon he consented to send Saul.* And their prophet said unto them, Verily God hath set up Saul as your king. They said, How shall he have the dominion over us, when we are more worthy of the dominion than he, (*for he was not of the royal lineage, nor of the prophetic, and he was a tanner, or a tender of flocks or herds,*) and he hath not been endowed with ample wealth? He replied, Verily God hath chosen him *as king* over you, and increased him in largeness of knowledge and of body, (*for he was the wisest of the children of Israel at that time, and the most comely of them, and the most perfect of them in make,*) and God giveth his kingdom unto whom He pleaseth; and God is ample *in His beneficence,* knowing *with respect to him who is worthy of the kingdom.*—And their prophet said unto them, *when they demanded of him a sign in proof of his kingship,* Verily the sign of his kingship *shall be* that the ark shall come unto you (*in it were the images of the prophets: God sent it down unto Adam, and it passed into their possession; but the Amalekites took it from them by force: and they used to seek victory thereby over their enemy, and to advance it in the fight, and to trust in it, as He—whose name be exalted!—hath said*); therein [shall be] tranquillity from your Lord,[1] and relics of what the family of Moses and the family of Aaron have left: *namely, the two shoes (or sandals) of Moses, and his rod, and the turban of Aaron, and a measure of the manna that used to descend upon them, and the fragments of the tables* [of the Law]: the angels shall bear it. Verily in this shall be a sign unto you *of his kingship,* if ye be believers. *Accordingly the angels bore it between heaven and earth, while they looked at it, until they placed it by Saul; whereupon they acknowledged his kingship, and hastened to the holy war; and he chose of their young men seventy thousand.*

And when Saul went forth with the troops *from Jerusalem, and it was violently hot weather, and they demanded of him water,* he said, Verily God will try you by a river, *that the obedient among you, and the disobedient, may appear,* (*and it was between the Jordan and Palestine,*) and whoso drinketh thereof, he is not of my party (but he who tasteth not thereof, he is of my party), excepting him who taketh forth a draught in his hand, *and is satisfied therewith, not adding to it; for he is of my party;*—then they drank thereof *abundantly,* excepting a few of them, *who were content only with the handful of water. It is related that it sufficed them for their own drinking and for their beasts, and they were three hundred and somewhat more*

---

[1] That is, because of the great confidence the Israelites placed in it, having won several battles by its miraculous assistance. I imagine, however, that the Arabic word 'sekeeneh,' which signifies 'tranquillity' or 'security of mind,' and is so understood by the commentators, may not improbably mean the 'divine presence' or 'glory,' which used to appear on the Ark, and which the Jews express by the same word 'Shekinah.'—S.

than ten. And when he had passed over it, he and those who believed with him, they (*that is, those who had drunk* [plentifully]) said, We have no power to-day *to contend* against Goliath and his troops. *And they were cowardly, and passed not over it.* They [however] who held it as certain that they should meet God *at the resurrection* (*and they were those who had passed over it*) said, How many a small body of men hath overcome a great body by the permission (*or will*) of God! And God is with the patient, *to defend and aid.*—And when they went forth to battle against Goliath and his troops, they said, O our Lord, pour upon us patience, and make firm our feet, *by strengthening our hearts for the holy war*, and help us against the unbelieving people!—And they routed them by the permission (*or will*) of God, and David [Dáwood, vulg. Dáood], *who was in the army of Saul*, slew Goliath. And God gave him (*David*) the kingship *over the children of Israel*, and wisdom (*that is prophecy*), *after the death of Samuel and Saul, and they* [namely these two gifts] *had not been given together to any one before him;* and He taught him what He pleased,[1] *as the art of making coats of mail, and the language of birds.* And were it not for God's repelling men, one by another, surely the earth had become corrupt *by the predominance of the polytheists and the slaughter of the Muslims and the ruin of the places of worship:* but God is beneficent to the peoples, *and hath repelled some by others.* (ii. 247–252.)

---

[1] Sale observes that Yahya most rationally understands hereby the divine revelations which David received from God, and not the art of making coats of mail.—The cause of his applying himself to this art is thus related in the Mir-át-ez-Zemán: —He used to go forth in disguise; and when he found any people who knew him not, he approached them and asked them respecting the conduct of David, and they praised him and prayed for him; but one day, as he was asking questions respecting himself as usual, God sent to him an angel in the form of a human being, who said, 'An excellent man were David if he did not take from the public treasury:'—whereupon the heart of David was contracted, and he begged of God to render him independent: so He made iron soft to him, and it became in his hands as thread; and he used to sell a coat of mail for four thousand [pieces of money—whether gold or silver is not

Hath the story of the two opposing parties come unto thee, *O Moḥammad*, when they ascended over the walls of the oratory *of David, having been prevented going in unto him by the door, because of his being engaged in devotion?* When they went in unto David, and he was frightened at them, they said, Fear not: *we are* two opposing parties. *It is said that they were two parties of more than one each; and it is said that they were two individuals, angels, who came as two litigants, to admonish David, who had ninety-nine wives, and had desired the wife of a person who had none but her, and married her and taken her as his wife.*[1] [One of them said,] One of us hath wronged the other; therefore judge between us with truth, and be not unjust, but direct us into the right way. Verily this my brother *in religion* had nine-and-ninety ewes, and I had one ewe; and he said, Make me her keeper. And he overcame me in the dispute.—*And the other confessed him to have spoken truth.*—[David] said, Verily he hath wronged thee in demanding thy ewe *to add her* to his ewes; and verily many associates wrong one another, except those who believe and do righteous deeds: and few indeed are they.—*And the two angels said, ascending in their* [proper or assumed] *forms to heaven, The man hath passed sentence against himself. So David was admonished.* And David perceived that We had tried him *by his love of that woman;* wherefore he asked pardon of his Lord, and fell down bowing himself (*or prostrating himself*), and repented. So We forgave him that; and verily for him [was ordained] a high rank with Us (*that is, an increase of good fortune in this world*), and [there shall

---

said], and with part of this he obtained food for himself, and part he gave in alms, and with part he fed his family.—Hence an excellent coat of mail is often called by the Arabs 'Dáwoodee,' *i.e.*, 'Davidean.' See my translation of 'The Thousand and One Nights,' chap. viii. note 5.

[1] For David, they say, divided his time regularly, setting apart one day for the service of God, another day for rendering justice to his people, another day for preaching to them, and another day for his own affairs.—S. (B.)

be for him] an excellent retreat *in the world to come.* (xxxviii. 20–24.)

We compelled the mountains to glorify Us, with David, and the birds *also, on his commanding them to do so, when he experienced languor;* and We did *this.* And We taught him the art of making coats of mail (*for before his time plates of metal were used*) for you *among mankind in general,* that they might defend you from your suffering *in warring with your enemies.*—Will ye then, *O people of Mekkeh,* be thankful *for My favours, believing the apostles?* —And *We subjected* unto Solomon [Suleymán] the wind, blowing strongly, *and being light at his desire,* which ran at his command[1] to the land that We blessed (*namely Syria*);[2] and We knew all things (*knowing that what We gave him would stimulate him to be submissive to his Lord*). And *We subjected,* of the devils, those who should dive for him *in the sea and bring forth from it jewels for him,* and do other work besides that; *that is, building, and performing other services;* and We watched over them, *that they might not spoil what they executed; for they used, when they had finished a work before night, to spoil it, if they were not employed in something else.* (xxi. 79–82.)

We gave unto David Solomon *his son.* How excellent a servant *was he!* For he was one who earnestly turned himself unto God, *glorifying and praising Him at all times.* [Remember] when, in the latter part of the day, *after the commencement of the declining of the sun,* the *mares* standing on three feet and touching the ground with the edge of the fourth foot, swift in the course, were

[1] They say that he had a carpet of green silk, on which his throne was placed, being of a prodigious length and breadth, and sufficient for all his forces to stand on, the men placing themselves on his right hand, and the spirits [or jinn] on his left; and that when all were in order the wind at his command took up the carpet and transported it with all that were upon it wherever he pleased; the army of birds at the same time flying over their heads and forming a kind of canopy to shade them from the sun.—S.

[2] Whither the wind brought back Solomon's throne in the evening, after having carried it to a distant country in the morning.—S.

displayed before him. *They were a thousand mares, which were displayed before him after he had performed the noon-prayers, on the occasion of his desiring to make use of them in a holy war; and when nine hundred of them had been displayed, the sun set, and he had not performed the afternoon-prayers. So he was grieved,* and he said, Verily I have preferred the love of [earthly] goods above the remembrance of my Lord, (*that is, the performance of the afternoon-prayers,*) so that *the sun* is concealed by the veil. Bring them (*namely the horses*) back unto me. *Therefore they brought them back.* And he began to sever *with his sword* the legs and the necks, *slaughtering them, and* [then] *cutting off their legs, as a sacrifice unto God, and gave their flesh in alms; and God gave him in compensation what was better than they were and swifter, namely the wind, which travelled by his command whithersoever he desired.*—And We tried Solomon *by depriving him of his kingdom. This was because he married a woman of whom he became enamoured, and she used to worship an idol in his palace without his knowledge. His dominion was in his signet; and he pulled it off once and deposited it with his wife, who was named El-Emeeneh; and a jinnee came unto her in the form of Solomon, and took it from her.* And We placed upon his throne a [counterfeit] body; *namely that jinnee, who was Ṣakhr, or another. He sat upon the throne of Solomon, and the birds and other creatures surrounded him; and Solomon went forth, with a changed appearance, and saw him upon his throne, and said unto the people, I am Solomon:—but they denied him.* Then he returned *unto his kingdom, after some days, having obtained the signet and put it on, and seated himself upon his throne.*[1] He said, O

[1] After the space of forty days, which was the time the image had been worshipped in his house, the devil [or jinnee] flew away, and threw the signet into the sea: the signet was immediately swallowed by a fish, which being taken and given to Solomon, he found the ring in its belly, and, having by this means recovered the kingdom, took Ṣakhr, and, tying a great stone to his neck, threw him into the Lake of Tiberias.—S. (B., A.F.)

my Lord, forgive me, and give me a dominion that may not be to any one after me (*or beside me*); for Thou art the Liberal Giver. So We subjected unto him the wind, which ran gently at his command whithersoever he desired; and the devils [also], every builder *of wonderful structures*, and diver *that brought up pearls from the sea*, and others bound in chains *which connected their hands to their necks. And We said unto him*, This is Our gift, and bestow thou *thereof upon whomsoever thou wilt*, or refrain *from bestowing*, without *rendering* an account. And verily for him [was ordained] a high rank with Us, and an excellent retreat. (xxxviii. 29–39.)

We bestowed on David and Solomon knowledge *in judging men and in the language of the birds and other matters;* and they said, Praise be to God who hath made us to excel many of His believing servants, *by the gift of prophecy and by the subjection of the jinn and mankind and the devils.* And Solomon inherited from David *the gift of prophecy and knowledge;* and he said, O men, we have been taught the language of the birds,[1] and have had bestowed on us of everything *wherewith prophets and kings are gifted.* Verily this is manifest excellence.—And his armies of jinn and men and birds were gathered together unto Solomon, and they were led on in order, until, when they came unto the valley of ants, (*which* [was] *at Eṭ-Ṭáïf, or in Syria, the ants whereof* [were] *small or great*,) an ant (*the queen of the ants*), *having seen the troops of Solomon*, said, O ants, enter your habitations, lest Solomon and his troops crush you violently, while they perceive not. And *Solomon* smiled, *afterwards* laughing at her saying, *which he heard from the distance of three miles, the wind conveying it to him: so he withheld his forces when he came in sight of their valley, until the ants had entered their dwellings: and his troops were on horses and on foot in this expedition.*

[1] See note 30 to the Introduction of my translation of the 'Thousand and One Nights.'

And he said, O my Lord, inspire me to be thankful for Thy favour which Thou hast bestowed upon me and upon my parents, and to do righteousness which Thou shalt approve, and admit me, in Thy mercy, among Thy servants, the righteous, *the prophets and the saints.*

And he examined the birds,[1] *that he might see the lapwing, that saw the water beneath the earth, and directed to it by pecking the earth, whereupon the devils used to draw it forth when Solomon wanted it* [to perform the ablution] *for prayer; but he saw it not:* and he said, Wherefore do I not see the lapwing? Is it [one] of the absent?—*And when he was certain of the case he said,* I will assuredly punish it with a severe punishment, *by plucking out its feathers and its tail and casting it in the sun so that it shall not be able to guard against excessive thirst;* or I will slaughter it; or it shall bring me a manifest convincing proof *showing its excuse.*—And it tarried not long *before it presented itself unto Solomon submissively, and raised its head and relaxed its tail and its wings: so he forgave it; and he asked it what it had met with during its absence;* and it said, I have become acquainted with that wherewith thou hast not become acquainted, and I have come unto thee from Seba (*a tribe of El-Yemen*) with a sure piece of news. I found a woman reigning over them, *named Bilḳees,* and she hath been gifted with everything *that princes require,* and hath a magnificent throne. (*Its length was eighty cubits; and its breadth, forty cubits; and its height, thirty cubits: it was composed of gold and silver set with fine pearls and with rubies and chrysolites, and its legs were of rubies and chrysolites and emeralds: upon it* [were

---

1 The Arab historians tell us that Solomon, having finished the Temple of Jerusalem, went in pilgrimage to Mekkeh, where having stayed as long as he pleased, he proceeded towards El-Yemen; and leaving Mekkeh in the morning he arrived by noon at Ṣan'a, and being extremely delighted with the country rested there; but wanting water to make the ablution, he looked among the birds for the lapwing which found it for him.—S. (B.)

closed] *seven doors: to each chamber* [through which one passed to it was] *a closed door.*) I found her and her people worshipping the sun instead of God, and the devil hath made their works to seem comely unto them, so that he hath hindered them from the *right* way, wherefore they are not rightly directed to the worship of God, who produceth what is hidden (*namely the rain and vegetables*) in the heavens and the earth, and knoweth what they [that is, mankind and others] conceal *in their hearts*, and what they reveal *with their tongues.* God: there is no deity but He, the Lord of the magnificent throne, *between which and the throne of Bilḳees is a vast difference.*

Solomon said *to the lapwing,* We will see whether thou hast spoken truth or whether thou art of the liars. *Then the lapwing guided them to the water, and it was drawn forth* [by the devils]; *and they quenched their thirst and performed the ablution and prayed. Then Solomon wrote a letter, the form whereof was this:—From the servant of God, Solomon the son of David, to Bilḳees the queen of Seba. In the name of God, the Compassionate, the Merciful. Peace be on whomsoever followeth the right direction. After* [this salutation, I say], *Act ye not proudly towards me; but come unto me submitting.—He then sealed it with musk, and stamped it with his signet, and said unto the lapwing,* Go with this my letter and throw it down unto them (*namely Bilḳees and her people*): then turn away from them, *but stay near them,* and see what *reply* they will return. *So the lapwing took it, and came unto her, and around her were her forces; and he threw it down into her lap; and when she saw it, she trembled with fear. Then she considered what was in it, and* she said *unto the nobles of her people,* O nobles, an honourable (*sealed*) letter hath been thrown down unto me. It is from Solomon; and it is *this*:—In the name of God, the Compassionate, the Merciful. Act ye not proudly towards me: but come unto me submitting.—She said, O nobles, advise me in mine affair. I will not decide upon a thing unless ye bear me witness.—They replied, We are endowed with strength and endowed with great valour; but the command [belongeth] to thee; therefore see what thou wilt command *us to do, and we will obey thee.* She said, Verily kings, when they enter a city, waste it, and render the mighty of its inhabitants abject; and thus will they do *who have sent the letter.* But I will send unto them with a gift, and I will see with what the messengers will return, *whether the gift will be accepted, or whether it will be rejected. If he be* [merely] *a king, he will accept it; and if he be a prophet, he will not accept it.—And she sent male and female servants, a thousand in equal numbers* [five hundred of each sex], *and five hundred bricks of gold, and a crown set with jewels, and musk and ambergris and other things, by a messenger with a letter.*[1] *And the lapwing hastened unto Solomon, to tell him the news; on hearing which, he commanded that bricks of gold and silver should be cast, and that a horse-course should be extended to the length of nine leagues from the place where he was, and that they should build around it a wall with battlements, of gold and silver, and that the handsomest of the beasts of the land and of the sea should be brought with the sons of the jinn on the right side of the horse-course and on its left.*

And when *the messenger* came *with the gift, and with him his attendants,* unto Solomon, he [Solomon] said, Do ye aid me with wealth? But what God hath given me (*namely the gift of prophecy and the kingdom*) is better than what He hath given you, *of worldly goods;* yet ye rejoice in your gift, *because ye glory in the showy things of this world.* Return unto them *with the gift that thou hast brought;* for we will surely come unto them with forces with which they have not power [to contend], and

[1] Some add that Bilkees, to try whether Solomon was a prophet or not, drest the boys like girls and the girls like boys, and sent him in a casket a pearl not drilled and an onyx drilled with a crooked hole; and that Solomon distinguished the boys from the girls by the different manner of their taking water, and ordered one worm to bore the pearl, and another to pass a thread through the onyx.—S. (B.)

we will surely drive them out from it, (*that is, from their country, Seba, which was named after the father of their tribe,*) abject and contemptible, *if they come not unto us submitting. And when the messenger returned unto her with the gift, she placed her throne within seven doors, within her palace, and her palace was within seven palaces; and she closed the doors, and set guards to them, and prepared to go unto Solomon, that she might see what he would command her to do. She departed with twelve thousand kings, each king having with him many thousands, and proceeded until she came as near to him as a league's distance; when he knew of her* [approach,] he said, O nobles, which of you will bring unto me her throne before they come unto me submitting? An 'efreet, of the jinn, answered, I will bring it unto thee before thou shalt arise from thy place *wherein thou sittest to judge from morning until mid-day;* for I am able to do it, [and] trustworthy *with respect to the jewels that it compriseth and other matters. Solomon said, I desire it more speedily.* [And thereupon] he with whom was knowledge of the *revealed* scripture (*namely* [his Wezeer] *Áṣaf the son of Bàrkhiya, who was a just person, acquainted with the most great name of God, which ensured an answer to him who invoked thereby*[1]) said, I will bring it unto thee before thy glance can be withdrawn *from any object. And he said unto him, Look at the sky. So he looked at it; then he withdrew his glance, and found it placed before him: for during his look towards the sky, Áṣaf prayed, by the most great name, that God would bring it; and it so happened, the throne passing under the ground until it came up before the throne of Solomon.* And when he saw it firmly placed before him, he said, This is of the favour of my Lord, that He may try me, whether I shall be thankful or whether I shall be unthankful. And he who is thankful is thankful for *the sake of* his own soul, *which will have the reward of his*

[1] Others, however, suppose it was El-Khidr, or else Gabriel, or some other angel; and some imagine it to have been Solomon himself.—S. (B.)

thankfulness; and [as to] him who is ungrateful, my Lord is independent [and] bountiful.

[Then Solomon] said, Alter ye her throne so that it may not be known by her, that we may see whether she be rightly directed *to the knowledge thereof,* or whether she be of those who are not rightly directed *to the knowledge of that which is altered. He desired thereby to try her intelligence. So they altered it, by adding to it, or taking from it, or in some other manner.* And when she came, it was said *unto her,* Is thy throne like this? She answered, As though it were the same. (*She answered them ambiguously like as they had questioned her ambiguously, not saying, Is this thy throne?—and had they so said, she had answered, Yes.*) *And when Solomon saw her knowledge, he said,* And we have had knowledge bestowed on us before her, and have been Muslims. But what she worshipped instead of God hindered her *from worshipping Him;* for she was of an unbelieving people.—It was said unto her *also,* Enter the palace. (*It had a floor of white, transparent glass, beneath which was running water, wherein were fish. Solomon had made it on its being said unto him that her legs and feet were* [hairy] *like the legs of an ass.* And when she saw it, she imagined it to be a great water, and she uncovered her legs, *that she might wade through it; and Solomon was on his throne at the upper end of the palace, and he saw that her legs and her feet were handsome.* He said *unto her,* Verily it is a palace evenly spread with glass. *And he invited her to embrace El-Islám,* [whereupon] she said, O my Lord, verily I have acted unjustly towards mine own soul, *by worshipping another than Thee,* and I resign myself, with Solomon, unto God, the Lord of the worlds. *And he desired to marry her; but he disliked the hair upon her legs; so the devils made for him the depilatory of quick-lime, wherewith she removed the hair, and he married her; and he loved her, and confirmed her in her kingdom. He used to visit her every month once, and to remain with her three days; and her reign expired on the expiration of the reign of Solomon. It is related that he began to reign when he was thirteen years of age, and died at the age of three and fifty years. Extolled be the perfection of Him to the duration of whose dominion there is no end!* (xxvii. 15–45.)

We subjected unto Solomon the wind, which travelled in the morning (*unto the period when the sun began to decline*) *the distance of* a month's *journey*, and in the evening *from the commencement of the declining of the sun into its setting*) a month's *journey*. And We made the fountain of molten brass to flow for him *three days with their nights* [in every month], *as water floweth*;[1] *and the people worked until the day* [of its flowing], *with that which had been given unto Solomon.* And of the jinn [were] those who worked in his presence, by the will of his Lord; and such of them as swerved from *obedience to* Our command We will cause to taste of the punishment of hell *in the world to come* (*or, as it is said by some, We cause to taste of its punishment in the present world, an angel beating them with a scourge from hell, the stripe of which burneth them*). They made for him whatever he pleased, of lofty halls (*with steps whereby to ascend to them*), and images (*for they were not forbidden by his law*[2]), and large dishes, like great tanks for watering camels, *around each of which assembled a thousand men, eating from it*, and cooking-pots standing firmly *on their legs, cut out from the mountains in El-Yemen, and to which they ascended by ladders. And We said,* Work, O family of David, *in the service of God*, with thanksgiving *unto Him for what He hath given you*:—but few of My servants are the thankful. And when We decreed that he (*namely, Solomon*) should die, *and he died, and remained standing, and leaning upon his staff for a year, dead, the jinn mean-*

---

[1] This fountain they say was in El-Yemen.—S. (B.)

[2] Some say these spirits made him two lions, which were placed at the foot of his throne; and two eagles, which were set above it; and that when he mounted it, the lions stretched out their paws; and when he sat down, the eagles shaded him with their wings.—S. (B.)

while performing those difficult works as they were accustomed to do, not knowing of his death, until the worm ate his staff, whereupon he fell down, nothing showed them his death but the eating reptile (*the worm*) that ate his staff.[1] And when he fell down, the jinn plainly perceived that if they had known things unseen (*of which things was the death of Solomon*), they had not continued in the ignominious affliction (*that is, in their difficult works*), *imagining that he was alive, inconsistently with their opinion that they knew things unseen. And that the period was a year was known by calculating what the worm had eaten of his staff since his death in each day and night or other space of time.* (xxxiv. 11–13.)

[1] The commentators to explain this passage tell us that David, having laid the foundations of the Temple of Jerusalem, which was to be in lieu of the tabernacle of Moses, when he died, left it to be finished by his son Solomon, who employed the genii in the work; that Solomon, before the edifice was quite completed, perceiving his end drew nigh, begged of God that his death might be concealed from the genii till they had entirely finished it; that God therefore so ordered it that Solomon died as he stood at his prayers, leaning on his staff, which supported the body in that posture a full year; and the genii, supposing him to be alive, continued their work during that term, at the expiration whereof, the temple being perfectly completed, a worm, which had gotten into the staff, ate it through, and the corpse fell to the ground and discovered the king's death.—S. (B., Jelál.)

JONAH.

Verily Jonah [Yoonus] was one of the apostles. [Remember] when he fled unto the laden ship, *being angry with his people, because the punishment wherewith he had threatened them did not fall upon them; wherefore he embarked in the ship; and it became stationary in the midst of the sea: so the sailors said, Here is a slave who hath fled from his master, and the lot will discover him:*—and he cast lots *with those who were in the ship*, and he was [the] one upon whom the lot fell. *They therefore cast him into the sea*, and the fish swallowed him; and he was reprehensible, *for having gone to the sea, and embarked in the ship, without the permission of his Lord.* And had he not been of those who glorified God (*by his saying often in the belly of the fish, There is no god but Thou! I extol Thy perfection! Verily I have been of the offenders!*), he had remained in his belly until the day of resurrection.[1] And We cast him on the plain land, *the same day, or after three or seven days, or twenty or forty days;* and he was sick; and We caused a gourd plant[2] to grow up over him, *to shade him. It had a trunk, contrary to what is the case of gourds in general, being miraculously produced for him.*[3] *And a wild she-goat came*

---

[1] It is said that the fish, after it had swallowed Jonah, swam after the ship with its head above water, that the prophet might breathe; who continued to praise God till the fish came to land and vomited him out.—S.

[2] Sale states that some imagine Jonah's plant to have been a fig; and others, the móz (or banana), which bears very large leaves and excellent fruit.

[3] The commentators add that this plant withered the next morning, and that Jonah being much concerned at it God made a remonstrance to him in behalf of the Ninevites, agreeably to what is recorded in Scripture.—S.

to him evening and morning, of whose milk he drank until he became strong. And We sent him *after that, as before,* unto *his people in Nineveh, in the land of El-Moṣil,* a hundred thousand, or they were a greater number by *twenty or thirty or seventy thousand;* and they believed *on beholding the punishment wherewith they had been threatened;*[1] wherefore We allowed them enjoyment *of their goods* for a time, *until the expiration of their terms of life.* (xxxvii. 139–148.)

[1] When he first began to exhort them to repentance, instead of hearkening to him, they used him very ill, so that he was obliged to leave the city, threatening them at his departure that they should be destroyed within three days, or, as others say, within forty. But when the time drew near, and they saw the heavens overcast with a black cloud which shot forth fire and filled the air with smoke and hung directly over the city, they were in a terrible consternation, and getting into the fields, with their families and cattle, they put on sackcloth and humbled themselves before God, calling aloud for pardon and sincerely repenting of their past wickedness. Whereupon God was pleased to forgive them, and the storm blew over.—S. (B., Jelál, A.F.)

EZRA.

[Hast thou not considered] him who passed by a city (*which was Jerusalem*), *riding upon an ass, and having with him a basket of figs and a vessel of the juice of grapes* (*and he was 'Ozeyr* [Ezra]), and it was falling down upon its roofs, *Nebuchadnezzar having ruined it?* He said, *wondering at the power of God*, How will God quicken this after its death?—And God caused him to die for a hundred years. Then He raised him to life: [and] He said *unto him*, How long hast thou tarried *here?*—He answered I have tarried a day, or part of a day.—*For he slept in the first part of the day, and was deprived of his life, and was reanimated at sunset.* He said Nay, thou hast tarried a hundred years: but look at thy food and thy drink: they have not become changed by time: and look at thine ass. —*And he beheld it dead, and its bones white and shining.*—*We have done this that thou mayest know*, and that We may make thee a sign *of the resurrection* unto men. And look at the bones *of thine ass*, how We will raise them; then We will clothe them with flesh.—*So he looked at them, and they had become put together, and were clothed with flesh, and life was breathed into it, and it brayed.* Therefore when it had been made manifest to him he said, I know that God is able to accomplish everything. (ii. 261.)

THE MESSIAH.

Remember when the wife of 'Imrán [1] said, (*when she had become aged, and desired offspring, wherefore she supplicated God, and became sensible of pregnancy,*) O my Lord, verily I devote unto Thee what is in my womb, to be dedicated *to the service of Thy holy house:* then accept [it] from me; for Thou art the Hearer *of prayer*, the Knower *of intentions. And 'Imrán perished while she was pregnant.* And when she gave birth to it, (*namely her daughter; and she was hoping that it might be a boy; since none but boys were dedicated,*) she said, O my Lord, verily I have brought forth a female, (and God well knew what she had brought forth,) and the male is not as the female, *the latter not being fit for the service* [of the temple]; and I have named her Mary [Maryam]; and I beg thy protection for her and her offspring from the accursed devil.[2] (*In the traditions* [it is said], *No child is born but the devil hath touched it at the time of its birth, wherefore it first raiseth its voice by crying, excepting Mary and her son.*[3]) And her Lord accepted her (*that is, He accepted Mary from her mother*) with a gracious acceptance, and caused her to grow with an excellent growth, *as though she grew in a day as a child* [generally] *groweth in a month. Her mother took her to the doctors, the keepers of the Holy House, and said, Receive*

---

[1] 'Imrán, as observed by Sale, is the name of two several persons according to the Muslims: one was the father of Moses and Aaron, and the other was the father of the Virgin Mary. The latter is here meant, and his wife's name was Hannah.

[2] Or the devil driven away with stones.—See note I., p. 7.

[3] And for this reason, they say, neither of them was guilty of any sin, like the rest of the children of Adam.—S. (Ḳatádeh.)

ye this devoted child. And they eagerly desired her, because she was the daughter of their chief. But Zechariah said, I am more worthy of having her; for her maternal aunt is with me. They however replied, Nay, but we will cast lots.—So they departed (and they were nine and twenty) to the river Jordan, and cast their divining arrows on the understanding that he whose arrow should become steady in the water and rise should be [acknowledged] *most worthy of her; and the arrow of Zechariah became steady, and he took her, and built for her a chamber in the temple, with stairs to which no one ascended but himself. And he used to bring her her food and her drink and her ointment; and used to find with her the fruits of winter in summer, and the fruits of summer in winter, as He—whose name be exalted!—hath said,* And Zechariah maintained her. Whenever Zechariah went in to her in the chamber, he found with her provisions. He said, O Mary, whence came to thee this? She answered, (*being then a little child,*) It is from God: *He bringeth it to me from Paradise:* for God supplieth whom He pleaseth without reckoning.

Then, *when he saw this, and knew that He who was able to produce a thing out of its season was able to give a child in old age, (and the people of his house had become extinct,)* Zechariah supplicated his Lord, *when he had entered the chamber to pray in the latter part of the night.* He said, O my Lord, give me from Thee a good offspring (*a righteous son*); for Thou art the Hearer of prayer.—And the angels (*by which is meant Gabriel*) called to him as he stood praying in the chamber (*that is, the temple*), saying, God promiseth thee John [Yaḥyá], who shall be a verifier of [the] Word *which cometh* from God, (*that is, Jesus* ['Eesa]; *for he is the Spirit of God, and was named* [the] *Word because he was created by the word Be,*) and a chief, (*or one followed,*) and chaste, and a prophet, of the righteous. (*It is related that he neither did any sin nor intended any.*)—He said, O my Lord, how shall I have a son, when old age hath come upon me, *when I have attained the utmost age, a hundred and twenty years,* and my wife is barren, *and hath attained the age of eight and ninety?*—He answered, *It shall be* thus. God will do what He pleaseth.—He said, O my Lord, give me a sign.—He replied, Thy sign [shall be] that thou shalt not speak unto men for three days, except by signal; but remember thy Lord often, and glorify [Him] in the evening and in the morning. (iii. 31–36.)

And he went forth unto his people from the chamber, and made a sign unto them, [as though he would say] Glorify [God] in the morning and in the evening *as usual. And he knew by his being prevented from speaking unto them that his wife had conceived John. And after his birth, by some years, God said unto him,* O John, receive the book (*that is, the Law*) with resolution. And We bestowed on him wisdom (*the gift of prophecy*) [when he was yet] a child, *three years of age,* and compassion from Us *for mankind,* and [a disposition to bestow] alms *upon them.* And he was pious, and dutiful to his parents, and was not proud [nor] rebellious *toward his Lord;* and peace *from Us* [was] on him on the day when he was born, and on the day of his death, and [shall be] on the day when he shall be raised to life. (xix. 12–15.)

And *remember* when the angels (*that is, Gabriel*) said, O Mary, verily God hath chosen thee and hath purified thee and hath chosen thee above the women of the peoples *of thy time.* O Mary, be devout towards thy Lord and prostrate thyself and bow down with those who bow down: *pray with those who pray.*—This is [one] of the announcements of things unseen *by thee:* We reveal it unto thee, *O Moḥammad;* for thou wast not with them when they cast their divining arrows *that it might appear to them* which of them should rear Mary, and thou wast not with them when they disputed together *as to rearing her.*—*Remember* when the angels (*that is, Gabriel*) said, O

Mary, verily God promiseth thee [the] Word from Him, whose name [shall be] the Messiah [El-Meseeḥ], Jesus the son of Mary, honourable in this world *by his prophetic office,* and in the world to come *by his intercession and high stations,* and of those admitted near *unto God;* and he shall speak unto men in the cradle, and when of full age,[1] and [he shall be] of the righteous.—She said, O my Lord, how shall I have a son, when a man hath not touched me?—He answered, *It shall be* thus; God will create what He pleaseth: when He determineth a thing, He only saith unto it, Be,—and it is. And He will teach him writing and wisdom and the Law and the Gospel, and *constitute him* an apostle to the children of Israel, *in youth or after adolescence. And Gabriel breathed into the bosom of her shift; whereupon she conceived; and those events of her history which are related in the Soorat Maryam* [Ḳur. xix.] *happened.* (iii. 37–43.)

Relate in the book (*that is, the Ḳur-án*) *the history of* Mary, when she retired from her family to a place towards the east, *in the house,* and she took a veil [to conceal herself] from them; and We sent unto her our spirit *Gabriel,* and he appeared unto her as a perfect man. She said, I beg the Compassionate to preserve me from thee! If thou be a pious person, *thou wilt withdraw from me.*—He replied, I am only the messenger of thy Lord [to inform thee] that He will give thee a pure son, *endowed with the gift of prophecy.* She said, How shall I have a son, when a man hath not touched me, and I am not a harlot? He answered, Thus *shall it be: a son shall be created unto thee without a father.* Thy Lord saith, This is easy unto Me; and *thus shall it be* that We may make him a sign unto men, *showing Our power,* and a mercy from Us *unto him who shall believe in him:* for it is a thing decreed.—And

---

[1] That is, between thirty, or thirty-four, and fifty-one: and the passage may relate to Christ's preaching here on earth. But as he had scarce attained this age when he was taken up into heaven, the commentators choose to understand it of his second coming.—S.

she conceived him; and she retired with him [yet unborn] to a distant place *far from her family;* and the pains of childbirth urged her to repair to the trunk of a palm-tree *that she might lean against it. And she gave birth to the child, which was conceived and formed and born in an hour.*[1] She said, Oh! would that I had died before this *event,* and had been a thing forgotten [and] unnoticed!—But he who was below her (*namely Gabriel, who was on a lower place than she*) called to her, Grieve not. God hath made below thee a rivulet: and shake thou towards thee the trunk of the palm-tree (*which was dried-up*); it shall let fall upon thee ripe dates, fresh-gathered: therefore eat *of the dates,* and drink *of the water of the rivulet,* and be of cheerful eye *on account of the child:* and if thou see any one of mankind, *asking thee concerning the child,* say, I have vowed unto the Compassionate an abstinence *from speech with mankind respecting him and other matters;* therefore I will not speak to-day unto a man *after this.*

And she brought him [namely the child] unto her people, carrying him. They said, O Mary, thou hast done a strange thing. O sister of Aaron, (*he was a righteous man; and the meaning is, O thou who art like him in chastity,*[2]) thy father was not a man of wickedness, nor was thy mother a harlot. *Then whence gottest thou this child?*—And she made a sign *to them,* [pointing] towards him, [namely the child, as though she would say,] *Speak ye unto him.* They said, How shall we speak unto him

[1] The age of the Virgin Mary at the time of her conception was thirteen, or, as others say, ten; and she went six, seven, eight, or nine months with him, according to different traditions; though some say the child was conceived at its full growth of nine months, and that she was delivered of him within an hour after.—S. (B., Yahya.)

[2] Some say the Virgin Mary had really a brother named Aaron, who had the same father but a different mother: others suppose Aaron the brother of Moses is here meant, but say Mary is called his sister either because she was of the Levitical race, (as, by her having been related to Elizabeth, it should seem she was,) or by way of comparison: others say that it was a different person of that name who was contemporary with her and conspicuous for his good or bad qualities, and that they likened her to him either by way of commendation or of reproach.—S. (B., Z., &c.)

who is in the cradle, an infant? He [however] said, Verily I am the servant of God:[1] He hath given me the book *of the Gospel*, and hath appointed me a prophet; and He hath made me blessed wherever I shall be, and hath commanded me to observe prayer and give alms as long as I shall live, and *hath made me* dutiful to my mother, and hath not made me proud [nor] wicked. And peace *from God* [was] on me on the day when I was born, and [will be] on the day when I shall die, and on the day when I shall be raised to life.—This [was] Jesus the son of Mary. *I have spoken* the saying of truth, concerning which they (*namely the Christians*) doubt, *saying that Jesus is the son of God.* It is not [meet] for God to get a son. Extolled be His purity *from that* [imputation]! When He decreeth a thing *that He desireth to bring into existence,* He only saith unto it, Be,—and it is: *and thus He created Jesus the son of Mary without a father.*—And *say,* Verily God is my Lord and your Lord: therefore worship ye Him: this is a right way, *leading to Paradise.* But the sects have differed among themselves; *that is, the Christians have differed concerning Jesus, as to whether he be the son of God, or a deity with Him, or the third of three.* And woe unto them who have disbelieved *in that which hath been stated, or in other matters,* on account of the assembly of a great day, *the day of resurrection, and its terrors.* How will they hear, and how *will they* see, on the day when they shall come unto Us *in the world to come!* But the offenders to-day (*that is, in the present world*) are in a manifest error: *they are deaf, so that they hear not the truth; and blind, so that they see it not.* And do thou, *O Moḥammad,* warn them (*namely the unbelievers of Mekkeh*) of the day of sighing (*the day of resurrection, when the evil-doer shall sigh for his having neglected*

[1] These were the first words which were put into the mouth of Jesus, to obviate the imagination of his partaking of the divine nature or having a right to the worship of mankind on account of his miraculous speaking so soon after his birth.—S. (B.)

to do good in the present world), when the command *for their punishment* shall be fulfilled, while they (*in the present world*) are in a state of heedlessness *with respect to it*, and while they believe not *therein*. Verily We shall inherit the earth and whomsoever are upon it (*the heedless and others; they being destroyed*); and unto Us shall they be brought back *to be recompensed*. (xix. 16–41.)

And when God sent him [Jesus] *to the children of Israel, he said unto them, Verily I am the apostle of God unto you;* for I have come unto you with a sign from your Lord; for I will make for you of earth the similitude of a bird, and will breathe into it, and it shall be a bird,[1] by the permission (*or will*) of God;[2] (*and he made for them a bat; for it is the most perfect of birds in make; and it flew, while they looked at it; but when it had gone out of their sight, it fell down dead;*) and I will cure the blind from his birth, and the leper; (*and he cured in one day fifty thousand, by prayer, on the condition of faith;*) and I will raise to life the dead, by the permission of God; (*this he repeated to deny his divinity: and he raised to life 'Áriz* [Lazarus] *a friend of his; and a son of the old woman, and the daughter of the publican; and they lived, and children were born to them; and Shem the son of Noah, who died immediately;*) and I will tell you what ye eat and what ye store up in your houses. Verily therein will be a sign unto you, if ye be believers. And *I have come unto you as* a verifier of that which was before me, of the

---

[1] It is related in the spurious Gospel of the Infancy of Christ that Jesus being seven years old and at play with several children of his age, they made several figures of birds and beasts of clay for their diversion; and each preferring his own workmanship, Jesus told them that he would make his walk and leap; which accordingly at his command they did. He made also several figures of sparrows and other birds, which flew about or stood on his hands as he ordered them, and also ate and drank when he offered them meat and drink. The children, telling this to their parents, were forbidden to play any more with Jesus, whom they held to be a sorcerer.—S.

[2] The commentators observe that these words are added lest it should be thought Jesus did these miracles by his own power, or was God.—S. (B.)

Law, and to make lawful unto you part of what was made unlawful to you *therein; (and he made lawful to them, of fish and fowls, whatsoever is without fin or spur; and it is said that he made lawful all, and that 'part' is used in the sense of 'the whole:')* and I have come unto you with a sign from your Lord; therefore fear ye God, and obey me *in that which I command you, as to the confession of the unity of God and the service of Him.* Verily God is my Lord and your Lord; therefore worship Him. This is [the] right way. *But they accused him of falsehood and believed not in him.* And when Jesus perceived their unbelief, he said, Who [will be] my helpers for God? The apostles [1] answered, We [will be] the helpers of God. We have believed in God; and bear thou witness, *O Jesus,* that we are Muslims [or resigned]. O our Lord, we have believed in that which Thou hast sent down *of the Gospel,* and we have followed the Apostle, *Jesus;* therefore write us down among those who bear witness *of Thy unity and of the truth of Thine apostle.*—And they (*that is, the unbelievers among the children of Israel*) devised a stratagem *against Jesus, to slay him treacherously;* but God devised a stratagem *against them; for He put the likeness of Jesus upon one who intended his slaughter, and they slew him; and Jesus was taken up* [into heaven],[2]

---

[1] In Arabic, 'el-Ḥawáreeyoon;' which word they derive from 'ḥára,' 'to be white' [or rather, 'to whiten' clothes], and suppose the apostles were so called either from the *candour* and *sincerity* of their minds, or because they were princes and wore white garments, or else because they were by trade fullers.—(B., Jelál.) According to which last opinion, their vocation is thus related: That as Jesus passed by the sea-side, he saw some fullers at work, and, accosting them, said, 'Ye cleanse these clothes, but cleanse not your hearts;' upon which they believed on him. But the true etymology seems to be from the Ethiopic verb 'hawyra,' 'to go;' whence 'hawârya' signifies 'one that is sent,' a 'messenger,' or 'apostle.' —S.

[2] The person crucified some will have to be a spy that was sent to entrap him; others that it was one Titian, who by the direction of Judas entered in at a window of the house where Jesus was; to kill him; and others that it was Judas himself, who agreed with the rulers of the Jews to betray him for thirty pieces of silver, and led those who were sent to take him.—They add, that

and God is the best of those who devise stratagems. . . *It is related that God sent a cloud to Jesus, and it took him up; but his mother clung unto him and wept: whereupon he said unto her, Verily the resurrection will unite us.—It is also related that he will descend shortly before the resurrection and judge according to the law of our prophet* [Mohammad], *slay Antichrist and the swine, break the cross, and impose the capitation-tax* [on unbelievers].—*Also, that he will remain, according to one tradition, seven years; according to another, forty years; and die, and be prayed over: but it is probable that* [by the latter period] *is meant the whole time of his tarrying upon the earth, before the ascension and after.* (iii. 43–47.)

Remember when the apostle said, O Jesus, son of Mary, is thy Lord able to cause a table to descend unto us from heaven?[1] He replied, Fear God, *in demanding signs,* if

Jesus, after his crucifixion in *effigy*, was sent down again to the earth to comfort his mother and disciples and acquaint them how the Jews were deceived, and was then taken up a second time into heaven.

It is supposed by several that this story was an original invention of Mohammad's; but they are certainly mistaken: for several sectaries held the same opinion long before his time. The Basilidians, in the very beginning of Christianity, denied that Christ himself suffered, but [asserted] that Simon the Cirenean was crucified in his place. The Corinthians before them, and the Carpocratians next (to name no more of those who affirmed Jesus to have been a mere man), did believe the same thing, that it was not himself, but one of his followers, very like him, that was crucified. Photius tells us that he read a book entitled 'The Journeys of the Apostles,' relating the acts of Peter, John, Andrew, Thomas, and Paul; and among other things contained therein this was one, that Christ was not crucified, but another in his stead, and that therefore he laughed at his crucifiers, or those who thought they had crucified him.—S.

[1] This miracle is thus related by the commentators. Jesus having at the request of his followers asked it of God, a red table immediately descended in their sight between two clouds and was set before them; whereupon he rose up, and, having made the ablution, prayed, and then took off the cloth which covered the table, saying, 'In the name of God, the best provider of food.' What the provisions were with which the table was furnished is a matter wherein the expositors are not agreed. One will have them to be nine cakes of bread and nine fishes; another, bread and flesh; another, all sorts of food except flesh; another, all sorts of food except bread and flesh; another, all except bread and fish; another, one fish which had the taste of all

ye be believers. They said, We desire that we may eat therefrom, and that our hearts may be at ease *in consequence of additional evidence*, and we may know, *with increased knowledge*, that thou hast spoken truth unto us *in asserting thyself to be a prophet*, and may be witnesses thereof.—Jesus the son of Mary said, O God, our Lord, cause a table to descend unto us from heaven, that it (*namely the day of its descent*) may be unto us a festival,[1] unto the first of us and the last of us (*or those who shall come after us*), and a sign from Thee *of Thy power, and of my prophetic office*; and provide us with food *thereby*; for Thou art the best of providers.—God said, *in reply to him*, Verily I will cause it to descend unto you; but whosoever of you shall disbelieve after *its descent*, I will surely punish him with a punishment wherewith I will not punish any [other] of the peoples.—*And the angels*

---

manner of food; another, fruits of Paradise: but the most received tradition is that when the table was uncovered there appeared a fish ready dressed, without scales or prickly fins, dropping with fat, having salt placed at its head, and vinegar at its tail, and round it all sorts of herbs except leeks, and five loaves of bread, on one of which there were olives, on the second honey, on the third butter, on the fourth cheese, and on the fifth dried flesh. They add that Jesus at the request of the apostles showed them another miracle by restoring the fish to life and causing its scales and fins to return to it; at which the standers-by being affrighted, he caused it to become as it was before: that one thousand three hundred men and women, all afflicted with bodily infirmities or poverty, ate of these provisions and were satisfied, the fish remaining whole as it was at the first: that then the table flew up to heaven in the sight of all; and every one who had partaken of this food were delivered from their infirmities and misfortunes: and that it continued to descend for forty days together, at dinner-time, and stood on the ground till the sun declined, and was then taken up into the clouds. Some of the Mohammadan writers are of opinion that this table did not really descend, but it was only a parable; but most think that the words of the Ḳur-án are plain to the contrary. A further tradition is that several men were changed into swine [and apes] for disbelieving this miracle and attributing it to magic art; or, as others pretend, for stealing some of the victuals from off it. Several other fabulous circumstances are also told, which are scarce worth transcribing.—S. (B.)

[1] Some say the table descended on a Sunday, which was the reason of the Christians' observing that day as sacred. Others pretend this day is still kept among them as a very great festival; and it seems as if the story had its rise from an imperfect notion of Christ's last supper and the institution of the Eucharist.—S.

descended with it from heaven: upon it were seven cakes of bread and seven fishes; and they ate of them until they were satisfied. And in a tradition related by Ibn-'Abbás it is said that the table brought down from heaven bread and flesh, and they were commanded not to act deceitfully, nor to store up for the morrow; but they [that is, some of the people] *did so, and were transformed into apes and swine.* (V. 112–115.)

Propound unto them, as an example, the inhabitants of the city *of Antioch*, when the apostles *of Jesus* came unto it;[1] when We sent unto them two,[2] and they charged

---

[1] To explain this passage, the commentators tell the following story:—The people of Antioch being idolaters, Jesus sent two of his disciples thither to preach to them; and when they drew near the city, they found Ḥabeeb, surnamed En-Nejjár, or The Carpenter, feeding sheep, and acquainted him with their errand; whereupon he asked them what proof they had of their veracity, and they told him they could cure the sick and the blind and the lepers; and to demonstrate the truth of what they said they laid their hands on a child of his who was sick and immediately restored him to health. Ḥabeeb was convinced by this miracle and believed; after which they went into the city and preached the worship of one true God, curing a great number of people of several infirmities; but at length, the affair coming to the prince's ear, he ordered them to be imprisoned for endeavouring to seduce the people. When Jesus heard of this, he sent another of his disciples, generally supposed to have been Simon Peter; who, coming to Antioch, and appearing as a zealous idolater, soon insinuated himself into the favour of the inhabitants and of their prince, and at length took an opportunity to desire the prince would order the two persons who, as he was informed, had been put in prison for broaching new opinions to be brought before him to be examined; and accordingly they were brought: when Peter, having previously warned them to take no notice that they knew him, asked them who sent them; to which they answered, God, who had created all things and had no companion. He then required some convincing proof of their mission, upon which they restored a blind person to his sight and performed some other miracles, with which Peter seemed not to be satisfied, for that according to some he did the very same miracles himself, but declared that if their God could enable them to raise the dead he would believe them; which condition the two apostles accepting, a lad was brought who had been dead seven days, and at their prayers he was raised to life; and thereupon Peter acknowledged himself convinced, and ran and demolished the idols, a great many of the people following him and embracing the true faith; but those who believed not were destroyed by the cry of the angel Gabriel.—S. (B., Z., &c.)

[2] Some say these two were John and Paul; but others name different persons.—S.

them with falsehood; wherefore We strengthened *them* with a third;[1] and they said, Verily we are sent unto you. They replied, Ye are not [aught] save men like us, and the Compassionate hath not revealed anything: ye do nothing but lie. They said, Our Lord knoweth that we are indeed sent unto you; and naught is imposed on us but the delivering of a plain message, *shown to be true by manifest proofs, namely the cure of him who hath been born blind and of the leper and the sick, and the raising of the dead.* [The people of Antioch] said, Verily we presage evil from you; *for the rain is withheld from us on your account:* if ye desist not, we will assuredly stone you, and a painful punishment shall surely betide you from us. [The apostles] replied, Your evil luck is with you *because of your unbelief.* If ye have been warned, *will ye presage evil and disbelieve?* Nay, ye are an exorbitant people.—And there came from the furthest part of the city a man (*namely Ḥabeeb the carpenter, who had believed in the apostles*) running: he said, O my people, follow the apostles: follow those who ask not of you a recompense, and who are rightly directed. *And it was said unto him, Art thou of their religion? He replied,* And why should I not worship Him who hath created me, and unto whom ye shall be brought back *after death?* Shall I take deities beside Him? If the Compassionate be pleased to afflict me, their intercession will not avert from me aught, nor will they deliver. Verily, in that case (*if I worshipped ought but God*), I should be in a manifest error. Verily I believe in your Lord; therefore hear ye me.—*But they stoned him, and he died;*[2] *and* it was said *unto him at his death,* Enter thou into Paradise. *And it is said that he entered it alive.* He said, O would that my people knew my Lord's forgiveness of me and His having made me [one] of those who are honoured?—

---

[1] Simon Peter.

[2] His tomb is still shown near Antioch, and is much visited by the Moḥammadans.—S.

And We sent not down against his people after him (*that is, after his death*) an army *of angels* from heaven *to destroy them,* nor were We sending down *angels to destroy any one.* It (*namely their punishment*) was naught but one cry *which Gabriel uttered against them;* and lo, they were extinct. (xxxvi. 12–28.)

We have cursed the Jews . . . for their disbelief *in Jesus* and their uttering against Mary a great calumny and their saying, We have killed the Messiah, Jesus the son of Mary, the apostle of God,—Yet they killed him not nor crucified him; but one (*namely the person whom they crucified*) was made to appear to them like *Jesus;* and verily those who disagreed respecting him were in doubt concerning him, *or his slaughter; for some of them said, when they saw the slain person, The face is the face of Jesus; but the body is not his body:—and others said, It is he:* [1]—they had no knowledge of him; but only followed an opinion. And they did not really kill him; but God took him up unto Himself; and God is mighty [and] wise. And there is not of the people of the Scripture *one* but he shall assuredly believe in him (*namely Jesus*) before his death; *that is, before his own death, or before the death of Jesus, when he descendeth shortly before the resurrection;* [2] and on the day of resurrection

[1] Also some said he was taken up into heaven; and others, that his manhood only suffered, and that his godhead ascended into heaven.—S. (B.)

[2] Some, referring the relative *his* to the first antecedent, take the meaning to be that no Jew or Christian shall die before he believes in Jesus; for they say that when one of either of those religions is ready to breathe his last, and sees the angel of death before him, he shall then believe in that prophet as he ought, though his faith will not then be of any avail. According to a tradition of El-Hajjáj, when a Jew is expiring the angels will strike him on the back and face, and say to him, 'O thou enemy of God, Jesus was sent as a prophet unto thee, and thou didst not believe on him;' to which he will answer, 'I now believe him to be the servant of God:' and to a dying Christian they will say, 'Jesus was sent as a prophet unto thee, and thou hast imagined him to be God, or the son of God;' whereupon he will believe him to be the servant of God only and His apostle. —Others, taking the above-mentioned relative to refer to Jesus, suppose the intent of the passage to be that all Jews and Christians in general [the

he (*namely Jesus*) shall be a witness against them (iv. 155–157.)

When God shall say, *on the day of resurrection,* O Jesus, son of Mary, hast thou said unto men, Take me and my mother as two deities, beside God?—*Jesus* shall answer, *after being agitated* (*or after it shall have thundered*), Extolled be Thy purity *from the imputation of aught that is unsuitable to Thee, as the having a partner, and other things!* It is not for me to say that which is not right for me. Had I said it, Thou hadst known it. Thou knowest what is in me; but I know not what is in Thee; for Thou well-knowest things unseen. I said not unto them aught but that which Thou commandedst me; *namely* Worship ye God, my Lord and your Lord;—and I was a watcher over them, *commanding them to abstain from what they said,* while I remained among them: but since Thou hast taken me to Thyself,[1] Thou hast been the watcher over them, and Thou art the witness of all things. If Thou punish them, (*that is, such of them as have continued in unbelief,*) they are Thy servants *and Thou mayest do with them as Thou pleasest;* and if Thou forgive them, (*that is, such of them as have believed,*) Thou art the Mighty, the Wise. (v. 116–118.)

When the son of Mary was proposed as an instance (*when the saying of God was revealed, Verily ye and what ye worship beside God* [shall be] *fuel of hell* [Kur. xxi. 98], *and the polytheists said, We are content for our gods to be with Jesus, for he hath been worshipped beside God,*[2])

dead being raised to life in their graves] shall have a right faith in that prophet before his death, that is, when he descends from heaven and returns into the world, where he is to kill Antichrist and to establish the Mohammadan religion and a most perfect tranquillity and security on earth [where he will remain forty years, and then die.—Others again suppose that the words 'believe in him' signify 'believe in God.']—S. (B., Z., Jelál, &c.)

[1] It is a dispute among the Mohammadans whether Christ actually died or not before his assumption.—S. (B.)

[2] Some, however, are of opinion it [this passage] might have been revealed in answer to certain idolaters, who said that the Christians, who received the Scriptures, worshipped

lo, thy people, *the polytheists,* cried out *in joy* thereat, and they said, [Are] our gods better, or [is] he? *We are content for our gods to be with him.*—They proposed not it (*namely the instance*) unto thee otherwise than as a cause of dispute (*knowing that the word 'what' applieth to that which is not endowed with reason; so that it doth not reflect upon Jesus, on whom be peace!*): yea, they are a contentious people. He (*namely Jesus*) is no other than a servant whom We favoured *with the gift of prophecy;* and We proposed him, *by reason of his having come into existence without a father,* as an instance *of the divine power* unto the children of Israel. And if We pleased, We would substitute for you angels to succeed in the earth.[1] And verily he (*namely Jesus*) *shall be* a sign of the [last] hour:[2] *it shall be known by his descending:* wherefore doubt not thereof.—And *say unto them,* Follow ye me *in confessing the unity of God:* this, *which I command you to follow,* is a right way. And let not the devil turn you away *from the religion of God;* for he is unto you a manifest enemy.—And when Jesus came with manifest proofs (*with miracles and ordinances*), he said, I have come unto you with wisdom (*with prophecy and with the ordinances of the Gospel*), and to explain unto you part of [the things] concerning which ye disagree: therefore fear ye God, and

---

Jesus, supposing him to be the son of God; whereas the angels were more worthy of that honour than he.—S. (B.)

[1] As easily as we produced Jesus without a father [B.]. The intent of the words is to show how just and reasonable it is to think that the angels should bear the relation of children to men rather than to God, they being His creatures as well as men, and equally in His power.—S.

[2] For some time before the resurrection Jesus is to descend on earth according to the Moḥammadans near Damascus, or as some say near a rock [or rather a mountain-road] named ['Aḳabet] Afeek, with a lance in his hand, wherewith he is to kill Antichrist, whom he will encounter at Ludd, or Lydda, a small town not far from Joppa. They add that he will arrive at Jerusalem at the time of morning-prayer, that he shall perform his devotions after the Moḥammadan institution, and officiate instead of the Imám, who shall give place to him; that he will break down the cross, and destroy the churches of the Christians, of whom he will also make a general slaughter, excepting only such as shall profess El-Islám.—S. (B.)

obey me. Verily God is my Lord and your Lord; wherefore worship ye Him: this is a right way.—But the parties disagreed among themselves *respecting Jesus, whether he were God, or the son of God, or the third of three:* and woe unto them that transgressed *in that which they said respecting Jesus,* because of the punishment of an afflicting day! (xliii. 57–65.)

Verily the similitude of Jesus in the sight of God is as the similitude of Adam. He created him (*Adam*) of earth: then He said unto him, Be,—and he was. *In like manner he said unto Jesus, Be, without a father,—and he was. This is* the truth from thy Lord: therefore be not thou of those who doubt. And whosoever *of the Christians* argueth with thee respecting him, after the knowledge that hath come unto thee *concerning him,* say, Come ye, let us call our sons and your sons and our wives and your wives, and ourselves and yourselves *will assemble:* then we will invoke, and will lay the curse of God on those who lie, *saying, O God, curse the liar respecting the nature of Jesus!—And the prophet invited a company from Nejrán to do so, when they had argued with him respecting Jesus; and they said,* [Wait] *until we consider our case: then we will come unto thee. And their counsellor said, Ye know his prophetic office, and that no people have execrated a prophet but they have perished. They however quieted the man, and departed, and came unto the prophet. And he had come forth, having with him El-Ḥasan and El-Ḥoseyn and Fáṭimeh and 'Alee; and he said unto them, When I pray, say ye Amen. But they refused to execrate, and made peace with him on the condition of their paying tribute.*—Verily this is indeed the true history, and there is no deity but God, and verily God is indeed the Mighty, the Wise. (iii. 52–55.)

O people of the Scripture (*that is, of the Gospel*), exceed not the just bounds in your religion,[1] nor say of God

[1] Either by rejecting and contemning Jesus, as the Jews do; or raising

[aught] but the truth. The Messiah, Jesus the son of Mary, [was] only the apostle of God, and His Word, which he transmitted unto Mary, and a spirit (*that is, a being possessing a spirit*) from Him. (*He is mentioned in conjunction with God, in order to show him honour, and is not, as ye assert, the son of God, or a God with Him, or the third of three; for the being possessing a spirit is compound, and the Deity must be confessed to be pure from the imputation of composition and the relationship of a compound being to Him.*) Therefore believe in God and His apostles, and say not, *There are* three *gods, God and Jesus and his mother.*[1] Abstain *from this, and say what will be* better for you; *that is, assert the unity of God.* God is only one god. Extolled be His purity from the imputation of His having a son! To Him belongeth whatsoever is in the heavens and whatsoever is in the earth: and God is a sufficient witness *thereof.* The Messiah doth not disdain to be a servant unto God, nor do the angels who are admitted near *unto Him.* (iv. 169, 170.)

---

him to an equality with God, as do the Christians.—S. (B.)

[1] For the Eastern writers mention a sect of Christians which held the Trinity to be composed of those three; but it is allowed that this heresy has been long since extinct.—S.

INDEX OF CHAPTERS.

GENERAL INDEX.

Erratum.—P. 36, line 1, *for* should *read* shall.
P. 122, line 21, *after* illiterate *add* [or Gentile, *i.e.*, Arab].